Words of a Monster

ALSO BY REBECCA FROST

*The Ripper's Victims in Print:
The Rhetoric of Portrayals Since 1929*
(McFarland, 2018)

Words of a Monster

*Analyzing the Writings
of H.H. Holmes,
America's First Serial Killer*

Rebecca Frost

Exposit
Jefferson, North Carolina

Library of Congress Cataloguing-in-Publication Data

Names: Frost, Rebecca, 1985– author.
Title: Words of a monster : analyzing the writings of H.H. Holmes, America's first serial killer / Rebecca Frost.
Description: Jefferson, North Carolina : Exposit Books, 2019 | Includes bibliographical references and index.
Identifiers: LCCN 2019015958 | ISBN 9781476677040 (paperback : acid free paper) ∞
Subjects: LCSH: Mudgett, Herman W., 1861–1896. | Serial murderers—Illinois—Chicago—Case studies. | Serial murders—Illinois—Chicago—Case studies.
Classification: LCC HV6248.M8 F76 2019 | DDC 364.152/32092—dc23
LC record available at https://lccn.loc.gov/2019015958

British Library cataloguing data are available

ISBN (print) 978-1-4766-7704-0
ISBN (ebook) 978-1-4766-3740-2

© 2019 Rebecca Frost. All rights reserved

No part of this book may be reproduced or transmitted in any form or by any means, electronic or mechanical, including photocopying or recording, or by any information storage and retrieval system, without permission in writing from the publisher.

On the cover: H.H. Holmes in 1895; *background* layout of Holmes Castle, Chicago; all images from *Holmes Own Story* (Philadelphia: Burk & McFetridge Co., 1895; Library of Congress, Rare Book and Special Collections Division)

Printed in the United States of America

Exposit is an imprint of McFarland & Company, Inc., Publishers

Exposit
Box 611, Jefferson, North Carolina 28640
www.expositbooks.com

To my parents,
who understand roots and wings

Acknowledgments

I would like to thank my colleagues Lynn Aho, Denise Cadeau, Megan Haataja, Jesse Koenig, Andrew Kozich, Cheryl LaRose, and Lori Ann Sherman; the KBOCC lunch crew and their tolerance for strange topics of mealtime conversation; UP-Write members past and present; Susan Kilby; my parents, who have been putting up with me the longest; and, of course, Eric, who continues to endure my enthusiasm for topics in which he personally has no interest.

Table of Contents

Introduction: Establishing "America's First Serial Killer"	1
Part I: Introducing H.H. Holmes	9
ONE. Separating the Man from the Myth	11
TWO. The Start of a Legend	31
Part II: *Holmes' Own Story*	49
THREE. Troubled Youth	53
FOUR. Of Wives and Mistresses	67
FIVE. Holmes, Pitezel and Hatch—Facets of Manhood	78
SIX. Holmes the Storyteller	95
SEVEN. Protestations of Innocence	110
Part III: Moyamensing Prison Diary Appendix	127
EIGHT. "My Wife"	130
NINE. Life Behind Bars	143
TEN. Hatch, Miss Williams and the Children	157
ELEVEN. Evidence and Motive	173
Part IV: Holmes Confesses 27 Murders	191
TWELVE. The Transformation from Innocent to Confessor	196
THIRTEEN. Details Revealed and Concealed	205
FOURTEEN. Those Hurt the Most	225

Conclusion: A Man of Mystery	241
Chapter Notes	267
Bibliography	271
Index	273

Introduction: Establishing "America's First Serial Killer"

In late 2016 I received an email from my dad with an Excel spreadsheet listing the contents of his Grandma Frost's coin collection. Dad asked if there were any coins I'd be especially interested in. I told him that yes, I would love to have the 1889 British sovereign, although of course it wasn't perfect—it was from the year after the Jack the Ripper murders. I also asked for the Columbian Exposition half dollars, one dated 1892 and the other 1893. "H.H. Holmes might have touched these," I told him when he gave them to me.

He sighed. "That's some other serial killer, isn't it?"

Well, actually…

Setting the Standards

Herman Webster Mudgett has been consigned to history under many names. Some of them, such as Dr. Henry Howard Holmes, are aliases of his own choosing. Others, like the Devil in the White City, have been bestowed upon him decades after his death. Executed in 1896 for a single murder, he has been figuratively—and literally—dug up again because of the recent fascination with "America's first serial killer."

H.H. Holmes, as he is most commonly called, was meant to have moved to Chicago prior to the Columbian Exposition and constructed a "Murder Castle" in which he housed—and murdered—patrons of the World's Fair. The vast majority of his murdered customers are said to have been young women experiencing their first taste of freedom, whom he murdered for his own pleasure alongside the money he might earn by selling their bodies as medical specimens. His hotel was meant to have numerous secret passageways and rooms that could be sealed off and filled with gas, along with cremation ovens in the basement for when his supply exceeded the demand for bodies. Apparently he murdered hundreds of people during the Columbian Exposition, although he was not suspected of such crimes until years later when he was arrested for insurance fraud and then charged with the murder of a single man: his friend and longtime employee, Benjamin Pitezel. The rumors swirled after Holmes' arrest as he was accused of any number of murders, some—such as those of Pitezel's children, Alice, Nellie, and Howard—quite likely, and others journalistic fantasy. Executed for a single murder, Holmes stood accused in newspapers if not in court of being so monstrous as to have killed hundreds.

The term "serial killer" was not in popular use until the latter half of the twentieth century, long after Holmes was hanged. The origin of the term is itself contested, often attributed to FBI Special Agent Robert Ressler in 1974, although further investigation has suggested that approximations of the term were used in English and non–English language documents previously.[1] Holmes, like Jack the Ripper a decade previously, was not called a serial killer during his lifetime. Newspaper reporters and even Holmes himself, in his letters and autobiographies, had to make do with other language, calling him deviant, a monster, or the arch fiend. Holmes, put on trial in Philadelphia in October 1895, was something brand new for the American reading audience, an enigma that needed a new kind of explanation. There was no framework upon which to build Holmes' story.

Today, in the twenty-first century, audiences who wish to read about criminals may peruse the true crime section in any given bookstore or library. Newly emerging criminals who have their stories unfolding in print or digital media have a ready set of referents for authors to choose from. Newly emerging criminals might be termed the next Ted Bundy or compared to Jeffrey Dahmer or John Wayne Gacy. If a spate of killings seems particularly unbelievable, those references can move beyond the true to the fictional, drawing comparisons to Hannibal Lecter, Dexter Morgan, or any number of fictional killers created to provide a rich fantasy text of good versus evil, however blurred those lines might be.

America witnessed a true crime boom in the 1980s, paralleling the Federal Bureau of Investigation's move to position itself as the expert when it came to deviant behavior of the multiple offender. The task of interviewing imprisoned criminals in order to determine common factors has been documented not only in the official law enforcement texts that emerged from the study, but in retired Special Agent John Douglas' book *Mindhunter: Inside the FBI's Elite Serial Crime Unit* (1995) and in the Netflix dramatization of the book that first aired in October 2017. These have served to present a new generation with the results of the interview project Douglas and Robert Ressler undertook in the late 1970s and the 1980s. With this information presented in this way to the public, especially in a television series that serves more to entertain than to educate, the average readers or viewers of true crime narratives find themselves in possession of what might be called the typical story of a serial killer.

A survey of true crime books prompted Mark Seltzer to call the genre "writing by numbers" because of the amazing similarity of the various texts.[2] Jean Murley has made similar observations in her 2008 book *The Rise of True Crime: 20th-Century Murder and American Popular Culture*, documenting many of the elements recognized by Seltzer. Some of these similarities are based in formatting—most books open with a crime and begin to tell the criminal's biography in chapter two—but others very nearly dictate the criminal's life story: absent father, abusive mother, lonely childhood, and so on. The interviews Douglas and Ressler performed presented them with these commonalities in the backgrounds of the serial killers and sex offenders that had been caught—and would speak to them—and these commonalities were presented to the world as universal and therefore expected.

Within the Behavioral Science Unit, these predictable life stories assisted agents in creating profiles in order to help law enforcement capture active serial offenders. If the interview data showed that most of the criminals were white men in their late twenties or early thirties when they began committing crimes, then law enforcement could narrow their search to white men in the proper age range. If the interviews dictated that serial killers commonly chose victims of their own race and of the gender that sexually attracted them, a string of white female victims would lead them to look for a heterosexual white male. Bloodier, more violent crimes that left victims' bodies ripped open were, according to the interviews, more likely to be committed by men, while women, historically, stuck to poisoning or smothering. The publication of the data and insights gained from these interviews grew beyond the position of being a tool for use by law enforcement officials, however, and emerged into the realm of common knowledge and entertainment as true crime books grew in popularity and the figure of the serial killer moved from fact to fiction.

The Silence of the Lambs (1991) is often credited with introducing the general public to the idea of criminal profiling through the character of Clarice Starling, a role for which Jodie Foster won the Academy Award for Best Actress. The film won five Oscars, including Best Picture, and has since been placed on multiple must-watch lists. Criminal profiling in the form of Special Agents Starling and Jack Crawford, and serial killers with the allure of Anthony Hopkins' award-winning Hannibal Lecter, were now no longer limited to written true crime. There was clearly something about the narrative that reached a wider audience and opened the door for other movies and film media concerned with the hunt for, and capture of, serial criminals.

Public and popular fascination with nearly mythical and at times almost supernatural serial killers shown on the screen has led to a phenomenon known as "the CSI effect" in which jurors selected for a trial expect to see the sort of evidence and clear connections in the courtroom that they watched on the show *CSI: Crime Scene Investigation* and its multiple spinoffs. Although such shows share fictional plot lines, Murley, at least, categorizes them under her true crime spectrum[3] because so many elements of science and law must be factual. The information that the reading and viewing audience digests through true crime and crime fiction aligns with previously released information concerning criminals and serial criminals, following the data collected and then disseminated by the FBI.

The average twenty-first-century consumer of true crime, then, comes to a text with certain expectations not only for the way in which the narrative will unfold, but what information will be presented. The serial killer, almost always male, will be expected to report on a past that falls in line with these teachings. There must be something in his past, likely a combination of both nature and nurture, that has turned him into the sort of person who would murder a number of strangers for his own pleasure, returning to his normal life between each incident and continuing the charade of being just another man while seeking out his next victim. Although the killer himself is dangerous since he possesses this chameleon-like ability to be overlooked—how else would he manage to convince so many victims to go with him to their deaths?—he is ultimately not a threat because he will be captured and, when his story is told, it will confirm basic expectations. Daughters will be safe from becoming victims as long as they refuse to go with strangers, and sons will be safe from becoming serial killers as long as their fathers are present, their mothers are not abusive, and their childhoods are "normal."

This education of the public, however, also means that criminals themselves, including those who have not yet been identified, are likewise free to educate themselves on true crime narratives. It is possible for them to prepare their narratives in anticipation of capture, relying on the tried and true biographical elements that have already been established as being acceptable explanations for why a man would commit such crimes. The twenty-first century not only offers the average citizen a chance to play at being a profiler, but also provides criminals with a template for their own stories, in case they might be the next Ted Bundy. These men already know what aspects of a biography will appeal to audiences, which will be automatically accepted, and which would likely end up getting them dismissed or ignored.

H.H. Holmes, arrested in 1894, had no such template.

When Holmes wrote his confessions, he was doing so without the benefit of the established serial killer narrative, first attempting to convince others—law enforcement as well as the general public—of his innocence, and then doing his best to sell his "true" confession before he would be executed. There was not even a word for what he was. A reporter came up with the turn "multimurderer" in order to distinguish Holmes' crimes from those committed by the average, everyday one-off murderers.[4] His written confessions broke new literary ground.

They were not, however, the first written accounts of crime ever to appear in print on American soil. Some forms of crime narratives had preceded him, including the Puritan execution sermon and trial reports, and others ran concurrently with Holmes' own life, including newspaper articles. In fact, Holmes was allowed to read the newspaper every day in prison and was thus able to remain informed of how his own case was proceeding and how reporters were presenting him for their reading audience. This allowed him to not only keep a finger on the pulse of his current reputation, but also to react and respond to those changes in an attempt to manipulate the reading public into being convinced of his innocence. Holmes wrote not merely to explain, but to persuade.

This book begins with an overview in Part I of the life of Herman Webster Mudgett, more commonly known as H.H. Holmes. Chapter One investigates his life and presents readers with a recitation of the most commonly told elements of his biography. Because so many myths and apocryphal tales have grown up around Holmes, some of them at his own instigation, there are gaps and questions surrounding this retelling that will be addressed through Holmes' own variations. Chapter Two tackles the first of these variations: Holmes' two spoken confessions given at the end of 1894 after he was arrested for the final time and imprisoned pending charges in the death of his longtime friend and associate, Benjamin Pitezel.

Part II contains the close reading of *Holmes' Own Story*, his autobiography published in the fall of 1895 before he stood trial for the murder of Benjamin Pitezel. It is divided into themes, beginning with Chapter Three, a look at how Holmes presented his boyhood and, as he relates them, his first forays into mischief. Chapter Four showcases the ways in which Holmes presents the main female figures in his life, especially the Williams sisters, Minnie and Nannie, and the woman he most often refers to as simply "my wife," Georgiana Yoke. Since Holmes is accused of murdering scores, if not hundreds, of women, the way he presents those most central to his story warrants close scrutiny. The men are the subject of Chapter Five in which Holmes attempts to set himself apart from the figures of Benjamin Pitezel, whom he represents as an alcoholic bigamist, and Hatch, the supposed child murderer. Chapter Six confronts some of the more absurd, bizarre, and possibly amusing aspect of *Holmes' Own Story* that are most often glossed over and ignored as being nothing but make-believe. Their presence within the text, however, was meant to serve a purpose, which will itself be investigated. Chapter Seven surveys all the various methods Holmes uses within the text in order to convince the reader that he is not guilty and, indeed, is not the man who should be on trial, after all.

Part III investigates the appendix to *Holmes' Own Story*, known as the Moyamensing Prison Diary. With its dated entries, this supplement is meant to have been penned by Holmes as he sat in prison over a period of months, reflecting on his life and his current situation. Chapter Eight returns to the figure of Georgiana Yoke, often invoked by Holmes to appeal to the emotions of his audience. Rather than loving references, Holmes' constant worries over her condition and descriptions of their interactions are heavy-handed and tiresome, although he still intends them to serve a purpose for his defense. Chapter Nine focuses on the aspects of prison life that Holmes chooses to relate in his diary and thus to the general public. These are carefully curated in order to present Holmes in a certain favorable light. Chapter Ten returns to the question of the fate of Alice, Nellie, and Howard Pitezel as Holmes continues to explain how, as best he can imagine it, the children were murdered. Here he struggles with apparent frustration at the law enforcement officials who cannot find evidence of Hatch's existence or Miss Williams' continued life, ceaselessly painting himself as a man wrongfully accused and falsely imprisoned. Chapter Eleven covers the final pages of the Prison Diary in which Holmes shifts his argument from emotional to logical appeals and addresses his concerns involving photographic identification before systematically dismantling any and all claims to motive he has seen given in the newspapers. This approach comes in strong contrast to his continual references to his wife and his own current condition, and is positioned to leave readers with a fully rounded rational argument as to his innocence.

Part IV examines the confession published in the *Philadelphia Inquirer* in 1896, just weeks before Holmes' execution. Since he had been found guilty and sentenced to hang by this time, Chapter Twelve examines the changes not only in Holmes' narrative, but in his word choice and presentation. He is now no longer professing his innocence but expressing the desire to unburden himself before his death. Chapter Thirteen follows the twenty-seven confessions to critically examine how Holmes has decided to present his crimes. Although his introduction indicates that he wishes to tell everything, there are obvious moments when Holmes glosses over information indirectly or even directly, affecting the impact of his supposed tell-all confession. Chapter Fourteen comes back to the Williams sisters and the Pitezel family, whose stories have been changed with every retelling and whose reputations Holmes clearly tarnished in earlier iterations. Once again Holmes attempts to make amends before his impending death, and his word choice and attention to specific details present his audience with a new sort of Holmes: a penitent man wishing to right all his wrongs before his justifiable execution.

The Conclusion looks back over the many iterations of his past that Holmes curated in his lifetime, ending with the confession he spoke on the gallows prior to his execution. Holmes' biography is so difficult to piece together because the man himself was so willing to change it from one iteration to another, responding to changes in public feeling he discovered through newspapers first in an attempt to secure his own acquittal, and then because he was offered a substantial sum for his confession. Even though he rose to fame before the birth of the modern serial killer, Holmes was able to construct his own narrative that would ensnare public fascination and convince his audience to open their pocketbooks in order to discover how, exactly, he had grown into such a "monster."

It should be noted that the Holmes referred to in these pages is the public image produced through his spoken confessions and the writings attributed to him. *Holmes' Own Story* and his confession in the *Philadelphia Inquirer* are argued to have been either heavily edited or not in fact written by H.H. Holmes at all. This book focuses on the representation of the figure of Holmes and the marketing of Holmes as a viable product and thus does not concern itself with the veracity of the statements within the texts or whether or not they were single-author pieces written by the man himself. These pieces are examined as public representations of Holmes that shaped him in the minds of the reading audience and began the creation of Holmes, the myth, at a time when there was no solid framework for representing men who murdered in this way.

Part I

Introducing H.H. Holmes

In 1994 Harold Schechter published his book *Depraved: The Shocking True Story of America's First Serial Killer* and, in his afterword, marveled at the fact that Holmes had been all but lost to history. "America's first serial killer" had been far eclipsed by the "world's first serial killer," Jack the Ripper, who had murdered several prostitutes in London six years before Holmes' execution. The mystery of Jack the Ripper's identity has led to the publication of more than one hundred nonfiction books about the Whitechapel murders, but although Holmes generally deserves a mention in overviews of the phenomenon of serial killing, few such texts have been devoted solely to him.

Even Schechter's book did not open the floodgates. In 2003 Erik Larson published the more popular *The Devil in the White City: Murder, Magic, and Madness at the Fair That Changed America*, which paralleled Holmes' biography with the story of Daniel Burnham, the Director of Works for the World's Columbian Exposition. Larson, then, did not focus solely on the true crime elements of Holmes' story, but interwove it with a history of the World's Fair—during which Holmes is meant to have murdered attendees in the triple digits, yes, but the chapters on the Exposition concern themselves with architecture, the various attractions, and the first Ferris Wheel instead of bloodlust. The fact that the Fair was home to the famous White City allowed for Larson to create a perfect contrast to the dark city of Chicago, which better suited Holmes' dark heart. The charming blue-eyed physician must share the pages of the book with Burnham and his associates until the Fair ends and Larson can follow the murderer's life to the gallows.

Over a decade passed before Adam Selzer's 2017 book, *H.H. Holmes: The True History of the White City Devil*, was published. As might be inferred from the title, Selzer wishes to correct the misconceptions and dispel the myths that Larson included and perpetrated in *Devil*, following a long history of rumor being presented alongside, and eventually superseding, fact. Larson may have made a point to avoid the internet when doing his research, but even the newspaper accounts he discovered were not necessarily factual. Headlines and articles are, of course, written to sell, and retractions and corrections were not always given as prominent a place as the original declarations of horror. Selzer, then, sets out to separate provable fact from probable fiction, reducing Holmes to his humanity instead of inflating him to a mythic monster who could, indeed, stand alongside the figure of Jack the Ripper. Not that Holmes is always kept separate—Dane Ladwig's 2014 book *Dr. H.H. Holmes and the Whitechapel Ripper* argues that Holmes and the Ripper are one and the same.

It is best, perhaps, to keep in mind that Schechter, Larson, and Ladwig were writing in the age during which the serial killer's story has been solidified and presented by the FBI, which has made itself the authority on such figures. There are indeed gaps in what can be learned about Holmes, and these are not helped by the fact that he was willing to change his narrative as it suited him. Selzer, at least, presents himself as being less concerned with telling a good murder story and more willing to admit where there are gaps. Holmes himself, however, has already been tainted, not only by the previous, more complete story arcs printed about him but by figures such as Ted Bundy and John Wayne Gacy: those who came after him and became easy points of comparison.

ONE

Separating the Man from the Myth

Herman Webster Mudgett was born in Gilmanton, New Hampshire, on May 16, 1861. He was the middle of five children, although his siblings seemed to play little, if any, role in his childhood. His parents, Levi and Theodate, have been stressed as being devoutly religious and wonderful, therefore playing no role in their son's descent into deception and crime. Even Holmes himself made sure to argue for their innocence[1] and come to their defense.

His childhood is largely a mystery. In *Holmes' Own Story*, published in 1895 before his murder trial, Holmes—or perhaps a journalist who may have heavily edited his original words[2]—laid out a number of incidents that certainly seem to point toward an adulthood of swindling and murder. Two of these have been included in most versions of Holmes' biography.

First, there is the tale of the local doctor in Gilmanton. As a boy Holmes apparently had to pass by his office every day on the way to school, and he was also terrified of the skeleton that was on display. Older boys, seeing this weakness, grabbed Holmes when he was still quite young and, depending on the variation, either shut him in the cabinet with the skeleton until the doctor discovered him and let him out, or were in the process of propelling him toward the skeleton when the doctor interrupted their fun. As terrifying as this incident must have been for the boy, he later credited it with piquing his interest in becoming a physician.

A second incident involved a young Holmes watching, agog, as a man casually removed his wooden leg. Up until that point Holmes was unaware that such conditions existed and it seems the child believed he was watching some sort of bloodless dismemberment.

Considering Holmes' adulthood activities of murder, it is no surprise that these two stories, apocryphal or truthful, would be continually remembered and rehashed since their publication in *Holmes' Own Story*. They are partially an explanation for how a boy whose childhood was, according to all sources, "almost entirely normal"[3] could grow into a man accused of multiple murders and various gruesome methods of body disposal. Had Holmes simply remained a physician, then perhaps the tale of the skeleton would indeed be nothing more than a charming explanation for how his interest in anatomy was initially piqued, but Holmes is not known for his medical degree. Fully articulated skeletons and dismembered limbs took on a new meaning as soon as Holmes' name made national headlines accompanied by epithets such as "arch fiend."

All authors, including the more skeptical Adam Selzer, are in agreement that Holmes was an intelligent child. He clearly did well enough at school to graduate at sixteen years old, and there seem to be few, if any, indicators that he would have grown into "America's first serial killer." A century later the FBI would conclude that there are a trio of indicators that a child was on such a path—starting fires, torturing and killing small animals, and bed-wetting far past the usual age of toilet training—but none seem to be remembered from Holmes' childhood. Harold Schechter is the only one to suggest that Holmes engaged in "secret medical experiments"[4] on animals, and that these experiments allowed him to learn much about keeping his subjects alive for an extended time during the torture. At the time of Schechter's writing, in the mid–1990s, the path from animal torturer to serial killer had been clearly established. However, even in the 1890s—after Holmes' arrest and at the time when reporters would have been seeking out information about the mysterious blue-eyed swindler—it is possible that citizens of Gilmanton may have misremembered or expounded upon stories from Holmes' youth in that same search for an explanation of why his life took such a violent turn. Holmes himself did not report cases of animal mutilation in either of his autobiographies, although there were other, provable omissions from his written recollections, so this omission does not mean that these occurrences did not take place.

One notable omission came in the form of Clara Lovering, the woman Holmes convinced to elope with him when he was eighteen.

Clara became his first wife, taking the name Mrs. Mudgett. She would be the only woman to do so, as he married his two bigamous wives under pseudonyms. Clara also bore Holmes' first child, a son named Robert Lovering Mudgett, who barely knew his father. When Holmes went off to Michigan in 1882 to attend medical school, he discovered that having a family impinged on the lifestyle he wished to pursue. Clara and Robert first returned to live with Holmes' parents before moving on their own, and Clara found work to support them since visits from her husband became more and more sporadic.

At the University of Michigan's Department of Medicine and Surgery Holmes faced the issue of many medical students of the day: a shortage of specimens to dissect. Dismemberment, even in the name of education and science, was considered a horrifying end. Even murderers who had been convicted of doing much the same to their victims, albeit without the intent of forwarding medical knowledge, could have judges work clauses into their sentences such that their own bodies would not be donated to science after their executions. This did not necessarily, however, protect them from grave robbers who might then sell their bodies to science but, as shall be seen, Holmes had his own solution for this concern.

Because medical students worked with cadavers in such an environment, they were in a prime position to be accused of being resurrection men. Due to a shortage of bodies approved for use in medical lectures and anatomy labs, there were those who decided that they could make a quick profit by digging up graves and selling the bodies. Others, such as the famed William Burke and William Hare of Scotland, responded to this need by committing murders to supply the anatomical samples. Although physicians were respected members of society, they needed to engage in the distasteful task of working with cadavers in order to attain their degrees, and as a result there were few questions as to how those cadavers ended up in the medical schools in the first place.

Holmes insisted later in his life that he had never worked as a resurrection man, either while he was in medical school or afterward. If this is true, then, popular sentiment is that it is only because he chose the Burke and Hare method of procuring bodies instead of arming himself with a pick and shovel.

After graduating medical school in 1884, Holmes—still using his birth name of Mudgett—lived for a time in New York and then for a while in Philadelphia. He found that he was not suited to working at an asylum, and apparently even being a pharmacist was not a good match. When he moved away from New York and from Philadelphia, in each case it was because of a suspicious disappearance or death that may or may not have been able to be tied back to him. It was therefore in his favor when, upon arriving in Chicago under the name H.H. Holmes, his new employer did not carefully follow up with his references. It should be noted that, despite modern association, this was before Sir Arthur Conan Doyle had introduced the figure of Sherlock Holmes. Holmes himself did not indicate how he had selected his pseudonym, so any explanations as to why he chose that specific last name would only be speculation.

Holmes' arrival in Chicago is part of the story that has been warped by myth. According to Schechter and Larson, Holmes walked through the door of Dr. Holton's pharmacy and was greeted by Mrs. Holton, who was working while her elderly husband was upstairs slowly dying of cancer. Holmes was first hired as an employee for the grateful, overworked Mrs. Holton, and then ended up buying the pharmacy after her husband had died. When Mrs. Holton began complaining about the fact that Holmes was not keeping up on his payments, despite the continual string of pretty young customers more than willing to flirt with Dr. Holmes, Mrs. Holton suddenly moved away and was never heard from again. Holmes installed himself in the apartment above the pharmacy, and that was that.

Selzer, however, argues that "the Holtons were not an elderly doctor and his wife, but a young doctor and her husband."[5] Dr. Holton, then, was not dying of cancer but in the prime of life, wishing to sell her pharmacy so that she could get on with raising a family. Selzer also points out that Dr. Holton, like Holmes, was a graduate of the University of Michigan, and thus Holmes' choice of entering her pharmacy may not have been purely by chance. Since they were both alumni of the same program, it is possible that the exchange of ownership had already been suggested through mutual acquaintances. Further, far from dying and disappearing, the Holtons were each still living at the time of Holmes' arrest. The fact that no reporter interviewed Dr. Holton, while it makes sense in the mythical explanation due to his death, puzzles Selzer, since the woman in question was still very much able to provide her own opinion of Holmes.

As Dr. Henry Howard Holmes, new owner of the pharmacy on Sixty-third Street, he took a second wife. This was another whirlwind courtship, with Holmes traveling to Minneapolis in order to court Myrta Belknap and bring her back to Chicago with him. Holmes' practice of flirting with his female customers failed to abate even when she was present at the pharmacy, and eventually Holmes bought this wife a house where she could raise their daughter, Lucy Theodate Holmes, once again locating his family at enough of a distance so that they would not interfere with his marketing strategies. His name would, after all, be attached with far more women than the three he claimed as wives.

A String of Mistresses

Holmes, free of both of his current wives, was able to concentrate on those of other men. As he expanded his building to become what would in time be known as the Murder Castle, other shops took up residence on the first floor, and one of those shops hired a jeweler named Ned Connor. Ned moved in with his wife, Julia, and small daughter, Pearl, but their marriage was not a harmonious one. Soon enough Julia and Holmes were having an affair, one that was not even kept secret from customers or indeed Ned himself. Ned eventually left his wife, who confronted Holmes with the fact that she was pregnant. Julia demanded that Holmes leave his own wife—in this case, Myrta, the only wife Holmes was thought to have had in Chicago—and marry her. It seems that Holmes may have shared details of some of his less-than-legal dealings with Julia, since he appeared to acquiesce to her request. If Julia would allow him to perform an abortion, he would leave his own wife and marry her.

The date for this illegal operation ended up being Christmas Eve and, before long, both Julia and her daughter were dead. It is possible that Holmes accidentally killed Julia while attempting the operation, as he indicated in some of his confessions, although the story is generally presented to argue that Holmes did not intend Julia to survive. Schechter, for example, explains that Holmes killed Pearl before beginning the operation on her mother. However it happened, neither Julia nor Pearl were seen or heard from again.

Emeline Cigrand was another woman connected to Holmes as both a lover and a victim. She was lured away from her position as a stenographer for Dr. Keeley—who promoted a cure for alcoholism—with the promise of double the pay as Holmes' typist, and once again quickly became more to him than that. Despite the fact that she was the "prettiest"[6] of the women Holmes ended up seducing, her beauty did not secure her safety. She was believed to have been killed in his Castle, although her body was never found. Her disappearance was explained by way of marriage, although her family had not met her supposed suitor, Robert Phelps, and none were invited to witness the ceremony. It seemed to them as though she had simply disappeared with nothing but a wedding announcement in the newspaper to suggest that she was still alive.

Minnie Williams is perhaps the most famous of Holmes' mistresses because of the role he assigned to her in *Holmes' Own Story*. She appealed to Holmes much in the way many of his victims did, having inherited a large sum of money from her parents but being in possession of a naïve worldview. As such she could perfectly play her way into his hands, signing away property and other valuables without oversight from any family members who might have known better and cautioned her otherwise. Minnie was brought to the Castle as a typist, and initially lived in a boarding house on her own but soon enough took up with Holmes, who is meant to have rented them an apartment where— depending on the story—either he or Minnie herself insisted that they live as husband and wife.

This was well enough in the beginning, since Minnie had no relatives living close by, but as time passed her worldlier sister, Nannie, seemed to grow suspicious. This was during the time of the Columbian Exposition, when millions of people were flocking to Chicago in order to view the World's Fair, so Holmes apparently suggested to Minnie that she should invite her sister to visit, both to make her acquaintance and to see the White City for herself. Holmes apparently moved back to his Castle before Nannie arrived so as to remove the suggestion that he and Minnie were living as man and wife, although Nannie warmed up to him almost immediately and wrote letters back home referring to him as "Brother Harry." Brother Harry escorted them to the fair and even made plans to take the sisters with him to Europe.

Unfortunately for the women, Holmes' building developed the name "Murder Castle" because of the number of people he was meant to have killed inside it. There were supposedly secret passageways and hidden rooms—Selzer argues that, since many of the employees knew about them and even took naps in them, they could not have been overly secret[7]—as well as a large, soundproofed safe that was easily large enough for a person to enter. One after the other, Holmes apparently lured the sisters into the safe, perhaps asking them to fetch some of his important documents. As well as soundproof, the safe was airtight, and the sisters died. Newspapers reported that, once the Castle was investigated, the outline of a bare footprint was revealed on the inside of the door, suggesting that at least one of the women Holmes disposed of in this way fought valiantly for her life. Popular theory suggests that this is the last remaining evidence of the life of Emeline Cigrand.

Because of the way his Castle was constructed, and the busy time period surrounding the Columbian Exposition, Holmes has also been accused of murdering a number of guests who stayed in his Castle during the Fair. How many is uncertain, but the number tends to have three digits. While Holmes' motivation for his previous victims has centered around women he no longer had a use for, who perhaps threatened his reputation and who could be convinced to sign over large amounts of property or money to him, the supposed World's Fair victims might have been murdered purely because Holmes felt compelled to continue his homicidal activities. Schechter argues that Holmes pumped rooms full of gas while his customers slept or perhaps hanged them in the elevator shaft, and then removed their valuables and used them to make a profit, but this was not his only motive. It seems that, according to Schechter, Holmes chose a select few of his victims—"all of them female, none older than twenty-five"[8]—to satisfy him sexually in ways that his living wives and mistresses never could.

The Columbian Exposition opened to the public in May 1893 and closed in October of that same year. If, during that time, Holmes murdered at least one hundred people—estimates have at times ranged above double that amount—no one seems to have fully explained how he managed to not only explain the disappearance of so many of his customers, but how he disposed of their bodies at such a high rate. One of Holmes' schemes involved the installation of an oven ostensibly meant for glass bending, and it has been suggested that this would have functioned as a crematorium. Other sources indicate that Holmes discovered one of the men working for him was skilled at articulating skeletons and thus Holmes enlisted the man so that he could sell the remains of his victims to medical schools and make another profit. Some of his victims may have been buried in the basement of the castle which, although on a large corner lot, still presented him with only a finite amount of space. Although John Wayne Gacy, nearly a century later, was discovered to have buried multiple victims in his basement by layering the bodies, no such technique was revealed at the Murder Castle. While those searching the Castle years later, after Holmes' arrest, may have been said to have discovered the secret rooms and the odd oven, few human remains were found. Even the amount trumpeted in the first headlines would not lend itself to the thought that at least one hundred people had met their end at that address.

Selzer even argues that the entire idea of Holmes using his Castle as a hotel for Fair guests was patently ridiculous, since there was no evidence that the ostensible guest rooms were even open at the time. He points out the fact that, when there was a fire in the Castle's third level, few people were even in the building, which would not have been expected had the Castle actually been operating as a hotel at the time.

Larson suggests that many people, especially young women, who went to Chicago to attend the Fair did indeed disappear, although most of them likely used the opportunity to break free of their families and strike out on their own. This, he argues, would have helped Holmes escape suspicion for so long, since it would not have been only the young women staying at the Castle who appeared to vanish into midair. Again, though, their bodies would have needed to have been disposed of in ways that would have left little or no trace in the Castle, and ways that would have failed to rouse suspicion. Logic leans toward Selzer's conclusion that the newspapers grabbed onto the story of the odd building and blew it out of proportion in order to sell more copies and, since it was such a good story, the tale stuck.

The Case of Benjamin Pitezel

Despite the number of mistresses who disappeared after their public relationships with Holmes, his shady business dealings, and the illegal manner in which he managed the construction of his Castle, Holmes was not put on trial for anything that took place in Chicago. It seemed that he managed to escape from any possible prosecution through either charm or brute negotiations. For example, during the construction of his three-story Castle, Holmes oversaw an ever-changing group of workmen who were his employees for however long it took before they demanded payment and, instead of paying them, Holmes fired them and took on more men. In this way, no one other than Holmes himself—according to legend—had any idea of all of the secrets his building held, including its hidden rooms and various methods of murdering the occupants. When he purchased the large safe where so many of his victims supposedly met their end, so the story goes, Holmes had the walls quickly built up around it so that, when he was confronted with the issue of non-payment, he countered that they could come in and take the safe back so long as they did no damage to his building.

In Chicago Holmes was known as a womanizer and a swindler, yes, but he managed to wriggle out of any trouble he had not been able to outright avoid. Even if he was taken to court, his lawyer managed to keep him out of jail. It was only after his second arrest in the fall of 1894 that Holmes and his Castle were fully scrutinized, although Holmes had met the man who unwittingly helped him make those headlines while he was constructing his castle.

Benjamin Freelon Pitezel was, in many accounts, nearly the opposite of Holmes. He had one wife, Carrie, who was the mother of his five children. Their eldest child, according to Schechter, necessitated their marriage, and Schechter himself argues that Pitezel, at least in his youth, was clearly more than capable of charming a minister's daughter to engage in extramarital sex.[9] This charisma either faded as he aged, a process that may have been aided by his dual vices of alcohol and tobacco, or were perhaps only limited to a single specimen of the fairer sex. Between Holmes and Pitezel, Holmes cut a dashing figure and Pitezel very nearly slouched along in his shadow.

Pitezel was, however, useful to Holmes as he went about his dealings.

Where a tall, slender man might not intimidate those who had come to collect the money that was owed to them, the rougher Pitezel apparently served his purpose without even saying a word. Pitezel functioned clearly as the sidekick to Holmes' central role, and Holmes apparently valued the other man's presence. Indeed, he was willing to pay for Pitezel's "gold cure" treatment for his alcoholism, a not-inconsiderable sum for the day. The fact that Pitezel returned with tales of the pretty secretary Emeline Cigrand was an added bonus.[10]

It seems that Holmes involved Pitezel in enough of his dealings for the other man to become a threat to him, especially while he was drunk enough to forget to watch what he said. Due to his drinking—the gold cure was apparently only a temporary solution—Pitezel, it seems, could not be trusted to follow Holmes' orders, or even to keep ahold of the money Holmes gave him. In spite of his promises to Carrie that various proceedings would be his last scheme with Holmes, and that she and the children would be well provided for at its conclusion, Carrie was often left alone with her five children and found herself installed in a small rundown apartment in St. Louis, unable to even send for a doctor when the baby fell ill, as Pitezel prepared for the final con.

Holmes had managed to court and marry a third wife, Georgiana Yoke, who believed she was now Mrs. Henry M. Howard. Holmes had sold her a story to explain why they had to go to Texas so that he might be able to retrieve some of the money he had gotten from the Williams sisters. Holmes and Pitezel had to flee Texas to escape persecution for horse thievery, and it was shortly thereafter that Holmes ended up jailed for the first time in St. Louis, Missouri, for selling mortgaged goods. While his incarceration was a time of trial for his pretty new wife before she was able to procure his bail, Holmes made good use of his days behind bars in befriending his cellmate, wild west outlaw Marion Hedgepeth.

Holmes related a scheme that had apparently first been conceived in his medical school days—a scheme that Benjamin Pitezel was eager to put into practice. He explained to Hedgepeth that it would be easy enough for a medical man, such as himself, to procure a corpse in order to scam an insurance company. Pitezel would move to a new city—they chose Philadelphia, since it was home to the head office of the company that insured Pitezel's life for $10,000—under a pseudonym and, once the "material" was procured, Holmes would help Pitezel fake his death. The corpse would, of necessity, need to be injured enough so that it could indeed have been Pitezel. Pitezel himself would go into hiding while Holmes, with the assistance of an attorney, would make an identification of the body and assure the insurance company that it was indeed Pitezel, but this was the sticking point: did Hedgepeth know, perhaps, of an attorney who would play this part for a small fee?

In exchange for $500 of the insurance money, Hedgepeth directed Holmes to a young lawyer named Jeptha Howe, whom he was sure would be of service. Upon his release, Holmes consulted with Howe, who agreed to the plan in exchange for his own portion of the insurance money.

Pitezel moved to Philadelphia and opened a small patent shop under the name of B.F. Perry. Schechter indicates that Holmes was quite choosy about the location of the shop and selected a long-unoccupied building that was in such a condition because of its proximity to the city morgue.[11] Holmes anticipated that it might be some time before "Perry's" body was discovered, since he was a single man alone in a new city, and he wanted to be sure to stretch this period out as long as possible. The smell from the morgue, he concluded, would mean that the stench of a single rotting corpse would go unnoticed for longer than it would elsewhere. The longer the body remained undiscovered, the likelier it would be that decay would be advanced enough for a misidentification to be accepted. It should be noted that, although Schechter makes it a point to show the lengths to which Holmes would go in order to hide a dead body, he does not follow this reasoning back to Chicago to explain how Holmes could have hidden the smell of so many other victims in such an enclosed space without the benefit of a morgue nearby to explain the odor.

Unfortunately for Pitezel, Holmes never intended to procure a substitute cadaver, since that would mean he would have had to split the $10,000 with Pitezel. And, unfortunately for Holmes, Pitezel's business actually attracted a customer.

Eugene Smith visited B.F. Perry's patent office and had multiple dealings with Pitezel before the Monday when he arrived to find the front door unlocked but Perry absent. Since he had left the device he wished to patent with Perry and had been assured that Perry had found multiple possible sources of funding, Smith was persistent and returned the following day. This time, not content to wait downstairs, he investigated the second floor and found an odd sight: Perry, quite dead and burned a bit about the face, but laying almost peacefully on his back. His pipe was nearby, looking as though it may have been placed as an afterthought since it was unburned and therefore unlikely to have been the cause of an explosion that had killed Perry, despite the presence of various other chemicals in the room. Smith alerted the proper authorities and the process of identifying the body began.

Back in St. Louis, in her small apartment with her sick baby, Carrie Pitezel read the report of B.F. Perry's death in the paper and recognized her husband's pseudonym. Ill herself, with no money for a doctor and little enough to keep her children fed, she was in a state when Holmes arrived, apparently to deliver the news before she could read it. Carrie had known of the insurance scam and Pitezel had reassured her that, even if she read about his death, it was untrue, but she was quickly becoming desperate. She had not wanted her husband to participate in the scam in the first place, no matter what the payoff, and neither the money nor a reunion with her husband would be immediately forthcoming. Pitezel would have to remain out of sight in order for the scam to work, and the thought of traveling in order to identify his body was just too much for her when she was as ill as the baby.

Holmes stepped in, first sending one of the other children for a physician and then offering Carrie money to tide her over. Since Carrie was not well enough to travel and she needed her oldest child, Dessie, to help her take care of the baby, it was decided that Alice Pitezel, age fourteen, would accompany lawyer Jeptha Howe to Pennsylvania to make the identification. In order to legitimize the process, although Holmes met Alice and Howe on the train, he arrived in Pennsylvania and at the insurance office separately, posing as a mere acquaintance of Pitezel's. Prior to heading to the graveyard for the disinterment of the body, all parties agreed upon identifying features of Benjamin Pitezel, including a warty growth on the back of his neck.

Reports of what happened at the grave site differ, although Alice was allowed to hold back until the body was already on display. There was some difficulty in finding the identifying marks, considering the state of the corpse and how long it had been since the body was buried, but Holmes, ever the resourceful physician, was apparently more than willing to use a knife on his deceased friend. Reports differ as to whether or not he personally removed the warty growth from Pitezel's neck, but all are in agreement that, to a certain extent—and with a notable amount of pleasure—Holmes dissected his friend's body.

With the testimony of Alice Pitezel and H.H. Holmes, the insurance company agreed that the deceased was indeed Benjamin F. Pitezel and, despite some reservations about the manner of his death, wrote out the check to be delivered to his grieving widow. It was a decision based more on public relations than on certain fact, since circumstances surrounding Pitezel's death were strange, with many facets unanswered, but the man had left behind five children who would need to eat. Holmes himself was paid for his train ticket and thanked for taking the time out of his busy schedule in order to attend and provide his services.

There was one other man at the gravesite that day. Eugene Smith, the carpenter who had sought Pitezel's help with a patent, thought that Holmes looked familiar. He could not, however, be certain that the man present for identification purposes was the same one he had seen meet with Pitezel shortly before his death, and so, rather than cause potential embarrassment, Smith held his tongue. It has been often lamented that, had he chosen to speak up instead, he could have prevented Holmes' victim count from rising higher, adding a measure of blame to a man who himself committed no crime.

Final Bids for Freedom

Holmes' next move is one that has been highly publicized as a sign of his cunning based on his ability to manage such a thing, but also as a point of confusion as to whether or not he actually found himself in possession of a plan. Instead of sending Alice back to her mother, Holmes made the journey himself to meet Carrie and to relieve her of much of the insurance payment. Howe had already taken a large amount, and Holmes swindled the widow out of much of the rest, leaving her with $500 out of the original $10,000.[12] He then suggested that Carrie might like to visit her parents for a while, although perhaps not with the burden of all of her children. Holmes suggested that she send Nellie and

Howard, the other middle children, back with him where they could meet up with Alice under the care of a nice woman Holmes knew who would see to their schooling.

Carrie, operating under the assumption that Holmes would eventually reunite her with her husband and that Pitezel wholeheartedly agreed with the plans for the children and their education, surrendered two more children to Holmes' care. Those who required Holmes' attention were thus divided into three groups: Alice, Nellie, and Howard; Carrie and her two remaining children; and his third wife, Georgiana Yoke, who believed herself to legally be Mrs. Howard. Holmes proceeded to move these three groups independently of each other throughout the Midwest and even into Canada, at times boarding one group mere blocks from another, all without letting the family know where the others were. Georgiana remained entirely unaware of the Pitezels even as Holmes moved her from boarding house to hotel, generally with little notice and always with an excuse to leave her alone for a while in this new city.

Holmes continually fed Carrie lies that he had searched for a secluded house in which she could be reunited with her husband but that Pitezel had to leave the city quickly when the police seemed to have caught on. He also informed her that the children could not be told of their father's continued existence since, being so young, they would be apt to tell the truth to someone and the news would get back to the insurance company. Alice, Nellie, and Howard, he assured Carrie, were all in the care of a woman who may or may not have been his cousin, Miss Minnie Williams. They were being well provided for, since he and Miss Williams had bought them some nice new winter clothes, which they needed since the weather was growing colder.

Holmes had been searching out isolated houses in the various cities he occupied with his assorted captives, but not for a family reunion. More than one neighbor recalled being intrigued by the fact that a man moved in nearby with little furniture other than a stove that was really too large for the given house. Landlords were befuddled when the man who had rented a house for his sister and her children suddenly packed up and left after a handful of days even though he had paid a month in advance. The truth was that most of the houses were not isolated enough for Holmes' purpose.

In the meantime, as Holmes maneuvered seven other people through such cities as Indianapolis, Detroit, and Toronto in such a way that they all conformed to his plan, Marion Hedgepeth came to the conclusion that he was waiting for his $500 in vain. The outlaw had seen the newspaper headlines in his jail cell and was a bit surprised that Holmes had indeed gone ahead with the con, making full use of the lawyer that Hedgepeth had suggested. Now, though, as time passed, Hedgepeth decided that he could not remain silent. He penned a letter to the St. Louis chief of police outlining the plan as Holmes had presented it to him, making the argument that, although identified as Benjamin Pitezel, the body that had been examined was, in fact, an anonymous cadaver.

Although the insurance representatives were highly resistant to the idea that they had been swindled, the Pinkerton National Detective Agency was given the task of finding Holmes so that he might be arrested. He was taken into custody in Boston on November 17, 1894, although he was not alone—Carrie Pitezel was also arrested for her assumed role in the insurance fraud. Although she still had two of her children with her, her three middle children—and their caretaker, Miss Williams—were nowhere to be found. It would be almost a year before Detective Frank Geyer tracked down their bodies: Alice and Nellie were buried in the basement of a house in Toronto, and Howard was discovered behind the bricks of a chimney in a house outside of Indianapolis. There had been no Miss Williams, and the children had often been left alone under the care of the owners of boarding houses or hotels until Holmes separated them, taking Howard first because the ten-year-old boy was acting out and causing scenes, unable to cope with being cooped up for so long in strange places without his mother.

It was after the discovery of the girls' bodies in Toronto that attention turned back to Chicago and Holmes' "Castle" was scrutinized—and, in resulting headlines, turned into the Murder Castle. Newspapers kept audiences enthralled with daily updates of the findings on Sixty-third Street, blaring gruesome headlines and, later, publishing smaller retractions. H.H. Holmes was making headlines, and he knew it.

Holmes had given his first confession on November 19, 1894, after his arrest in Boston. In this account, which will be discussed more in depth in the next chapter, Holmes argues that the children had been taken abroad by their father who was, of course, still alive. This first confession was followed by "Confession No. 2"[13] in December, during which Holmes admitted that Pitezel was in fact dead by suicide, and that Holmes had moved and mutilated his friend's body in order to make the death appear to be an accident so that Carrie would receive the full amount of the insurance payment.

Holmes spoke again to police after the bodies of Alice and Nellie were found, although any hope they had of catching him off guard with this discovery was dashed. Reporters had already swarmed the jail and Holmes had sent out for the paper, which he was allowed to read. Because Detective Geyer's search had been making daily headlines in Toronto, Holmes knew exactly why the police would be interested in anything he had to say. He also knew what was already being said about him in public venues, thanks to the newspapers, and, before his trial in October 1895, he published his autobiography, marketed as *Holmes' Own Story*. This "confession," discussed at length in chapters three through seven, includes his so-called prison diary and was, indeed, an attempt to sway public opinion before his trial. *Holmes' Own Story* is often referenced quickly by authors addressing him and then dismissed as nothing more than fanciful propaganda, likely heavily edited, but it was still a document written purely to sell, and provides a unique insight into the sort of murder narrative expected to fly into the hands of the reading public in the last decade of the nineteenth century.

At his trial Holmes continued to show a flair for the dramatic, dismissing his lawyers and acting as his own attorney nearly a century before Ted Bundy called attention to himself by doing the same thing. Bundy had been a law student and thus carried his own defense with the support of his legal team, but Holmes appeared to not be up to the task. Although Holmes astounded reporters and even Judge Arnold in the initial days he was left to his own defense, requesting special accommodations so that he might do research in his cell, his energy suddenly flagged and the two lawyers—who had not so much been dismissed as begged to be allowed to leave—re-entered the courtroom as though nothing had happened.

In spite of the fact that he put questions to witnesses, at times eloquently and at times nonsensically, Holmes did not himself take the stand and thus did not offer any comments or explanations during his trial. Instead, his lawyers first moved that the judge should advise the jury to vote for acquittal, based on the lack of evidence provided by the state and then, when Judge Arnold refused, they chose to rest their defense, claiming that the prosecution had indeed not proven its case. The prosecution agreed to allow one of Holmes' lawyers the chance to give the final closing argument and then, before dismissing the jury, Judge Arnold instructed them on what, exactly was meant by "circumstantial evidence"[14] since it was true that the prosecution's case was built upon it.

In a matter of hours—with enough time to have dinner—the jury returned and declared that Holmes was guilty of the murder of Benjamin Pitezel.

It was the only murder for which Holmes would stand trial, and the only one mentioned in the courtroom. The prosecution had wanted to bring in evidence surrounding the deaths of Alice, Nellie, and Howard—even having brought along the boy's skull and teeth to display as evidence—but Judge Arnold refused, since being guilty of one crime was in no way proof of guilt in another. Speculation was rampant in the newspapers, but there was no way of proving exactly how many murders Holmes had committed.

Then, in April 1896, only a few weeks before his execution, Holmes published once again. The *Philadelphia Enquirer* advertised its exclusive two days before printing Holmes' self-proclaimed confession. This time, instead of a long and meandering argument against his guilt, he carefully laid out the twenty-seven victims who perished by his hand, ending with the four members of the Pitezel family (and lamenting that he could not add Carrie and her two remaining children to that total, as well). It seemed that Holmes had undergone a change of heart or conscience and wished to come clean before he hanged, although this version of events, too, was brought into doubt in less than a week. A number of the people Holmes had confessed to murdering, most of them for money or to make sure they kept his secrets, in fact turned up alive and well.

Holmes was hanged on May 7, 1896, although his last words were yet another admission of guilt. This time his admitted body count was only two unnamed women who had died "as the result of criminal operations"[15] he had performed on them. Holmes went so far as to admonish his audience about the fact that the real murderer of Benjamin Pitezel—

not to mention the children—was still free and in need of being brought to justice. This was Holmes' final word on the subject, although it is doubted as much as any other "confession" he penned or spoke during his lifetime.

After being pronounced dead, Holmes' body was cut down and placed into a special coffin. His lawyers had apparently received numerous offers, most of them including payment, for the privilege of dissecting the body of the greatest criminal in history, and Holmes was adamant that his corpse would not be carved up for pleasure or for science. As further protection against graverobbers—a practice with which he was suggested to be intimately familiar—his coffin was half-filled with cement before his body was placed inside, and more cement was poured over top. This extra-large coffin was buried in a double plot and remained undisturbed until the History Channel's series *American Ripper*[16] in which Holmes' body was indeed disinterred, not for dissection but for positive identification. Despite the number of times he had managed to swindle others during his lifetime, Holmes had not managed to escape death.

America's First Serial Killer Narrative

Many authors have suggested that the fact of Holmes' death is what sets him apart from Jack the Ripper, who was never caught and has not yet left public fascination. Aside from surveys of serial killers that tend to list various historical figures before getting to what Peter Vronsky calls the "Golden Age" of serial killers[17] in the latter half of the twentieth century, Holmes remains a sort of footnote or afterthought. True, he might be billed as America's first serial killer, but those who followed him have left him far in their wake. Jack the Ripper has only gained books as time passed the century mark of his murders as authors attempt to ferret out the true identity of the man who, at the high end of estimation, murdered the lowest reasonable number of victims attributed to Holmes. The Ripper, generally thought to have murdered five prostitutes in the fall of 1888, has reached mythological status far above and beyond Holmes, his Murder Castle, and his schemes to kill an entire family.

The question of why certain criminals fascinate the public and others are largely ignored has long plagued those who write, and write about, true crime. What is it that ensures a newspaper or a book will sell? Why will people remember the name Ted Bundy but not recall who Gary Ridgway is, even though the men were born in the same decade, active in the same general region of the country, and killed more than thirty women each? Perhaps it is a question of victimology—Bundy preferred white college co-eds while the Green River Killer murdered prostitutes of various races—or simply the fact that Ridgway came after Bundy and thus there was nothing left to learn. But, if anything, it seems that Holmes' victims—from various classes, many of them apparently beautiful young women—and his timing as "America's first" would propel him toward center stage.

The main issue with Holmes, as Adam Selzer relates, is that the myth has far surpassed the man. His *True History of the White City Devil* set out to separate those long-held myths from provable fact and, indeed, to disprove much of what Erik Larson had published more than a decade earlier. The dismantling of a legend makes for far less entertaining reading than the myth, especially a myth that had been updated in the late twentieth century to make its central figure align more exactly with growing bodies of scholarship surrounding serial killers. But the myth of H.H. Holmes began while the man himself was still alive—and cunning enough to take full advantage of it.

In his lifetime Holmes offered multiple verbal and written accounts of his life and his crimes, but hardly any elements agreed from one telling to another. Holmes is clearly an unreliable narrator and researchers have to fall back on other means of gaining information about his life and his crimes, although that, too, is not without its pitfalls. The newspapers, like Holmes himself, were writing in order to sell and not concerned first and foremost with accuracy. Thus, information that Holmes imparted, from his spoken confessions to *Holmes' Own Story* in 1895 and his printed confession to twenty-seven murders in 1896, are briefly mentioned and quickly dismissed.

While they are unlikely to reveal any factual information regarding Holmes' life, a close rhetorical reading of his confessions can take full advantage of his "first" status. Whether or not the information Holmes disclosed was true, his selection of which elements to reveal and which to hold back, as well as his mode of communication, all took place with a purpose: to convince others of his innocence at first, prior to his trial, and then, after being found guilty and shortly before his execution, to confess his guilt in a paper that paid him for the story. Holmes found himself in a situation where he had to present himself verbally in such a way to law enforcement—and then chose to communicate to a much larger audience through his writing—as to convey his innocence in spite of the information that was continually discovered and published that would indicate the contrary. Holmes lacked both a known narrative of deviance that was already shown to be accepted by and acceptable to his contemporaries, as well as specific vocabulary surrounding his identity and actions.

Holmes' autobiography and confessions are interesting and worth examining not because they reveal the truth, but because of what they reveal about attempts of America's first serial killer to establish his own narrative in a way that would resonate with his audience and respond to their expectations when they had never seen anything like him before.

Two

The Start of a Legend

From the time Holmes arrived in Chicago, there has been evidence that he did not hesitate to change his story in a way that would benefit him. Through lies, half-truths, and outright reversals of his past and his identity, he received a job, numerous items for his newly purchased building, labor to construct his Castle, and even training on how to use the glass-bending oven that he was suspected of turning into a crematorium. There are numerous accounts that mirror the abovementioned case of the large safe that Holmes installed and then refused to pay for, some traceable to lawsuits at the time and others that surfaced after Holmes' arrest, but in none of these cases were Holmes' words themselves transcribed. He may have signed a promissory note—and he may have used any number of names—but there was no stenographer present either during the agreement or the later arguments in order to record what, exactly, was said.

Holmes made full use of the oral nature of these statements, both in Chicago and during the months in which he maneuvered members of the Pitezel family and his own wife from city to city, all without knowing of the others' presence. Georgiana had already been shown to be obedient and acquiescent to her husband's apparently random itinerant lifestyle, and accepted his reasons for having to leave her alone in her room. She had already accepted a rather convoluted explanation that, in order to receive the inheritance his uncle had left him, Holmes had to legally change his name to Howard, so being moved from city to city as her husband tended to business deals was apparently completely understandable.

It cannot be corroborated that Holmes kept the children under control—for the most part, at least—with promises that they would see either their mother or father after this next train ride, but this explanation is one of his more reasonable ones. He clearly held enough power over them to keep them indoors unless he came to take them out, since there were multiple accounts of people reporting that the children did just that. Those who delivered the children their meals often found them sad and assumed, since they were of course not given an entire explanation for the situation, that they were orphans, missing their mother. Even Howard, who eventually became an annoyance and perhaps a risk for Holmes, followed instructions at the beginning, in spite of the fact that Holmes' orders meant being cooped up and unable to release the energy usually found in ten-year-old boys.

Carrie Pitezel did not hold Holmes in the same respect as Georgiana did, but she still followed Holmes' orders readily enough. Although she later confessed to having tried to stand up for herself, demanding to know where her husband was and what he was doing, she was too terrified of the insurance scam being found out by the police to be too much of a threat to Holmes' plot. After all, Holmes had three of her children and was the only one who knew where her husband was. Without Pitezel she was a widow, left to care for their children on her own, and in her grief and shock she had already lost three of them. Holmes' earlier dealings also meant that, instead of being set for life as the scheme was meant to have concluded, Carrie ended up with only $500 after Holmes and Howe had taken their share, and thus she found herself unable to care for Dessie and the baby for long, even on that sum. The train rides and hotels were clearly taking their toll so that, by the time she and Holmes were taken into custody, Carrie was quickly convinced to tell her story and confessed to the insurance scam and all she had endured since.

Most of what Holmes had said in the course of his various scams and schemes was not written down but, following his capture on November 17, 1894, his words began being recorded not for posterity, but as evidence to be used against him.

The First Confession

On November 19, 1894—two days after his arrest—Holmes was interviewed by the Deputy Superintendent of Police, Massachusetts,

O.M. Hanscom, and John Cornish, the Superintendent of the Pinkerton Detective Agency of Boston, Massachusetts. Although Holmes had officially been arrested for the charge of being a horse thief in Texas, he quickly surmised that this was not, in fact, the reason he had been so detained. The questions and answers recorded in his first confession and presented as part of Frank Geyer's publication *The Holmes-Pitezel Case: A History of the Greatest Crime of the Century and of the Search for the Missing Pitezel Children* (1896) show that Holmes was well aware that their main concern was insurance fraud. This interview covers thirty-eight pages in Geyer's account and reveals the foundations of Holmes' initial narrative of his innocence.

At this point the facts could be laid out thusly: there had been a body found in B.F. Perry's patent office, although the manner of death and the identity of that body were both under question. The insurance company had paid money to Carrie Pitezel under the assumption that "Perry" was her husband, it was indeed Pitezel's body, and the death was accidental. Carrie had two of her children with her in Boston, but the remaining members of the Pitezel family were nowhere to be found. They had been tracked in their various movements through Indiana, Michigan, and Canada, but there was no obvious explanation for these odd moves.

At this point Holmes admitted to the insurance scam, relating it to his interviewers along the lines of the plan Hedgepeth had passed on to the chief of police in St. Louis. Holmes and Pitezel had plotted together, with Pitezel setting up shop in Philadelphia and Holmes procuring the body from a connection in New York. Holmes admitted that he would "rather not answer"[1] the question of that contact's identity, as though there might be honor among resurrection men. Suffice it to say that no, the body found on the second floor above the patent shop was not actually Benjamin F. Pitezel's. Pitezel himself was abroad somewhere with the three children not currently with their mother, and he was meant to remain in hiding so that the insurance scam would not be discovered. Holmes, though, being faced with murder charges, declared he was more than willing to have Pitezel found and identified, despite the loss of money. "While I am bad enough on smallest things," he told them with apparent sincerity, arguing against the murder accusations, "I am not guilty of that."[2] Enough other aspects of Holmes' personality had already come forward so that he could not claim complete innocence in every facet of his life, but at this point Holmes was still almost charming in his reputation as a swindler, nearly a figure worthy of respect for how much he had been able to procure for himself and how many people he had bamboozled.

Pitezel in this case was not one of these people. He and Holmes were unequal partners, and Holmes told the others "I acted under him."[3] The odd bouncing of the children and Mrs. Pitezel from place to place came about because Pitezel himself ordered it to be so. He desperately missed his wife and children and wanted to see them. Carrie wished to see her husband, as well, but this had to be arranged so that none of the children were aware that their father was still alive, since they could not reliably keep such a secret. If it were to be revealed that Pitezel had not died, then the scam would be off and the Pitezel family would not have inherited the money they desperately needed.

Unfortunately the men kept being foiled in their attempts to reunite the married couple, thanks to the observant policemen in any town they had chosen for the meeting. Carrie was continually told that she would see her husband soon, perhaps even that very night, only to have her hopes spoiled and be forced to face another move. All communication from Pitezel to his wife had to pass through Holmes so as not to leave a trail. Aside from the ever-so-alert police force that seemed to shadow them everywhere, Pitezel was also undone by his drinking: in spite of his plan, and against the wishes of both Holmes and Carrie, a drunk Pitezel revealed himself to the children before too much time had passed. Since he had promised Carrie that he would do no such thing, the only sensible course of action, according to what Holmes and Pitezel had then discussed, was to make sure that Carrie did not see either her three middle children or Pitezel, since all would be revealed.

During the interview Holmes agreed when they asked him if Carrie was "rather an illiterate, plain person"[4] and also insisted that Carrie not only knew about the scheme to defraud the insurance company, but wholeheartedly supported it. She had sent her children on with Holmes of her own free will, and she knew that she could not reveal any element of the plot for fear of losing the insurance money. Carrie was therefore a full participant in the fraud, and it was right that she had also been arrested. This was the opinion not only of Holmes but of the police, as well, who held Carrie for months until deciding that, whatever she had known, she was as much a victim of Holmes as her children had been.

Holmes was grilled further about his movements since, in this version of the tale, he was manipulating four groups of people: his own wife, whom he insisted had no idea what was happening with either the Pitezel family or the insurance scam; Pitezel himself, who had to remain hidden so he would not be recognized; Alice, Nellie, and Howard; and Mrs. Pitezel and her eldest and youngest children. The assumption was that, with all his running about and locating various rooms at multiple establishments in each city, there had to be at least *one* person who had seen him with Pitezel and could offer corroboration that the man was still alive. His interviewers were looking not only for evidence of Pitezel's continued living, but also attempting to form a proper timeline of all the events so that they might understand what, exactly, had been happening all this time. Holmes, coming across as a bit peevish even in the simple written texts, insists that he could place all events in order if he could only speak with his wife, Georgiana. He even shows confusion in his answers with immediate corrections, such as "Yes, sir. No, it was the other hotel"[5] without apparent pause or any sort of extra prompting from his interviewers.

It seems that Holmes wanted to plant the idea that he had been moving around so frequently that yes, it was indeed difficult to keep track of where and when they had all been present in various parts of which city. If many of these moves and locations were prompted by Pitezel, then it would make sense that Holmes himself might not be able to construct a proper timeline, since the master plan was not his and his alone. By mentioning his wife he was reminding his interviewers that there was a poor woman out there dependent on him for her own continued welfare—a woman who, along with being of a higher class than Carrie Pitezel, had no role in any of this and thus was being tortured needlessly by his imprisonment.

It is also possible that, at this juncture, Holmes had not had enough time to fully construct an explanation for what had happened that would follow his apparently erratic decisions while also proving his own innocence. He was hammered with questions from his two interviewers, unable to fully control the direction or speed of the conversation. In this instance, Holmes was clearly not the one in command. He had to endure the pacing, topic, and requests for details from two live audience members whose intent was completely at odds with his own: Holmes argued for his own innocence, while Hanscom and Cornish sought to catch him in a lie and force him to incriminate himself.

Holmes walked the line between appearing to reveal pieces of information, such as the fact that he had dressed Nellie as a boy so that they would attract less attention[6] when traveling together—a move that would be imitated by Dr. Hawley Harvey Crippen's mistress, Ethel Neave, during their trans–Atlantic crossing in 1910—and withholding information, such as the previously mentioned contact in New York. Yet even Holmes' deliberately withheld information might be offered up if the threat to his own skin became too great, since Holmes indicated that he might, in time, reveal the name of this contact and assured his interviewers that he no longer cared if Pitezel were discovered and joined him to face consequences resulting from their scam. The purposefully withheld information, it seemed, did not need to remain permanently unsaid. Given the right conditions—say, the threat of the noose—Holmes would be willing to reveal all.

There is more verbal floundering surrounding the moments in which Holmes seems to be honestly confused and unsure of what to say. When he is asked to pin down a date and location at which others could confirm his presence, or the fact that he was with Pitezel, he brushes them off irritably and insists that he would need to speak to his wife in order to better remember the timeline. If his interviewers were given concrete information, then they might send others from the Pinkerton Detective Agency to check for corroborating information, which Holmes knew they would not find. No one would recall seeing him with Pitezel, and anyone who remembered the children would also likely remember their emotional states and, as the weeks wore on, that they had seen the two girls, yes, but not their brother.

In spite of the interference from his interviewers, Holmes still did manage to emphasize the salient points of his story: Pitezel was still alive, the children were with him, and much of the plan had been enacted based on Pitezel's orders. Carrie was a fully participating member of their little scheme, and if Holmes did not offer much as to why Pitezel would have taken three of their children and gone into hiding without her, well, this was the same man who had decided he did not want to face her once he had slipped up and revealed himself to Alice, Nellie, and Howard. Clearly the Pitezels did not inhabit a perfect marriage, although Carrie was enough of a dutiful wife to support her husband in enacting the insurance scam. Once again, however, and most important, Pitezel was still very much alive.

Geyer himself notes that this first interview was very much concerned with the location of Benjamin Pitezel at, perhaps, the exclusion of other questions that would soon come to light as being of greater importance. It was suggested that the absent Pitezel children were with their father, wherever he happened to be—London, perhaps, or South America, depending on when Holmes and Pitezel had been making plans—but the interview ended still focused on their father. It was true that Holmes stood accused either of desecrating a corpse provided by that contact in New York, or perhaps even of killing Pitezel, but surely he would have done nothing to harm the children. "That they had been murdered," Geyer concludes somberly, "was not yet dreamed of"[7]—and it would be months before suspicions truly set in.

Confession No. 2

Although he remained in jail, Holmes was not out of contact with the outside world. He had been moved to Philadelphia after a preliminary hearing in Boston and sat in Moyamensing Prison, an experience he later related in his prison diary appendix to *Holmes' Own Story*, discussed here in chapters three through seven. Although prisoners were limited in the number of letters they might receive each day, Holmes was able to read the newspaper and keep abreast of what was happening and what was being printed—including how newspaper readers were experiencing his own case. He was able to follow along with popular opinion and reports on what the police might pursue as their next move, and it was a worrisome one: disinterring the body of "B.F. Perry" for a second time in order to determine with more reliable witnesses whether or not the dead man was in fact Benjamin Pitezel.

A fully identified Pitezel would mean that Holmes was clearly lying in his first confession, and thus he called for the Superintendent of Police of the Department of Public Safety of Philadelphia on December 27,

1894, to admit that he had previously told lies. He then dictated a new statement to a stenographer which has come to be called Confession No. 2. This is a much shorter statement, stretching to just under seven pages in Geyer's book, although this time Holmes was allowed to speak without interruption. By admitting to the fact that the dead man discovered above the patent shop was indeed Pitezel, Holmes had to reconstruct his story so that the inarguable elements—the strange movements of various people from hotel to boarding house and the current absence of Alice, Nellie, and Howard, for example—would still be explained in a way that led to his innocence.

Although Pitezel was indeed dead, Holmes' second confession was not that he killed the man. Instead, Holmes, Pitezel, and Carrie had once again all agreed to the plot to scam the insurance company, and of course Holmes had related this idea to Marion Hedgepeth while they were in jail. Because Hedgepeth had written his own letter, this, like the children's absence, was another inarguable occurrence that had to find its place in his new tale. With Pitezel in Philadelphia, financed by money Holmes obtained from Miss Minnie Williams,[8] they were all set to enact the plan as Holmes had previously related it: by substituting a cadaver for Pitezel.

Once again it was Pitezel's drinking that led to the downfall of this plan. Not only did Pitezel need to keep borrowing money from Holmes to tide himself over, but he also fell into periods of despair. Holmes adds in the detail that Pitezel received a telegram informing him that his baby was sick—and, presumably, that Carrie did not have the funds to provide for a doctor's care—and the two men made plans to be sure that the patent shop would be looked after while Pitezel was away. Holmes indicates that travel arrangements were made, but he refused to give Pitezel any more money, considering how quickly the rest of it had gone. There was a last-minute change in which Holmes should be the one to return to Chicago, presumably to procure the body for the scam, and that discussion was the last time Holmes saw Pitezel alive.

The next morning Holmes did not find his friend until after he had discovered first a note in cipher and then a longer letter hidden in the cupboard that indicated Pitezel had committed suicide. When Holmes ran up to the third floor, above Pitezel's living quarters, the small room was apparently so filled with chloroform fumes that Holmes had to wait for it to air out before he could enter. His next actions are illogical, but once again had to conform to the facts as they had already been laid out: instead of simply leaving Pitezel where he was, Holmes moved not only the body but also the furniture from the third floor down to the second, and made sure to destroy the suicide note—which, of course, no one had seen but him. Because there would be no insurance payout for a suicide, and because Pitezel had left behind his wife and five children, the youngest one so ill that Carrie had paid for a telegram to inform him of it, Holmes set about using chemicals Pitezel had obtained as stage dressing for his patent shop to make it appear that he had died during an accidental explosion. Part of this process involved burning some of Pitezel's body, which Holmes reports frankly. There is no indication that he had any strong reaction to either finding Pitizel dead or to mutilating his corpse.

Once he had Pitezel's body and belongings arranged to his satisfaction, Holmes left the patent office, apparently ensuring the front door was slightly ajar to encourage someone to find his friend before too much longer. The lack of impact the entire situation had on him is also evident in that he reports returning to where he was staying with Georgiana and, because she was not feeling well, Holmes sensibly spent the evening packing so that they would be able to leave Philadelphia.

According to this confession, Holmes did not decide to work with the lawyer, Howe, until after he had seen a report in the paper concerning "Perry's" death. This is apparently meant to indicate a lack of premeditation for what happened next. When Holmes was able to talk to Howe, he let the lawyer think that the scam was still in place, and did not tell him that the dead body was, in fact, Pitezel. Howe had the presence of mind to suggest that there should be a delay before Carrie contacted him, lest she seem too eager to collect the insurance money.

At this point the narrative seems to break down. Holmes perhaps recalls that there was another inarguable fact that he had to acknowledge. Although his description indicated that the room where Pitezel died was full of chloroform, the autopsy revealed that there was also chloroform in Pitezel's stomach. Holmes gives a vague description of a setup involving a tube, a bottle, a cork, and a quill, all of which Pitezel presumably used to flow the chloroform into his stomach and cause his own death. Holmes adds that he took the tube with him, lest someone recall that no such item was found in the room where Pitezel's body was discovered. There is one last addendum in which, in response to a question that was put to him, Holmes insists that he did not give Pitezel chloroform. The question "Then who did?" goes unasked.

Although Holmes was allowed to speak this confession more freely, with the single question for clarification only coming at the end, it still lacks a solid narrative throughline that follows the proper chronology of the events. The confusion present while answering specific questions in his first confession still remains in this second confession, shown in how Holmes had to backtrack to the day of his discovery of Pitezel's body to tie up the loose ends of chloroform, and then to make sure he explained why there was no such tube found among Pitezel's belongings or in his mouth. His presentation of the information makes it seem as though he catches these omissions only on the fly and must then remember to fill in the details before his confession is over.

The disjointed, fragmented narrative calls up even more questions. With the order of events as Geyer presented them, this would not be the first time Holmes had spoken his entire confession. Geyer says that Holmes first called for the Superintendent of Police, and he must have already related the story once before the stenographer was called. What is not presented is the content of Holmes' conversation with the Superintendent, so we do not know if the Superintendent asked him questions, pointed out the gaps in his story, or guided him in any way. There are also no transcriptions of Holmes' previous dealings in Chicago and elsewhere, which might indicate whether this tactic of either attempting to avoid answering an undesired question or the practice of catching up all the loose ends in one fell swoop were common to Holmes and had perhaps worked for him before. Previously, of course, his audience had rarely been law enforcement officials questioning or listening to him in an official context. Perhaps the transcription we see is a poor method of transmitting Holmes' silver-tongued negotiations.

In spite of these possible shortcomings, Holmes did manage to change the course those law enforcement officials were taking against him. First, by shifting his story to indicate that Pitezel was really dead, Holmes put the plans to disinter the body once more on hold. He also took some of the pressure off of the young lawyer, Jeptha Howe, by declaring that yes, perhaps Howe had agreed to the scam when it involved a cadaver, but Howe was in no way aware that Pitezel was really dead. Carrie, too, had full knowledge of the scam and was a willing participant, but she, along with the children, had honestly thought Pitezel was still alive.

Second, the accusation that Holmes, Carrie, and Howe had scammed the insurance company by using a substitute body would now no longer work in court. If such a charge were to be leveled against them and the body proven to be Pitezel's, it would have to be dropped. Holmes remained in prison for months while various law enforcement and insurance officials attempted to verify this new version of the story, although now they were not looking for evidence that someone had seen Holmes with Pitezel during his strange travels that autumn. Now, among other aspects, they were attempting to verify that Pitezel had indeed committed suicide—and likely commenting ironically on what a pity it was that Holmes had destroyed the suicide note. Had he kept it, he could have proven his innocence, at least as far as murder.

Months passed, but there was no word from Pitezel, which led them to think that he was honestly dead, and no reports of the whereabouts of the children, which was much more distressing. Alice, Nellie, and Howard were supposedly in the care of Holmes' friend, Miss Minnie Williams, who likely had taken them abroad, perhaps to London. In May 1895 Holmes wrote a short, apparently helpful, letter to the district attorney suggesting that an advertisement be put in the *New York Herald* using a specific cipher in order to contact Miss Williams—who may have also been using the pseudonym of Adele Covelle or Geraldine Wanda[9]—to inform her that she must send a telegram at once so that this entire ordeal might be resolved.

It is suspicious Holmes first mentioned that the children were with Miss Williams in December 1894 and yet apparently did not inform anyone of how he was meant to remain in contact with her until the end of May 1895. Although Minnie was meant to be in hiding, she still had the children with her, and Holmes would need to be able to provide for them and reassure himself that all was well. Further, the name of Minnie Williams, connected with her sister Nannie, was associated with a number of rumors in Chicago, none of which pointed to the truth of Holmes' story. It was suspected that the Williams sisters were dead, and the fact that the only streets Holmes could name as the possible current address for Minnie in London did not exist was a further blow. The law was beginning to think that the only truthful element of Holmes' second confession was that the body found above the patent office was indeed Benjamin F. Pitezel.

In June of 1895 Holmes was put on trial for "having conspired to cheat the Insurance Company,"[10] a charge that would cover either of Holmes' confessions thus far. Even if his second confession were proven, Holmes had still already admitted to changing the scene of a suicide in order to make Pitezel's death appear accidental. Although Holmes entered the trial claiming innocence, on the second day he changed his plea to guilty, apparently under the assumption that, with time served, he would soon be on his merry way.

A Living Victim

Just as Holmes had been in jail for months, so had Carrie Pitezel. Dessie and the baby had been cared for by a women's group in Philadelphia, so the widow who did not know the whereabouts of three of her children had been left completely alone. She had also cooperated with the police, giving her first full confession in Boston. Despite the fact that her story was at times as unbelievable as Holmes' concoction—what mother would possibly send her children off with such a man?—legal and public opinion quickly centered on the feeling that Carrie had been conned by Holmes and was deserving of empathy, not judgment. Still, she remained behind bars until June 17, 1895, when she was finally allowed to see her remaining children again and to speak freely to the press.

In a rather grisly coincidence, it was on the day of her release that Holmes sent Carrie a letter he had written from jail. Holmes' missive begins by reminding her of the fact that he had done "all I could do for you and yours,"[11] fairly admonishing Carrie for allowing the police to convince her otherwise. He emphasizes how much he had done not only for Pitezel, but for his entire family, with a clear stress on how freely money flowed from Holmes' pockets to theirs. If Holmes cared for the Pitezel family this much, and was always willing to pass on what he could, then clearly he would not have murdered Pitezel, scammed Carrie out of her insurance money, and harmed the children.

He lays out his story once more, this time in writing. Pitezel, it seems, had already set out to kill himself with laudanum at an earlier date and, in contrast to his first confession, Holmes provides the location of the hotel and the name of the proprietor, in case Carrie should like to confirm this information. Holmes also points out, in gentle rebuke of his dead friend, that much of the money he gave to Pitezel was quickly drunk away. Pitezel's alcoholism was so much of a problem that Holmes believed he would reveal the scam himself, so Holmes decided to tell Pitezel that he wanted nothing more to do with the scam and thus it could not be completed, since Holmes would not supply the cadaver. Although Holmes' intention was purportedly to encourage Pitezel to stop drinking, Pitezel committed suicide that very night. Holmes, apparently out of guilt, decided to follow Pitezel's orders and enlist the help of Miss Williams to move the remaining Pitezels to Cincinnati, "on ac. of good schools."[12] Clearly Holmes was a good man and a good friend since he went far out of his way to assist the family in spite of their father's death—a death that, if fully and truthfully explained, would mean that they never would have received any insurance money.

Since more facts had come to light indicating that Howard had been separated from his sisters at some point before they arrived in Toronto—or rather, that Alice and Nellie arrived in Toronto and were not known to be with Howard the entire time they were there—Holmes used Miss Williams to explain the children's separation, as well. There is another rebuke, this time against Howard, who was said to need adult supervision at all times so he would not continually fight with his sisters. So that she could maintain order, Miss Williams took Howard with her when she moved away from Detroit, leaving Holmes to follow with the girls. The fact that Holmes mentions one of the children's notable quarrels had to do with their father's watch, and that he bought the children their own cheaper versions, is a theme that will recur later in *Holmes' Own Story*.

Even the idea that Howard was with Minnie Williams was not in fact a comfort, either to Carrie or to others who had heard it in detail, since Holmes had provided her with an unsettling backstory. According to him, Minnie was responsible for killing her sister, Nannie, and Holmes himself had helped her get rid of the body. The remaining Miss Williams was thus in hiding and would do her best to not be recognized by anyone, which made it all the more difficult to find her and prove that all three absent Pitezel children were thriving under her care. By the time Holmes penned this letter to Carrie, the newspaper ad, asking in cipher for Minnie Williams to contact him, had already been printed, although there had been no response. This new story of sororicide, then, is how Holmes explains this long silence from a kindhearted woman who would by no means wish to cause the children's mother undue worry.

Holmes also reassures Carrie of his own feelings toward the rest of her family, once again using money as proof. Concerning Pitezel himself, Holmes stresses that "he was worth too much to me for me to have killed him,"[13] perhaps indicating that the possible $10,000 gain—less Howe's fees and the money Carrie would receive—was laughable in comparison with Pitezel's life, even though it was a large sum for the day. Pitezel was such a good friend to Holmes that he could not measure his confidence and usefulness against money, and he seems shocked that Carrie, having been a witness to their friendship, would not have known this without having to be told. As for the children, Holmes reminds her that he bought them warmer clothes and even insists he can prove he bought underwear for Howard in Toronto. This is important because Howard himself could not be placed in Toronto and was assumed to be dead. If, though, Howard had been elsewhere with Miss Williams, then it would make perfect sense for Holmes to buy him some underthings and send them along, since the act of spending money on Howard would prove not only that Holmes cared for the boy, but that he was still alive.

The question of money comes up again near the end of this letter, although this time it is a more practical matter only belatedly tied to care. Although much of the insurance money was taken from Carrie, a large amount of it by Holmes himself, he insists this was because of debts her husband had owed, some of it to Miss Williams. Certainly Carrie would have wanted her husband to pay off those debts, especially to the person who was taking charge of their children. Holmes then attempts to appeal to his audience's emotions further when he assures Carrie that, as he has taken care of her family in the past—since apparently the alcoholic, suicidal Benjamin was unable to do so—he would naturally continue to care for them in the future. This was, of course, difficult considering his current position in jail, but Holmes assured her

Two. The Start of a Legend

that he could manage it somehow and give her not only money but also other possessions, such as letters from Alice and Pitezel's watch.

Although he must have known that others would indeed be reading this letter, in this instance Holmes' main audience was intimately tied up in the story he was telling. This letter was not a case of explaining one's actions to a stranger or even reporting on them in the context of a police interview. Holmes is not speaking about his friend, Benjamin Pitezel, a stranger to his audience, or about some theoretical children. This is Holmes writing to someone who has had interactions with him before, explaining about her own husband's death and the situation involving the mysterious absence of three of her own children, last known to be in his care. In the interview that she gave in Boston, Carrie could not even give the name of the woman Holmes said had her children, reporting, "I asked him the name and he simply told me who they were with, said she was a widow, a nice woman."[14] The fact that a mother would not only let someone like Holmes take her children, but could not name the woman who was caring for them, had at first been met with incredulity but now, six months into the quest for answers, changing public opinion meant that Carrie was treated with all manner of sympathy. At the time of her arrest she even admitted that she "could not find them if it was a case of life and death,"[15] and here, in his letter, Holmes comes close to stating the same thing. Indeed, the only reason he wishes Miss Williams to be found is to exonerate him from accusations of child murder.

This is not a letter in which Holmes can make up the details entirely out of his own imagination. He is writing to someone who has actually been involved in this entire incident, and, whether or not he was well acquainted with Carrie, Carrie must have heard about him through her husband. She certainly knew that Pitezel was seemingly always embarking on the next scheme for easy income, assisted by Holmes, and she had her own interactions with the man surrounding the collection of the insurance money. Carrie was dragged from place to place, told which trains to board, and where she should remain all but imprisoned indoors, but it is also important to note what she was not told at the time: Miss Williams' name.

There certainly needed to be someone looking after the children during their frantic weeks of travel, since Carrie did not think that the children knew Pitezel was alive and would herself not have been told Holmes' previous story, which put them in Pitezel's care. However, she was entirely reliant on Holmes as far as their itinerary and any word she received from her husband or her children—everything they would have told her passed through him. Although the letters the children wrote their mother and other family members were found later, Holmes had merely collected them instead of mailing them. All Carrie had was Holmes' word that he was passing on messages from her family members, and that someone—a stranger—was caring for her children.

As much as Holmes attempts to clear his name of any and all suspicion, including reporting Pitezel's death as a suicide and the children's absence due to their being in London with Miss Williams, Holmes does little in his letter to endear himself to Carrie—or indeed, anyone else who may have read it. His intent seems less to reassure her as to chide her for allowing herself to have her thoughts turned against him when he has clearly wanted nothing but the best for her family. If she has been convinced otherwise by the men who have come to interview her, then Holmes is largely disappointed in her—the way he was disappointed by Pitezel's alcoholism and Howard's inability to behave himself. If Carrie believes that Holmes has in any way harmed her children, this must be chalked up to a personal character weakness, since she has known Holmes for years. If she could only remember properly instead of listening to what everyone else has been saying, she would remember the truth instead of these horrible lies.

It seems as though Holmes thinks that, if Carrie accepts his letter as the truth, he might be released from jail. If she agreed that Pitezel would have committed suicide and then perhaps decided to set off for London in order to find her children herself, Holmes might emerge without a stain on either his soul or his record. Although the abundance of charm in his written words seems doubtful, he may have had a lot of prior experience with offering angry opponents alternative explanations for the current situation and then having any accusations against him dismissed, either out of bewilderment or because his challengers simply did not have the time and money to pursue the questions further.

Holmes even points out a bit self-righteously that, although he has written this letter to Carrie, he has not asked her any questions lest he be seen as taking advantage of her. He also offers to answer any she may have for him, promising that his responses would merely be those answers and nothing to concern lawyers or complicate matters further. He closes by informing her that "I, at least, hope your suffering here is nearly ended,"[16] as though she were surrounded by others who only wished to increase that suffering. Indeed, since she had first been imprisoned and then had her other children taken away, Carrie may well have felt that way. If Holmes had managed to catch her in the proper emotional moment, as he had when he managed to take away most of the insurance money, he may have once again emerged on top.

Unfortunately for Holmes, after the district attorney read this letter, he began the process of setting Detective Frank Geyer, a member of the Philadelphia Detective Bureau, on the case.

Another Change in the Story

Although many had tried before him to follow Holmes' odd journey and to track down what had happened to the Pitezel children, Geyer remained undaunted. He learned that, wherever Holmes went, he wished to rent a house and often told the story that it was for his newly widowed sister. After a long and trying day of having to repeat his mission to every agent he came across, Geyer decided to meet with reporters so that the story might be the leading headline. The following day Geyer was able to visit realtors at speed, since they were already aware of his quest and would be able to tell him immediately if someone answering Holmes' description had come by. The newspapers updated the story daily until they were able to report that two bodies had been found buried in a cellar of a house Holmes had rented the previous year.

After having discovered the girls relatively quickly, Geyer ran into trouble tracking down what had happened to Howard. He was aided by the letters the children had written to their mother, since they included the city and date at the top of each page.[17] With a lot of footwork and help from the local police, Geyer was able to identify one rented house after another, finally ending up in a suburb outside of Indianapolis where two boys, playing detective themselves, found the remains of little Howard. Carrie's children had all been located, and she had identified them—the girls by their teeth and hair, and Howard through his favorite toy.

Through it all, there were the headlines. Holmes, in his prison cell, was allowed to read the daily newspapers. On the day they announced that Nellie and Alice had been found, Holmes heard reporters shouting for him and sent out for the paper, which arrived before the police who wished to interview him. The press coverage meant that they could not catch Holmes off guard and he knew exactly why they had come.

Once again Holmes was confronted with new information that put his current narrative in peril. While previously he had been forced to make changes through the mere threat of a single body, he was now confronted with the fact of three of them, all of them children, and all of them discovered in the cities he had already confessed to recently occupying. His photograph had been shown around to many hotel and boarding house owners, and he had been identified at many locations, whether he was alone, or with some set of the children, or with Georgiana Yoke. Further aliases were uncovered in the guest books as more pieces of the puzzle were brought to light, and Holmes' letter to Carrie could not account for all of them.

Those newspapers that had alerted Holmes would continue to print his name and he would not be tried for Pitezel's murder for months yet. His story, with all its lurid details and wild rumors, would be repeated again and again, by strangers, in a format over which he had no control. The purpose of the journalists would be to sell their newspapers, and those papers had long since established the fact that murder would sell. If Holmes were accused of murdering children over and over again in the press, by the time he went on trial for the death of their father, public opinion would already be against him. Holmes needed to present the public with another side of the narrative—and indeed, another side of himself—if he hoped to achieve an acquittal. And, of course, there was the additional benefit of the money he could earn by penning and selling his own story.

PART II

Holmes' Own Story

As he sat in prison through most of 1895, awaiting his trial for the murder of Benjamin Pitezel, H.H. Holmes could not reasonably hope that his name and the charges against him would not be published. Six decades earlier journalists had discovered that murder made headlines and sold accounts in various formats, from newspapers to trial reports. Even the fact that Holmes was a physician and therefore presented the world with an upper-class defendant did not mean that he would be represented kindly in the headlines.

The first case in America to have garnered extensive media attention was that of the murder of prostitute Helen Jewett, who was found dead in a brothel early one morning in April 1836. The room was filled with smoke, as though someone had attempted to start a fire in order to disguise the fact that Jewett's head had been struck multiple times with a sharp object. Her client of the previous evening, nineteen-year-old Richard Robinson, was not in the room at the time, although he was quickly located and charged with her murder.

Reporters were allowed into the brothel to view the scene, including *New York Herald* editor James Gordon Bennet, who described Jewett's dead body as "a work of art perpetrated by her murderer."[1] Indeed, Jewett's beauty and her mysterious history—like Holmes, she had been living under an assumed name that was only one of many—intrigued the reading public. This past included multiple accounts of the fact that she was a fallen woman who had surrendered her dignity even before living as a prostitute in New York City, which tarnished her reputation. Since she was also older than Robinson, the fact that this was not his first night at the brothel as one of her clients was framed as a case of a predatory woman corrupting an otherwise upstanding young man who seemed to have everything else in life going for him, including his marriage.

Robinson was backed by numerous supporters at his trial, many of whom showed their allegiance by wearing the same style of cap the accused sported. Men and women alike called for his acquittal, which the jury awarded him after half an hour of deliberation—not because they believed he was truly innocent, but because the evidence, all of it circumstantial, came largely from prostitutes. A man who outclassed his victim, then, might earn acquittal even if the case had already been tried in the headlines before he ever entered a courtroom, and the evidence against Holmes was like that against Robinson: circumstantial.

Less encouraging, but also the subject of headlines, had been the case of the murder of Dr. George Parkman in 1849. Parkman had gone missing one afternoon after going about errands which included visiting John Webster, a lecturer at Harvard Medical College—in chemistry, whereas Holmes concentrated on anatomy—and requesting that Webster repay a debt. A dismembered and partially burned body was found in two locations at Webster's laboratory: a sewage tank and a furnace. Although the contents of the furnace had been burned, there remained a dental plate identified at Webster's trial as belonging to Parkman, recognizable because of the molds that had been made so recently of his unique jaw. Webster was found guilty and executed, although this verdict remains in doubt.

The headlines made by the Parkman-Webster case would have had more bearing on Holmes' perception of himself and his worries about how his own trial might play out, not so much concerning Benjamin Pitezel—although the two were known friends and associates, as were Parkman and Webster—but because of Howard Pitezel. Howard's remains had been found partially burned and identifiable through means of the teeth, much in the same way Parkman's dental work had been discovered. While Parkman was in the furnace in Webster's laboratory, Howard had been found in the basement of a house rented by Holmes. Webster had come forward to say that yes, Parkman had been by to see him on the afternoon he had disappeared, and Holmes, too, was known to have been with Howard before the boy went missing. Although the evidence condemning Webster was circumstantial, and although Webster was a well-educated member of the upper class, he still hanged.

Granted, Holmes was only set to go on trial for the murder of Benjamin Pitezel since the charges were brought against him in Philadelphia and Howard had been discovered outside of Indianapolis, but there were the newspapers to consider. Although a judge should—and, in this case, did—bar any mention of other possible crimes, since guilt in one does not point to guilt in another, Holmes could not enter the courtroom without bringing the children's names with him by association. Alice, especially, would have to be mentioned, since she was the other witness, along with Holmes himself, who identified the disinterred body as being that of her father. It was all very well that the gentlemen of the jury would swear that they had not been swayed by the headlines and that they would determine their verdict based solely on the evidence presented to them in the courtroom, but Holmes could not allow the journalists to take hold of his story and be the only voices presenting it.

Newspapers and their competing headlines with lurid facts on the front pages and smaller retractions within were not the only threat. Journalist Robert L. Corbitt rehashed those headlines into a small book in 1895, after the "Murder Castle" had burned to the ground but before Holmes published his own version of his story. Corbitt claimed to have in his possession various letters and documents taken from the Castle, and he also personally explored the building and looked on as the basement was excavated. As a man who held Holmes' own handwriting in his hands and had seen the evidence being unearthed with his own two eyes, Corbitt may have seemed to his readers to have been a fairly reliable source.

Corbitt did, however, make some mistakes in his reporting—or his copying of others' articles—and at least one such detail threatened Holmes' innocence greatly. Corbitt reported that "the charred remains of three of his victims, Annie [Nannie] Williams, Minnie Williams and Howard Pitezel, were discovered in the house which was built by the arch-criminal"[2] in Chicago. Although Corbitt struggles with Nannie's first name, the presence of her body in the cellar of the castle would likely be the least of Holmes' worries. Holmes had already admitted that she was dead, murdered by Minnie in a jealous rage, and if her body happened to be in the cellar instead of in a trunk at the bottom of Lake Michigan, at least Holmes himself had not killed her. Holmes' most recent confession, though, had placed the children safely with Minnie

Williams in London—a claim that fell apart once their bodies had been found. If Minnie happened to have been buried in his cellar the whole time, it would certainly cast doubts on his claims of innocence, although the most problematic of these declarations was, in fact, the passing on of misinformation.

Had Howard Pitezel's body been discovered buried in the basement of the Castle in Chicago, then the case against Holmes would have looked very grim indeed. It had not been—Howard had been found in Indiana in a house Holmes had merely rented instead of built—but the association of guilt had already been printed. Newspapers were happy to report any number of bodies discovered in and under Holmes' Castle, but the supposed identification of these three especially challenged Holmes' explanation of what had happened to the children, which in turn would complicate the questions about how Pitezel himself had died. Holmes may have been a swindler who was willing to use his silver tongue to get himself out of tricky situations, but this was different. This time the story was in print, once again taken out of Holmes' control, and so he countered by using his long hours in jail to write his own autobiography as a means of setting the record straight—or at least a means of muddying the waters before his murder trial began.

Three

Troubled Youth

When unnatural deaths occur, the question is not simply one of what has happened, but *why* it has happened. Part of this points to the audience's next question: how can I prevent this from happening to me? The same follows along with criminal acts, whether or not they involve murder: why was this person compelled to commit such crimes in the first place? What sort of person would it take in order to commit this crime?

In the earliest days of printed crime narratives in America, the answer to this was simple. These narratives took the form of Puritan execution sermons—although not all were preached and penned by Puritan ministers once the form caught hold[1]—which described the condemned criminal's actions as stemming from original sin. Since these explanations took place within religious communities, this was all the clarification that was needed. The sermon itself did not dwell on the final crime of the condemned man or woman, but rather extoled the praises of God's mercy and reassured the listeners that the person about to be executed had repented and indeed accepted his or her execution as the price for those actions. Oftentimes the condemned would speak, as well, supporting this very narrative and fully confessing.

The Puritan execution sermon was therefore comforting to those who listened to it or those who later purchased copies and read them. Such sermons clearly spelled out the consequences for sin while reminding audiences that they, too, have sinned. Oftentimes the sermons would list all manner of sins that the condemned had confessed, from the most mundane that audiences might recognize as undertaking in their own lives up to the crime for which death was the only consequence. Since everyone sinned, and since most prisoners confessed before the noose was placed around their necks, there was no need to delve deeper into questions of why this person—and this person specifically—had committed such a crime. The sort of person who would murder was not an Other but could in fact be any of the audience members themselves, since no one was immune to sin.

The execution sermon was the only written narrative of crime up until the 1730s, when secular tales began to appear alongside them. Changing populations and cultural norms meant that the execution sermon died out in the mid-nineteenth century and the answers to questions of guilt were no longer so simple. Whereas the subjects of execution sermons generally confessed to their crimes, the rise of the adversarial trial meant that guilt now became not only a matter of doubt, but one of debate. Newspapers with their daily updates and trial reports, printed after a verdict had been reached, presented audiences with two different sides of the same story and offered arguments to support either the subject's guilt or his innocence. Audiences of these texts shifted from being able to passively digest the information presented to them to finding themselves in the position of having to make such decisions for themselves. As illustrated by the uproar that followed the verdict in the Parkman-Webster case, these readers did not always agree with the decision reached by the jury. When a man protested his innocence, there was still a need to be able to see him as the type of person who *could* have committed such a crime, especially if there were no direct evidence pointing his way.

By the late summer of 1895, Holmes had found himself in a peculiar position: he had already confessed to crimes such as swindling the insurance company, but he also staunchly stood by his claim that he had not committed murder. Part of his narrative, then, had to reveal him as the sort of man who might stoop to certain levels when it came to procuring money, but would never kill a man, much less a child. The man Holmes chose to make himself through these written words would also never commit bigamy—although others, like Corbitt, reported that he had married different women under different names, in *Holmes' Own Story* only Georgiana Yoke is mentioned. His first two wives—and their children—are ignored completely. Holmes very carefully crafts himself for presentation to a wider audience, making careful selections over what to include and what to leave out.

Holmes' tale of the man he is now grows out of the boy he was before. He begins his autobiography with a brief introduction into his current situation, explaining that he is writing these pages against all advice from friends and lawyers both. He may, perhaps, even be taking his readers into his confidence and revealing aspects of himself and his life that he has not told anyone else—and that they certainly would not read about through the words of anyone else. There would be no one with a better insight into Holmes than Holmes himself.

He hastens to reassure his readers that "any deviations in my after life from the straight and narrow way of rectitude are not attributable to the want of a tender mother's prayers or a father's control,"[2] immediately removing his parents from the equation. Whatever went wrong in Holmes' life cannot, and shall not, be traced back to anything they did, or did not do, during his childhood or beyond. He seems to view his childhood in religious terms, although Holmes does not specifically state whether or not religion was a central tenant in the Mudgett household. His parents, however, remain as untouchable and as blameless as saints.

Later, when he returns home as an adult—surprising his parents, who had thought he had been dead for years—Holmes describes his childhood room as "too sacred a place to be entered now."[3] The "now" he references could indicate any number of incidents that have occurred since he left New Hampshire so many years ago: the swindles and cons he committed in Chicago; his arrest in St. Louis; or even his staging of Pitezel's suicide to seem as though it were an accidental death. Holmes appears to hold his younger self, his child self, as separate and distinctly apart from the man he has grown to be. The innocence of childhood is not quite the same as the innocence of the wrongly imprisoned man, although that boy still resides somewhere deep inside Holmes.

Despite the pathos Holmes attempts to invoke during the reunion with his parents or the observation that he fears receiving his daily mail, lest it bring him news of their deaths—likely of shame over his current predicament—Mr. and Mrs. Mudgett do not cast long shadows in his autobiography. The "control" he spoke of concerning his father centers around a single story, an event that Holmes refers to as his "first falsehood and … first imprisonment."[4] Since Holmes later reveals that he feared imprisonment so much more than any other possible consequence, his choice of this language concerning a childhood incident gives it distinct weight.

According to Holmes, his first falsehood—or perhaps merely the first time he was caught in a lie—came when he casually made it seem as though an entire herd of cows belonged to him, personally, as opposed to the few that belonged to his family. Instead of writing it off as a slip of the tongue that made his comment less accurate than it should have been—even as a boy, his tongue never slips—Holmes presents it as a prideful boast, and thus his father's extreme reaction was apparently justified. After demanding to know why his son had lied about the cows, Holmes' father locked him in his room in a situation that seems to recall so many fairy tale figures wrongfully imprisoned in a high tower. His friends came to find him when they noticed he was missing, and thus the embarrassment could not be contained within the family circle. He had to explain to his friends what had happened, which made the experience all the more shameful.

In spite of the impact this "imprisonment" apparently had upon the boy, the lesson his father meant to impose was apparently all too short-lived—or perhaps merely twisted. It was likely that the father meant to teach his son not to tell lies and, to a lesser extent, not to misrepresent himself boastfully. Considering the fact that Holmes grew to be a self-confessed swindler and con man, if not a murderer, it seems that this apparently strict punishment meted out by his father was nowhere near strict enough. The message the boy took from the incident and carried with him into adulthood was one concerning how his choice of words could be interpreted and how, at all times, he would need to be on his toes in order to counter any apparent misinterpretations. Granted, in the future Holmes would be in a better position to come to his own defense with supposed righteous indignation, since he would not be a son confronted by his father but a man in his own right, fully backed by his university education.

With such minimal interaction shown between the young Holmes and his parents, it is easy enough for readers to follow his conclusion that his parents played no role in his turning to crime, since they seem to play little role in his childhood at all. His mother is simply a woman who has prayed for him when he was a boy, and she is hardly mentioned during his surprisingly quick return home as an adult. Indeed, Holmes seems more moved by the house itself and the changed landscape around it than his parents, protesting that first their meeting and then their sudden parting were too "pathetic and hard to bear"[5] to describe to his audience of strangers, should he even want to try. His interaction with his father consists of settling up monetarily, considering how his father had thought him dead and had already dispensed with what would have been Holmes' inheritance—although, until this point, it seems that Holmes had been an only child and that there would have been no brothers or sisters to receive it in his absence. Holmes even gives his father money in a scene that, like most of the instances in which he describes dispensing cash, is meant to show emotion and affection through the transfer. Although Holmes had not seen his parents in so long that they thought he must have died, he still means to show that he obviously cares for them and induce in his reader some sympathy for them, with their shortly-returned son so wrongly imprisoned and accused of such a heinous act as murder.

Holmes' brief representation of his family life runs counter to the serial killer narrative established nearly a century later. According to the FBI—and thus to many of the serial killers whose biographies line the shelves under "true crime"—the serial killer is most likely to have had an absent father, whether emotionally or physically, and a controlling, abusive mother. Indeed, according to the information gathered and then disseminated in the twentieth century, the seeds of a serial killer are planted in childhood in such a way that allows his parents to be blamed for either absence or an abusive presence. At times parents of such killers are allowed to throw up their hands and declare that they simply did not know what to do with their wayward sons, and some of them—Ted Bundy's mother and Jeffrey Dahmer's father, for example— are treated kindly by the press and allowed to be seen from a point of empathy. Although much is made over the fact that Bundy apparently did not begin killing until he found his birth certificate and realized that his father's name was left blank, Louise Bundy seemingly cannot be blamed for the fact that her own parents at first chose to raise Ted as their son and her own brother in order to cover up the fact that she had given birth out of wedlock. The pressures of the time period, as well as those of her parents, allow Louise to avoid accusations of blame even when it is acknowledged that perhaps this false family tree—and its abrupt dissolution when Louise took her son and left her parents' home—did indeed play a role in Bundy's development. Bundy, like Holmes, protested that it was nothing that Louise or his stepfather did, or had not done, that had led him to the electric chair.

But this granting of clemency when it comes to the role of the parents is rare. When it comes to the creation of the serial killer, the question of nature versus nurture leads to many complicated debates. If a man is a serial killer from birth, then there is nothing that his parents can do to prevent him from his slew of murders—although, on the opposite side of the coin, even terrible parents would not be able to turn their son into a serial killer if the condition is entirely genetic. If, on the other hand, serial killers are made instead of born, then the presence or absence of the parents plays a large role in setting up the child for his adult actions. Holmes begins with the insistence that his parents had nothing to do with the negative aspects of his adult character and thus removes the option that they caused his current predicament through either action or inaction.

Although the information is brief, Holmes further offers a reversal of the twentieth-century serial killer narrative in that it is his mother who seems to be passive, merely praying for him as a boy and weeping over his return as a man, while his father is, at least in one instance, the stern disciplinarian. This falls perhaps more in line with gendered expectations of the mid to late nineteenth century and allows Holmes to represent his parents as being "good" parents. He does not—and perhaps cannot—ignore them completely, as he chooses to do with people or events from his past that will not serve his overall narrative or will strike a blow against the person he wishes to present himself to be. Holmes finds his parents helpful as a tool to remind his audience of his own basic humanity since, however much he may be suffering from being wrongfully imprisoned, his parents—who themselves have done nothing wrong—must be suffering more.

Gruesome Boyhood Highlights

If nothing Holmes' parents did can be seen as the cause for his wayward path, then another explanation must be provided. Were Holmes to attempt to argue that his boyhood was like every other and there were no possible seeds of his current deviance, he would falter with the most basic question of the crime narrative: why did this happen? Contemporary language lacked not only the term "serial killer" but much of the discourse surrounding psychopathy that is generally used to discuss Holmes in more recent retellings, the same way that the twenty-first-century serial killer narrative is often applied to flesh out the gaps in Holmes' story. Holmes provides some of his own insights by relating three events—two of which are often mentioned in retellings of his biography, although they cannot be proven to have happened.

The first is an incidence of bullying that took place when Holmes was around five years old. He notes that the local doctor had a skeleton on display, and that he had to pass by this sight on his way to school. Some older boys noticed that Holmes seemed to be afraid of that skeleton and plotted to grab the boy and lock him up with it. Instead of turning this account of bullying into a childhood trauma, Holmes instead says that it not only cured his fear of that skeleton but instilled in him "a strong feeling of curiosity and, later, a desire to learn."[6] Presumably this curiosity was directed toward anatomy and his desire to learn pointed toward his later attendance at medical school.

The second event generally included in biographies of Holmes is one which he, still as a boy, watched with nothing less than amazement as a man remove his prosthetic leg. Holmes had not been aware that the man had one in the first place and thus, years later, writes that he would not have been surprised had the man removed his head next. Apparently there was nothing in the man's gait, nor in the appearance of the prosthetic leg and foot, that had alerted young Holmes to the man's condition. Holmes also possessed either the imagination or lack of anatomical knowledge at that point to assume that he might have been fooled by the man's false head, as well, as though a false leg should be just as difficult to overlook.

These incidents have likely made it into the more recent retellings of Holmes' story because they are traumatic moments, and childhood trauma is so expected in the biography of the serial killer that it is nearly a requirement. Since Holmes' trauma did not come from his parents, both by his own insistence and by a lack of provable information about his childhood, then it must have come from elsewhere. In these two stories, the traumatic events are brought about by older boys intent on giving Holmes a scare and by a man who may not have even thought of the effect he might have on the lad. His leg had simply been bothering him and he had to put it to rights.

Holmes himself, though, treats neither event as traumatic. They are instead amusing incidents that, in hindsight, can be connected to his medical degree and his focus on anatomy. Instead of continuing to be afraid of the articulated skeleton, he made a shift in perception that allowed him to become fascinated. The fact that he was accused of murdering women and selling their articulated skeletons to medical schools and doctors goes unmentioned in this narrative, although it seems to be a massive oversight on his part if he thought his audience would not think of it. Holmes could control what he put in his own words, but he could not control the other sources of information his audience came across, or which they were more likely to believe. With this outside knowledge, garnered from newspapers and other printed material, the tale of a young Holmes overcoming his fear of an articulated skeleton becomes gruesome and worrisome. If, perhaps, those other boys had not forced Holmes into that doctor's office and ended up making him so comfortable with the bones, would he have committed the sorts of crimes of which he stood accused in headlines if not in court?

The shock of seeing a man casually remove a body part is dismissed not as an educational beginning but rather as a joke. It would be absurd for a boy to be convinced that a man might then remove his head, but Holmes suggests it as a coda to the story to induce amusement in his readers. Perhaps it was meant to show them that he, too, was once a gullible and naïve young thing, although the consequences for his innocence hardly ranged beyond confusion. The moment in which a man disarticulates himself, observed by a boy who will grow to be accused of dismembering bodies, is one of only a handful of moments Holmes chooses to present from his childhood and it, like the story of the doctor's skeleton, does not seem to have been a wise selection.

Perhaps, if readers only learned about Holmes through this one text, these vignettes' intended purpose might be fulfilled. Within his own story, Holmes has never robbed a grave, much less murdered anyone, and his interactions with corpses outside of medical school are few: one during a botched insurance con and one being Benjamin Pitezel following his suicide, each discussed here in later chapters. The first becomes more a bumbling joke as Holmes proves his own ineptitude, while the second is overlain with the same sort of disgust that might be hinted at in the childhood stories. Holmes' aversion to the skeleton may have been meant to set him up as the sort of man who would never engage with bodies or their parts lightly, and he ties that incident to his desire for learning. The shock at seeing a man remove his prosthetic leg is countered with humor instead of leading to that same sort of disgust and horror, as though perhaps Holmes' boyhood was in need of a measure of levity between the life lessons.

The choice of these two stories shows a lack of understanding of how his audience would interpret them, as well as a lack of understanding of the traumatic events themselves. It may have been possible that his audience would have read about them and taken away only the lessons Holmes says he did—that spark of curiosity and moment of absurdity instead of the possibility of deep-seated emotional and mental trauma—but it still seems ill-conceived that, of all his childhood experiences, Holmes has chosen two that involve bodies in pieces. Surely a man who had been faithfully reading the daily newspaper and following his name in the headlines would have concluded that any reference to his supposed crimes, no matter how vague, would be better excluded from a biography meant to convince its readers of his innocence.

A Boy and His Money

As an admitted swindler and con man, it would seem reasonable that references to money—spent, lent, borrowed, or loaned—would also appear early in Holmes' story, and he provides his readers with a few references from childhood. The first involved a marvelous mail-order watch that young Holmes saved up his money to purchase and then eagerly awaited. Although it arrived just as shiny and picture-perfect as advertised, the finish soon wore off and the watch broke. It was, Holmes admitted, an affair that became a point of "ridicule for my companions and of self-reproach for myself,"[7] although it seems he may have learned a few lessons from the experience.

The recounting of this experience was meant, perhaps, to show his readers that he had indeed once been naïve and gullible. They would have encountered him as a suave, well-spoken, and well-groomed man through the newspapers and other accounts, the sort of person who took advantage of the naïve and gullible. The fact that such a man had once been a boy fooled by a mail order ad—as, no doubt, many boys were fooled—was perhaps meant to tug at the readers' heartstrings as they imagined Holmes in such a different light. The problem once again is that Holmes is introducing an event from his past that might seem harmless and amusing when taken on its own but, when put in context against everything that had been published about Holmes up until that point, it comes across as tasteless. When young Holmes found himself with the bad end of a deal, he only had a cheap watch to show for it. When others wound up at the bad end of a deal with Holmes, they ended up dead.

Money also plays a role in other small incidents Holmes nearly rushes over to get to his time at medical school. He recounts writing a note with his best friend, the contents of which he does not reveal, and leaving it for their teacher, whom the boys had heard had fallen on hard times. Unfortunately for the pair, who had anticipated that man's departure, this did not mean that they would have a new instructor in the fall. The consequences to Holmes were once again small, since that teacher simply changed his seat in the school room and put him next to "a very disagreeable and unpopular girl."[8] Again, when taken in context with all the rumors of Holmes' multiple wives and mistresses, his boyhood assessment is overshadowed with sinister meaning. After all, if the adult Holmes found himself attracted to a woman, their relationship generally ended quite poorly for her indeed. It might have been all the safer for a girl to have been thought disagreeable.

In yet another instance, writing a mocking note is only the first step in Holmes' plan. Again with that same friend—presumably, since the other boy is not named and in spite of his insistence that he had playmates, plural, only this one stands out—Holmes conspired against a farmer who, the boys thought, had mistreated them. The pair had bent their backs and blistered their hands clearing a field of weeds for this farmer, who, at the end of the day, refused to pay them. This time the anonymous note demanded to know who would pull the farmer's weeds the following year, and Holmes and his friend made sure to take the pulled weeds before they were burned and remove the seeds from them. These seeds were sprinkled back over that very field.

Holmes does not indicate exactly how old he was at this time, but he does remark that it only seemed suiting to include this event because it showed quite clearly how his conscious was lacking even then. His phrasing makes it seem as though he is referring solely to the incident with the weeds and does not include the letter to the teacher who was rumored to be in monetary distress. Perhaps he did not think it was such a bad thing to mock an adult who was in trouble, or perhaps being seated next to the disagreeable classmate meant that Holmes assumed he had paid his dues for that particular piece of fun. It seems that this is his first confession to the note left for the farmer and the seeding of the field, and so perhaps public penance must be undertaken.

The note to the farmer seems perhaps a bit more straightforward and explicable than the note to the teacher, since the farmer is said to have done something that directly slighted and offended the boys. It would be reasonable for a boy—or anyone, for that matter, including so many workers in Holmes' adult schemes—to be upset when pay was not forthcoming for a job already done. They directed their note against the very person who had inflicted this wrong, containing a rather reasonable question: indeed, if the farmer had refused to pay Holmes and his friend, and the boys were willing to tell the others in town, who would the farmer get to do that work the next year? He would already have the negative reputation and, although parents might shush their children for passing on such gossip, the tale would still spread. This, at least, would be more understandable to boys than the monetary predicament of an adult.

At this young age, whatever age it was, Holmes was already showing contempt for adults who were not financially stable. Even a man with the position of teacher was not respectable enough to escape ridicule. The boys must have heard of his troubles somewhere and may have only been repeating what the adults around them, likely their parents, had previously said. Already Holmes is showing himself to be someone who cannot respect a man apparently—and in this case not even provably—unable to support himself. Even if Holmes has simply made up the incident, or any of these incidents, to flesh out his tale, he is still presenting his readers with these impressions of his character as they move forward and follow this Holmes, factual or fictional, to adulthood.

As rude as the notes were, Holmes himself argues that what he and his friend did to the farmer's field clearly displays his own lack of conscience. As a boy he might not have known enough to see the connections between that field and the farmer's own monetary state, but now, reflecting on it as an adult, the deed seems far less a childish prank and more an act of vandalism. Again, though, this regret strikes a false note, since Holmes is willing to express it over a plot of land and a long-ago farmer but seems incapable of directing it toward the people who have mysteriously disappeared or turned up dead after their encounters with him.

Holmes quickly hops through two more brief experiences that had to do with money, first barely describing two different attempts at farming that each failed, and then recounting a day when he had found a purse containing forty dollars in cash. This must, of necessity, come after the explanation that he had failed at his own first attempts at making money. Holmes feels rather miserable at the fact that this meant he could not pursue his grand and glorious dreams, because a rich man would be far less tempted to remove the money before attempting to find the owner of the purse. Holmes admits that he did hesitate, but that he did return the purse and all its contents to its owner. He even refused the proffered reward, poor as he was, because at this time his moral compass still managed to point vaguely northward and Holmes felt that he did not deserve a single penny because he had indeed contemplated taking the money. The fact that the thought of a sin felt equal to sinning perhaps shows the religious influence of his parents although, again, the ethics displayed by a younger Holmes when the older has admitted to cons and swindling seem jarring. There is a great disconnect not only between the man on the page and the man writing the words, but also the man on these pages and the one he presents himself to be even a dozen further on.

Leaving Childhood Behind

These small instances in which Holmes shows himself doing the right thing—most of them involving passing money from his possession to someone else's—are meant to somehow rise above and overshadow his wrongdoings. If juries are instructed to determine a man's guilt beyond reasonable doubt, perhaps these moments are meant to instill that doubt. After all, if the more questionable moments of Holmes' childhood developed into his less desirable adult traits, then perhaps a measure of that goodness also remains.

Over the next couple pages, however, Holmes grows into a man who spends a year at college before going off to Michigan to attend medical school. This entails his initial encounters with bodies—first during his schooling, where he reassures the reader that, although he cannot give many details of his education, graverobbing was not part and parcel of it; and second, through a scheme concocted with a fellow medical student after they had graduated. It seemed that neither physician had found the immediate and immense riches he thought would come in the first year after schooling was completed, and so the friends plotted their first insurance scam. A friend of Holmes' friend, distant and unnamed, would take out insurance not only on himself but also his wife and child. Their deaths would be faked—it would seem as though the husband killed and dismembered the others in a drunken rage before killing himself—while the family relocated somewhere out West until such a time as the insurance money could be collected.

In order to fake these deaths, however, cadavers were necessary. Holmes specifically describes the scam as requiring "a considerable amount of material"[9] before he uses the word "bodies." He shows a clear aversion to continually reminding his readers that a dead person—or, in this case, three dead people—are being referenced, and often resorts to euphemisms that, at times, are meant to be humorous. At any rate, this initial scheme goes unfulfilled due to the difficulty of procuring three bodies—enough material—all at once without appearing suspicious. It was decided that such a collection would take time, with the friend acquiring and then storing his "portion" first, while Holmes managed to procure his own, which he then divided into two packages. All of this is described as though he were discussing bags of grain and not even sides of meat, much less human bodies.

Holmes does not indicate what happened to the "portions" thus obtained, since the scam was never realized. First he writes that the experience helped him learn exactly how difficult it would be to defraud an insurance company, suggesting that, even now, he would not be either intelligent enough to manage it or so stupid to believe that he could. Next came the death of his friend, and that was that. The scam, as well as the material, appears to have been forgotten as Holmes moved on with his life, arriving in Chicago and adopting his soon-to-be-famous moniker on a permanent basis.

It was in Chicago that his admitted misdeeds truly began.

Four

Of Wives and Mistresses

In Chicago Holmes found work at a pharmacy that he quickly bought from the previous owner, who had been both ill and looking to sell. For the first time one of his business endeavors thrived instead of collapsing, although even in success Holmes was apparently hounded. He said that the reason he bought the vacant lot across the street from the pharmacy and constructed his own building was so that he could avoid the ever-increasing rent his landlord levied upon him, seeing that his business was thriving and that such money could be demanded. This meant that his prosperity was at this point in time short-lived, and he recounts a day when a constable and lawyer came to make inventory of his new store because of the creditors who were after him.

At this point Holmes returns to the subject of the "material" procured for the insurance scam that did not take place, which he had apparently kept in two barrels among his other goods. By this time the material had been inside those barrels for more than a year, although there was nothing about them to arouse suspicion in Holmes' visitors. However, when Holmes decided to dispose of the contents of the first barrel through burning it in a furnace, it gave off such a "terrible odor"[1] that he knew he could not continue to take care of such items in the same way.

This story serves a double purpose. First, because Holmes reports that he chose to simply bury the contents of the second barrel, along with what had not been properly burned from the first, this explains the fact that human bones were indeed found in the basement of his Castle. He does not indicate whether his "portion" of the proposed scam involved the husband, wife, or child in the trio of supposed victims, and since he explains that he had "divided" his portion in the first place, it may well indeed have been a woman and a child—just the sorts of bodies reported to have been found in that basement in and among some animal bones.

Secondly, in this piece of the story Holmes shows himself to be well aware of how the details relate to the charges against him. Not only does he account for the bones reported beneath his Castle in a way that removes the stigma of murder—while maintaining that of fraud, which he has also admitted when it comes to Benjamin Pitezel—but he also presents readers with a logical puzzle: if burning the contents of a single barrel produced enough of a smell that he feared it would be noticed, how was he meant to have disposed of the bodies of all of the people he stood accused of murdering? This was also near the beginning of the Castle's creation, when there were far fewer people in and around it during the day. So later on, during the course of the Columbian Exposition, there would have been far more people threatening to sniff the air and raise the alarm.

At the time he was writing his own story, Holmes had been accused in the papers of murdering a number of women, most of whom had been connected to him romantically prior to their mysterious disappearances. Since his Castle had multiple stores at street level there were multiple employees working in the shops, and Holmes needed secretaries and assistants and such in order to help him keep track of all these businesses. In fact, he maintains that he has employed many young ladies, "most of whom are still living in and about Chicago, whose parents and friends know only too well that far from being their seducer I have done much to materially help them in their narrow lives,"[2] considering how difficult it was for anyone, much less young women attempting to attain some measure of independence, to find work. His argument, therefore, is that there are many young women he did not kill, so it makes little sense that he could be accused of murdering those who could not be found. Nearly a century later, when Gary Ridgway was active as the Green River Killer along the Sea-Tac Strip in Washington and preying on prostitutes, he employed much the same argument: Ridgway indeed did not kill every prostitute he hired, and thus they informed their friends that he was in fact safe and could not be the man they were all afraid of.[3] In each case the killer uses this argument to display his innocence when it in fact only makes a case for his caution.

Indeed, if every single young woman Holmes had been connected to had turned up missing, the suspicion would have begun much sooner.

As it was, the disappearances of the women who were clearly connected to Holmes romantically were indeed noticed. By this point in his narrative Holmes had conveniently left out two of his wives: Mrs. Mudgett back in New Hampshire raising their son, and Mrs. Holmes, whom he had moved to a nice house in the subdivision so she could raise their daughter while he continued pursuing other women. One of those women, Emenline Cigrand, is ignored as completely as his wives. Another woman, Julia Connor—wife to jeweler Ned and mother of daughter Pearl, who also disappeared—is mentioned only briefly. Holmes, in fact, seems to come to Julia's defense as he attempts to nip a rumor in the bud when he declares that, although she worked taking boarders after her husband's store closed, she was certainly not an "immoral"[4] woman. The way he positions this defense is meant to accuse the reader of thinking that Julia's boarders were a different sort of customer, and to shame them for even considering it. This is a distraction from the popular accusation that Holmes had taken Julia, a married woman, as his willing mistress.

For those who were worried about Julia's young daughter, Pearl, Holmes adds that he should not reveal the whereabouts of mother and daughter until Pearl is old enough to protect herself from the rumors surrounding her mother, perhaps, or maybe to stake a claim that she wishes to stay with her mother, who is indeed a good woman. Holmes indicated that Julia had been afraid of losing her daughter, after all, which also suggests that she might have been seen as an improper mother. Holmes, the accused murderer, argues for the moral rightness of a woman he has not seen in a number of years and once again shows some measure of an upright moral character himself. It helps, then, that he ignores both his bigamous marriage and his personal relationship with Julia.

Julia, however, comes off lucky in Holmes' written description of her if not in how their affair likely ended. Miss Minnie Williams fared much worse.

The Williams Sisters

Minnie Williams entered Holmes' life in January 1893 as a woman who "had seen much of the world."[5] This counters many other narratives of Minnie, in which she, even as an adult woman, is described as being as naïve and gullible as a child—say, as the child Holmes presented himself to be earlier. If this were the case, then her encounter with Holmes, who was by this time a full-grown adult well adept at swindling and charming to get what he wants, would have been greatly ruinous to her reputation as well as her pocketbook. The Minnie in *Holmes' Own Story*, however, comes to Holmes already with her own dark past and her own methods of coping with her situation. She supposedly told Holmes her entire story, which he relates in these pages so that his readers might know the Minnie that he did.

This Minnie is not a virginal woman when she meets Holmes, and indeed already has experience being a married man's mistress. At the time of this affair, Minnie further reported that she had been engaged to another man, and she had been forced to end the relationship with the first and break off the engagement to the second because the situation was weighing heavily on her conscience. Her former fiancé's accusations of heartlessness stuck with her, and Minnie sank into a deep depression in which she began to contemplate suicide. She will not be the only one of Holmes' companions reported to do so.

According to Holmes, Minnie relocated to Denver to get away not only from these two men, but from all of those who knew her. She alludes to the fact that she was pregnant, presumably by the married man and, since she could not bring herself to commit suicide, she confesses that "the life of my unborn child was sacrificed"[6] in order to preserve her sanity. Unfortunately for Minnie, even after undergoing the illegal procedure, effecting such a move, and introducing herself under an assumed name, she was unable to leave all of the stress and shame of her past behind her. In Denver Minnie once again gained attention from a man who was already attached—in this case, an engaged man who was willing to break that engagement to marry Minnie. Once again Minnie was forced to remove herself from a situation that proved far too embarrassing to endure.

In the papers it was Holmes who had been accused not only of bigamy but of taking mistresses as well as wives. In the case of Julia Connor, the popular narrative suggested that he had not only gotten his mistress pregnant but that her death had come perhaps by accident while he was performing the abortion. Holmes retains these elements of the popular story while placing them in Minnie's past instead of his own, preserving the essentials of sex and intrigue while removing them from his backstory. Holmes remains a rogue when it comes to business deals and he freely admits that he and Minnie had a relationship, although in this case Minnie comes to him already as a fallen woman. In the belief of the day a woman, once fallen, could not be resurrected— and neither could she fall further. If Minnie had already engaged in an affair with a married man and needed an abortion by the time she met Holmes, a relationship between the pair could not tarnish her reputation, although it might be a mark against his.

Once again Holmes uses money as a measure of the strength of an emotional commitment, although this time it is Minnie making Holmes the offer through her only remaining asset: a plot of land in Fort Worth, Texas. Holmes presents her as offering this valuable asset freely—perhaps as freely as she offered herself, fallen woman that she is—and insists that he would not accept it until he had "explained to her, at some length,"[7] more about his own business affairs. Once again he had found himself in the position of being able to make full use of any money she could offer him, but Holmes wanted to protect her—monetarily, at least. He even makes sure to tell his readers that he signed some of his own property in Illinois over to Minnie so that she would be financially stable even in the case of his own death. What Holmes does not mention is whether men of his age routinely protected women who were not their wives against their own deaths, or whether he had any reason to think that he might die and leave her so imperiled.

In an unfortunate sequence of events, Holmes follows his discussion of money with a report that Minnie had to be institutionalized shortly after this exchange because of a resurgence of the mania that had previously plagued her. Readers may have already doubted whether such a young woman, without the guidance of a father or other well-meaning family member, would have been able to properly negotiate land deals with even the most kindly and non-duplicitous of strange men, but Holmes does Minnie and himself a disservice when he stresses her instability. Her capacity for making good decisions for herself is again thrown in doubt when she wishes to be released from the institution and live in an apartment with Holmes, making it appear to her younger sister, Nannie, as though they were husband and wife. Once again this morally questionable suggestion comes from Minnie herself so that, rather than an older man preying upon the innocence of a younger woman, Holmes is simply accepting what has been offered to him by a woman who has already seen much of the world. Again, it may be unwise for a man to make such a decision, but the sexual double standard tends to forgive men who fall and allows them to pick themselves back up and resume their places in society afterward. Extramarital relations were always more detrimental to the woman.

Holmes and the Williams sisters shared an apartment quite companionably through June and the first part of July 1893. They attended the Columbian Exposition and did not speak of Minnie's recent illness, since she did not want her sister to know about it. Then came a day when Minnie had to be called away from Chicago, and she did not wish her sister to be left alone all evening in a strange city. Holmes had promised Minnie he would leave work early in order to sit with Nannie but, upon returning to the apartment, reached an agreement with the younger sister that he could indeed go out and enjoy some time to himself. Nannie promised not to tell Minnie that Holmes had left her alone and presumably vulnerable, and he returned to the apartment the next morning only shortly before Minnie did, with enough time to wave and be off.

What follows contains all the melodrama of a twentieth-century soap opera. Holmes returned from work to find Minnie in hysterics, declaring that Nannie was dead. Since Nannie had agreed to not tell Minnie Holmes had left her alone the previous night, and since Minnie had seen that Holmes' bed had not been slept in, Minnie seized upon "one thought in her disordered mind"[8] and accused Nannie of stealing her husband. Apparently in hot blood and not entirely in control of herself, Minnie hit her sister once in the head with a small footstool. Even though Holmes is a physician, he does not attempt to explain how one wild blow resulted in Nannie's immediate death, but rather focuses on Minnie's reaction. She, at least, calmed herself down after a moment of panic and decided that Nannie must have simply fainted, employing every method she knew to rouse her sister. By the time Holmes returned from work, it was clear that Nannie was dead and that the events of the day were understandably having a negative effect on Minnie's tenuous mental health.

Four. Of Wives and Mistresses 73

"It is useless for me to speak now of what should have been done,"[9] Holmes laments in his written account. He argues that his own reactions were apparently quite reasonable, in spite of the shock of returning home to find his mistress fretting over a dead body. He suggested to Minnie that they should call the police at once, reassuring her that he would make it known that she was not responsible for the act, thanks to her mental condition, but Minnie refused. She would not hear of any course of action that would bring on an investigation, perhaps because it would reveal her institutionalization as well as her affair with Holmes and, ever the gentleman, Holmes reports that he agreed to dispose of Nannie's body so that Minnie might calm down and not end up institutionalized once more. Further, he admits that he had been keeping his affair with Minnie a secret from the outside world, and it would be far more ruinous than he could stand to have this revealed along with the fact of Nannie's death.

Working alone, and with the motive of covering up for Minnie's sake as well as his own, Holmes managed to get Nannie's body into a trunk and find a boat so he could drop that trunk into Lake Michigan. He writes that the sight of that trunk disappearing has haunted him daily ever since. Holmes was so affected by the day's events, Minnie's role as much as his own, that, when he returned to her, he told her that their relationship was over. Minnie was removed to a private institution, and Holmes smoothed over both the murder of Nannie and Minnie's mental state by writing to their family to inform them that the sisters had gone off to Europe with Minnie's husband. Since Minnie had already been presenting Holmes as her husband in her letters and hinting at such a trip in the fall, Holmes shows himself as simply piggybacking on a lie that was already in place instead of making one up out of whole cloth. The deception would not have gone over at all had Minnie decided to tell anyone otherwise, but she was complicit in the lie, both because she did not want her current mental and physical condition to be revealed and because Minnie would certainly not want the question of Nannie's whereabouts raised. It served both parties to keep their relationship and the reason for its dissolution a secret, which explains to concerned readers why Miss Williams has not allowed herself to be heard from since.

Lest readers worry that Minnie's rumored death might be laid at

Holmes' feet as well in the midst of all the swirling accusations, he assures his audience that there have been multiple times when the two of them have been seen together since the day they parted ways after Nannie's death. Minnie's continued role in Holmes' life will be discussed in the next chapter when it combines with the narrative of one Edward Hatch.

An Admitted Wife

Although Holmes had in fact taken two wives by this point in his life, his biography refuses to address either woman or the children he had with them. The wife who is acknowledged, Georgiana Yoke, only enters the narrative in an offhanded way. In later 1893, when Holmes meets with Minnie Williams for the final time, she makes a scene when she discovers that Holmes will soon marry. This tantrum, during which Minnie threatened the lives of both Holmes and his intended, was apparently short-lived, and she and Holmes parted ways the following morning cheerfully enough. It was the last time Holmes says he saw Minnie personally, and she informed him that she was already thinking of moving to London to open a respectable massage parlor there. Although Minnie is physically out of Holmes' life, she continually returns in his narrative to support his argument that he, himself, is innocent.

Holmes' new wife, Georgiana Yoke, however, assumes the role of a token side character for much of his biography. Although he is finding her places to stay during his random trips across the country and managing to avoid her running across any members of the Pitezel family, the references to her are few, far between, and by title only. Holmes does not refer to her as Miss Yoke, since she is married to him, but he also does not call her Mrs. Holmes, since that was not how they signed the marriage certificate. He further refrains from calling her by her first name and continually references her as merely "my wife." In many cases this is a description of his wife's health and ability to travel, although there is one instance in which, charming husband that he is, Holmes reports on buying her a bouquet of flowers. Since the room they were renting was locked—and he apparently did not have a key—he simply threw them through the open transom for her to find later.[10] This is a

Four. Of Wives and Mistresses

rare moment in which he shows a measure of attention to Georgiana outside of her physical condition, whether her illness meant she was unable to move between cities as quickly as he wished, or whether he parades her physical health to his readers to invoke their empathy and pity.

After her long absence from the narrative during which Holmes constructs what he feels must have happened to the Pitezel family, Georgiana is reintroduced when, as a favor to the newly arrested Holmes, she is brought to him so that he might tell her what was happening himself. Since Georgiana had already suffered through his previous arrest in St. Louis, Holmes reports that it was quite kind of the inspector to give him time "to make it as easy for her—for us both, for that matter—as possible."[11] Georgiana had already been through much in their short marriage, thanks to Holmes' own actions, and he makes sure to note an apparent single kindness from the law enforcement officials who, thereafter, have endeavored to make Georgiana's life as difficult as possible.

Although she and her husband are able to exchange letters—one of which Holmes deigns to quote in his book, "sacred though it is to me"[12]—other promises made for the health and wellbeing of Georgiana are broken. In spite of this generous first moment of contact between newly arrested husband and wife, Holmes accuses the detectives and other officials in Philadelphia of conspiring to turn Georgiana against him so that she will not want to visit him and, overall, making her embarrassing situation worse. A room at a boarding house had been found for her, but Holmes reports that she is continually badgered by those attempting to make a case against him, to the point where he reports that "it seemed for a time after my imprisonment commenced that I should die from the effect"[13] of worrying about Georgiana and what the others, outside of his control, might say or do to her. This constant voicing of concern continues into his prison diary, discussed more in Chapter Eight.

Holmes' invoking of Georgiana is not meant purely to tug at readers' heartstrings, although they should certainly fear not only for Holmes as he sits wrongly imprisoned, but for his poor young wife. Even those who might be convinced of Holmes' guilt might find it in their hearts to pity Georgiana, since Holmes insists that she knew nothing of any of his business dealings and had not even met Mrs. Pitezel until after his arrest. The only mistake Georgiana Yoke made was in marrying a con man who here freely admits to his cons while professing love for his wife, and thus she deserves to be protected from all of the terrible things that have been happening to her. Readers might, in fact, be touched with the amount of concern Holmes shows for "my wife."

There is, however, another point to all this that emerges during Holmes' October trial. Holmes has barred himself from personally referring to Georgiana as "Miss Yoke" because he has married her, but he cannot properly call her "Mrs. Holmes" because that is not how she thinks of herself. On the marriage certificate she is Georgiana Howard, but Holmes wrote his autobiography under the name of Holmes and does not explain the taking of another pseudonym or how he used it in order to undertake yet more cons and swindle more people. There is, in fact, a Mrs. Holmes living outside of Chicago and raising Holmes' daughter, although that marriage is also bigamous and Holmes leaves it out of this narrative entirely. If Georgiana Yoke is not, in fact, Holmes' legal wife, then she is free to take the stand at his trial and give evidence against him.

In presenting his audience with the woman he calls his wife, Holmes wishes not only to evoke empathetic emotional responses but also to cast doubt on any testimony Georgiana might give at the trial. Her relationship with Holmes was the basis for arguments concerning whether or not she was a competent witness and indeed Judge Arnold instructed the jury to decide for themselves whether or not Georgiana was Holmes' legal wife. If they found her to be, then they had to disregard her testimony but, if the jury found that their marriage was yet another of Holmes' swindles, then she was in fact a competent witness for the prosecution and her testimony had to be considered.

Prior to this trial, including in a letter to Mrs. Pitezel and during his initial confessions, Holmes has stated that he would be able to account for all his time during the period between Benjamin Pitezel's death and his own arrest if he were able to consult with Georgiana. This would presumably allow him to fill in the gaps of locations and activities on the various days, since Georgiana would, in this case, be reliable. As a fine, upstanding young woman who is a credit to her class and a beauty besides, having her on his side as his one and only wife would not only mean that she would be unable to point out the gaps in time when he may indeed have been getting up to mischief, but that she would be a credit to him, as well. Such a young woman, it may be argued, would never marry the sort of man who could kill a child, and, even if unable to testify, Georgiana could be a mute supporter of Holmes' character.

This is not to say that there are no evil men in Holmes' world—men who would do worse than swindle and con. The presence of sweet, beautiful Georgiana as his dutiful wife is simply meant to indicate that Holmes is not one of them.

Five

Holmes, Pitezel and Hatch— Facets of Manhood

In composing his autobiography, Holmes wanted to present a very specific version of himself: one who was an admitted cad, yes, but also one against whom an accusation of murder would be laughable, much less child murderer. He was a man who had once been a very gullible and naïve boy but had grown up and learned to take charge of situations that did not seem to be in his favor, using his words to outwit his opponent and emerge from confrontations as the victor. These deals were not entirely above the law and they, along with his admission to living with an already-fallen woman as her husband, means that his morality comes across as gray rather than the purest white. There is, however, quite a distance between conning a swindler or allowing himself to be seduced by a woman of the world and committing homicide, and Holmes' narrative works to plant him more or less on the side of good.

The fact that such a fine, upstanding young woman as Georgiana Yoke would first marry and then stand by Holmes after not one but two imprisonments is meant to speak strongly in his favor. A woman of her class and with the morals and ethics that accompany said class would be thought of as degrading herself to marry someone who did not possess those same morals and ethics, and Holmes crafted his depictions of Georgiana carefully so that readers would be hesitant to cast such aspersions on her. He admits a number of lesser crimes willingly enough, but the man Holmes depicted himself to be was one who was able to approach the edge of the cliff without falling down the slippery slope.

As a depiction of an accused criminal, Holmes' representation of himself is a decidedly modern one. In the days of execution sermons all sins were arrayed on a slope and the commission of one, no matter how small, carried with it the threat that next, slightly larger sin would be all the easier. Readers of those sermons were meant to recognize that their own daily actions might contain within them the seeds of murder—indeed, of any sin large enough to merit the noose. Either the condemned or the minister who had worked with him or her prior to the execution would extol a litany of all sins, no matter how small, to show how they were interconnected and how easy it would be to continually toe the line, thus moving it far past contemporary ideals of morality.

Holmes, however, took full advantage of the fact that he was writing in the era of the adversarial trial, when the accused was no longer expected to make a full confession. He was entitled by law to be considered innocent until proven guilty and therefore seized upon the chance to instill reasonable doubt. While the Puritans may have treated the admission of one sin as evidence for another, the American legal system dictated that evidence of one crime could not be admitted while he was on trial for another. Holmes appears to have decided that admitting crimes of property would not, in his present day, be equated with an admission to crimes against people.

He also apparently felt it would be in his favor to admit to a number of those shady dealings, perhaps because so much evidence existed to support them. Even though he may have wished to refute the newspaper reports completely, the sense and sensation of them—illicit love affairs included—meant that the journalists' version of events was exciting and intriguing, and a plain and ordinary autobiography would be more likely to be overlooked than chosen as the favored narrative. Holmes' own story needed to include such interesting tidbits as his childhood fear of a skeleton or that time when his mistress murdered her sister in a jealous rage, but it also needed to address questions of manhood and its ideal. Once again Holmes was able to take accusations against himself and insert them into narratives of others—in this case, two men who, when placed on the moral gradient beside Holmes, each slide closer to black.

Benjamin F. Pitezel

In relating the story of Benjamin Pitezel, Holmes must take care to present him first as the sort of man who would commit suicide, since that is the cause of death Holmes had chosen for Pitezel. However, a suicidal man is not enough. Since Holmes concocted a story involving three of the Pitezel children that was based on what their father wanted for them, he also needed to convince his readers that Pitezel was also a man who cared about his family. There is a conflict, then, between Pitezel's apparent alcoholic depression and his concern for his wife and children and, just as Holmes did not have the language of the serial killer in order to explain himself, he also was not in possession of proper terminology to discuss Pitezel's mental state.

When Holmes first encountered Pitezel in Chicago, he seemed inclined to dislike the man who, despite being a carpenter and more than competent with his hands, was a "dreamer"[1] who had to be paid by the job instead of by the hour because of how much time he wasted. It was only after Pitezel related his history to Holmes, much in the way Minnie Williams seems to have done, that he inspired empathy in the other man. Pitezel, it seemed, had faced a string of misfortunes that very much mirrored Holmes' own history, although he had not then also had Holmes' apparent accompanying luck. Pitezel had married young and fathered a number of children so that, in his continued calamities, he had a half dozen others tethered to him and his fate. Holmes continued to keep Pitezel in his employ from the time they met until Pitezel's death, another gesture of care for a human being that centered around money, although this time in return for services.

Pitezel's bad luck was compounded first by his tendency to daydream, thus causing simple tasks to become a long and drawn-out process, and second by his alcoholism. Holmes noted that Pitezel would sink into bouts of melancholy during which he wanted nothing but drink, and he would waste his money on a bottle instead of putting it toward such necessities as food, shelter, and clothes either for himself or for his family, which included five children at the time of his death. Holmes had taken on a partner who could, in fact, not be trusted to follow even the simplest of instructions while he was drunk, which happened more and more frequently.

While in Fort Worth under orders from Holmes, Pitezel managed to not only fail to conduct himself as a gentleman of standing but also, during one of his fits of drunkenness, married "a woman of doubtful character."[2] As this was a bigamous marriage it would have been shameful enough, but Pitezel's apparent choice of a second wife made the situation all the worse. Upon sobering up he reported to Holmes and suggested that the solution would, in fact, be a murder/suicide. Holmes was able to convince his companion to reconsider and, while in Fort Worth, Pitezel lived with his new wife under an assumed name. Holmes does not indicate how this couple parted or what excuse Pitezel might have made when he returned to Chicago and his first wife, although this story provides Holmes with two narrative elements: first, that Pitezel had already suggested suicide as a solution to his drink-induced problems; and second, that the situation weighed heavily on Pitezel's mind.

Although these elements are meant to convince readers that Pitezel would have been more than capable of taking his own life if Holmes had not kept such a close eye on him, it also presents readers with information that is in fact less favorable to Holmes. Although he insists that he would not have taken Pitezel's life, backing this up with the fact that "during the previous years he had been worth to me much more than $10,000 per year"[3] and measuring life and caring in the only way he seems to know how, Holmes also offers his readers a motive for Pitezel's death. A man who would betray his wife and his marriage vows during a bout of drunkenness would surely also betray his good friend, no matter how supportive that man had been. Holmes reports that, while drunk, Pitezel not only spent money more freely than he should have but was also open to robbery. Since Holmes routinely paid Pitezel or gave him money for joint business ventures, and since Pitezel was then privy to information surrounding business ventures that were not all necessarily legal, then a living, talking, and especially drinking Pitezel would pose a threat for Holmes.

Money was as much or perhaps even more of a struggle for Pitezel then for Holmes, who had his own concerns about creditors calling, and, according to Holmes, it was Pitezel who fixed upon the idea of insurance fraud as the solution to their problems. He proposed a number of schemes to Holmes who found reasons to argue against them, most of which having to do with the diligence with which insurance companies investigated their claims so as to avoid becoming the victims of such frauds. Holmes makes it clear that he had to be gentle with these rejections, however, since Pitezel continued to drink heavily and show signs of depression. After one instance in which Holmes wrote to tell

Pitezel that he had been unable to obtain a substitute body for Pitezel's latest scheme, Holmes reported that he later learned Pitezel had tried to take his own life upon receiving that letter. At the time Holmes was not aware of this, although he might have been informed that Pitezel had fallen ill since he needed some time to recover from the attempt, which is itself not described. Holmes was himself shortly distracted by dint of his first arrest, which he insists was also a wrongful imprisonment.

Upon Holmes' release, he and Pitezel chose to relocate to Philadelphia since each was in need of an income and Holmes said he was being sought in both Fort Worth and Chicago. Here again Holmes plants the necessary seeds, mentioning that although he, personally, had allowed his insurance policy to lapse, Pitezel refused to do so. It had been a long while since Holmes had been able to spend time with his friend and he noticed that Pitezel "was not as pleasant as usual, and was more inclined to sit by himself and smoke and think and frown and worry."[4] Holmes asked him—rather reasonably considering the situation as he had related it—if Pitezel were having more trouble at home, but Pitezel said this was not the case. Aside from a lack of money, there seemed to be nothing wrong with Pitezel, even though he was in a new city and far from his wife and children.

Although Pitezel's melancholy remained, Holmes did allow his friend a measure of redemption in that Pitezel did seem to attempt to overcome his alcoholism while in Philadelphia. Holmes relates that Pitezel had sent away what money he had possessed so that he would be literally unable to afford drink when first in the city. Holmes himself did not know this at the time and thus had continued to treat his friend with caution, not wishing to give him money outright because of how quickly it would be spent, and on what.

The question of money and Benjamin Pitezel quickly becomes confusing, however, since Holmes argued that Pitezel had been solely in charge of renting the house in which he ran his patent shop. He also recounts one of his final interactions with Pitezel in which Holmes gave his friend around thirty dollars for such things as rent and advertising, mentioning that Pitezel had two larger bills in his possession that he did not wish to break, since he would spend it that much more quickly. The construction of this last exchange means that Holmes can once again show his care for another person through the transaction of money, while also emphasizing Pitezel's lack of responsibility concerning the same. Pitezel cannot manage money to care for himself, much less to send back to his wife and children. In fact, Holmes realizes that he must have a stern talk with Pitezel in which he declares that, from now on, instead of giving money to Pitezel, Holmes will have it sent directly to his family—a strong accusation of incompetence against Pitezel and an apparently angelic gesture from Holmes, who currently has little to spare.

Holmes further insults Pitezel's ability to care for his family when he points out that, because of Pitezel's drinking, even an insurance scam is beyond his abilities. Holmes predicted that it would take Pitezel less than a month after committing the scam to drunkenly own up to it. As a father, husband and provider, as well as a friend, Pitezel was a failure. Holmes, who had spent so much time detailing Pitezel's depression, was apparently too frustrated with Pitezel to sugarcoat his words or attempt to spare his friend's feelings. Holmes told him that they would form a plan to support Pitezel's family as much as they could, and then remarked "that is the last time I ever saw him alive."[5]

There is no guilt in this statement, nor much reflection about whether or not Holmes might have prevented Pitezel's suicide had he only provided a kinder listening ear or engaged in the sort of constant supervision that prevented a murder/suicide in Fort Worth. Indeed, later Holmes reflects that "I did not then, nor have I since felt the great horror concerning it that I experienced at the time of Nannie Williams' death in Chicago."[6] Holmes experienced guilt over Nannie's death and names himself as an indirect cause of it, but the responsibility for Pitezel's suicide, according to Holmes, falls on Pitezel and Pitezel alone. It is the alcoholism and depression, along with a possible lack of moral fortitude, that has led to Pitezel's death, and Holmes will accept no measure of the guilt. In this instance his conscience is clean and thus it is an even greater injustice that he currently sits in prison for Pitezel's murder. There is nothing Holmes could have done to prevent it, and certainly nothing he did to cause it.

Holmes' discovery of Pitezel's body falls largely under Chapter Seven of this book, Protestations of Innocence, but elements of his narrative continue to shape the figure of Benjamin Pitezel in the readers' minds. Although no such letter is produced, and Holmes makes no mention of destroying it, he explains to the readers that Pitezel had left him not so much a suicide note as a set of instructions, "poorly written"[7] as it was. Pitezel may have been drunk while composing it, or overcome with emotion, or perhaps merely unschooled. The contents of that letter directed Holmes to make it appear as though he had died in some manner of accident, thus securing the insurance money for his family. There were even instructions to ensure that other family members would not take that money away from his wife, which Holmes and lawyer Jeptha Howe had already been accused of doing through the newspaper reports. Although he was unable to face the thought of living another day, Pitezel's letter to Holmes made it quite clear that he was greatly concerned with his family's future.

Holmes did not possess the necessary psychological vocabulary to examine either Pitezel's state of mind or his request, and he does not try to do so. He simply describes the difficulty he had in following Pitezel's orders and the fact that he left the door to the patent shop unlocked to aid in the speed of the body's discovery. Urged on by his dead friend's wishes and the facts of the situation, Holmes left Philadelphia as soon as his wife was well enough to travel and met with the remaining Pitezels to, he presumed, pass on the news. Unfortunately they had already read it in the paper and Holmes had to begin the awkward dance of negotiating with Carrie, who believed her husband was alive, and Howe, who believed the same, to feign ignorance with each other long enough for Carrie to collect the life insurance. Holmes does not offer an explanation as to why he directed such a pantomime, although he does manage to work in the fact that he once again passed money to Carrie to tide her over. In the case of funds, Holmes presents himself as having been operating as the head of the Pitezel family for years already—another blow against Pitezel.

In life, it seemed, Pitezel could not care for himself, nor for his wife and children, and there was a question of whether or not he would be able to do so after death. Since Pitezel was living in Philadelphia under an assumed name—and indeed, Holmes admitted that he did not want to linger in Philadelphia or call attention to his dead friend because he, too, was using an assumed name—his identification was called into question, and it was determined that Alice, the second oldest Pitezel child, and Holmes himself would travel east in order to identify the body.

Up until this point Holmes was faced with the relatively simple narrative task of taking the factual information already disseminated to the public and aligning it with the idea that Pitezel had committed suicide and Holmes had used his friend's corpse to fake the cause of death in order to ensure a full insurance payout. Holmes himself had already admitted to the salient facts in his second verbal confession: the body was indeed Pitezel's. The argument his narrative needed to support was one that insisted that he himself did not kill Pitezel—or anyone at all—even though he was an admitted con man. The repeated mentions of Pitezel's depression, his various attempts at suicide, his alcoholism, and his irresponsibility with money all help point to a man who might indeed have decided that suicide was his best option for providing for his family. As Carrie Pitezel had been imprisoned for half a dozen months herself for her part in the conspiracy, Holmes may even have thought that this would lessen the strength of any protests she might give about her husband's mental state, especially since the pair had been apart at the time of his death. Holmes even offers the name of the innkeeper who could corroborate the story of Pitezel's suicide attempt in Texas.

In this narrative, Holmes appears to be the best—or possibly the only—friend Pitezel ever had. He kept him employed in spite of the amount of time it took Pitezel to complete a project due to how often his head was in the clouds. Instead of firing him, Holmes simply decided that he would make an exception and pay Pitezel by the task and not hourly. He then apparently took Pitezel under his wing, entrusting him with more and more aspects of his business and continuing to provide income for Pitezel to pass on to his family. When Pitezel drank too much of that money away, Holmes gave Carrie and the children his own money. Holmes even did his best to support Pitezel emotionally, persuading him that suicide was not the answer even when Pitezel was faced with the fact that he had committed bigamy during a drinking spree. With as many times as Pitezel failed—and failed him—Holmes was still there to support him, and turned out to be the sort of friend who would mutilate a corpse when instructed to do so. In this case, that is meant to make him the best sort of friend, since it ensures that Pitezel's death was not in vain and the family Holmes has long been supporting should be able to provide for themselves.

If Holmes' only task were to have convinced his readers that Pitezel's death was a suicide, he might still have been able to manage it. Carrie would have been able to corroborate much of the story since Pitezel had told her that he was moving to Philadelphia in order to defraud the insurance company—a plan that Carrie did not in fact support, but one she could not convince him to give up. This, too, would support Pitezel's continual badgering of Holmes with his various proposed schemes involving substitute corpses. The apartment in which she had been living, as well as the clothes she and the children were known to have been wearing at different points in time, would all have supported the fact that Pitezel was in great need of money. With his checkered past and his proven loyalty to Pitezel, it would have been understandable for Holmes to have stumbled upon his friend's body and followed the instructions Pitezel had left behind.

Unfortunately for Holmes and his chances of an acquittal, this was the easiest death to explain.

The Mysterious Mr. Hatch

By the time Holmes was writing his autobiography in the late summer of 1895, the bodies of Alice and Nellie Pitezel had been found in the basement of a house in Toronto and their brother Howard's body had likewise been located in a house outside of Indianapolis. Inspector Frank P. Geyer's hunt for, and discovery of, the children had made headlines in both Canada and the United States. Their mother had identified them, and thus the explanation that the children had been entrusted to Miss Williams and were living with her in London was no longer viable. Further, Geyer had uncovered evidence that a man who looked like Holmes had been the one seen renting the houses in question—as well as other houses in other cities he had admitted to visiting during the fall of 1894—at times with Howard in tow. As a final narrative constraint, all of the children had been known to have been in Holmes' care prior to their deaths. Holmes had thus set himself the task of offering his readers a tale that explained all of these publicized facts while maintaining his own position as a swindler and con man, yes, but not a murderer—and certainly not a murderer of children.

Holmes planted the seed of his explanation much earlier when he describes how, in late June 1893, "I met and was introduced by Miss Williams to a Mr. Edward Hatch, whom she had formerly known during her theatrical life."[8] Hatch then accompanied Holmes and the Williams sisters to the Columbian Exposition, although only Holmes was able to corroborate this fact at the time of his writing. Nannie had been murdered by her sister years earlier in a scenario that still plagued Holmes' conscience, and Miss Williams was then abroad and hiding, likely because he had revealed her to be a murderess. During the fall of 1894, however, both Hatch and Minnie Williams were in the United States and their paths—Hatch's especially—very closely followed that of Holmes, his wife, and the two groups comprised of the remaining members of the Pitezel family.

Following the wishes Pitezel had spoken to him as well as put in the letter, Holmes took custody of Alice after the identification of her father's body so that he might take her to meet Minnie Williams, who would see to Alice's schooling. Holmes expressed an almost uncharacteristic concern for Alice during the identification, which involved disinterring her father's body, although Holmes once again missteps when he observes that he "found the impression left upon her tender mind would remain as long as she lived."[9] Any concern for Alice is thus overshadowed by the thought of her impending death and the fact that "as long as she lived" was to be measured in mere weeks, although her body, buried with her sister's, would remain undiscovered for more than half a year.

Holmes makes it out to be Alice's choice to not return to St. Louis after identifying her father's body. He explains that, since she had told everyone she knew that she would be away all winter, it would have been rather embarrassing for her to suddenly show up again. Even though Holmes had not heard from Miss Williams at that point, he left Alice at a hotel in Indianapolis while he himself went on in order to pick up Nellie and Howard, the next two Pitezel children. This was ostensibly so that Carrie Pitezel could visit her parents without the distraction of having to care for her children since the oldest, Dessie, would look after the baby.

Since Miss Williams was apparently not as dependable as Holmes had expected, he ended up taking the children with him for a while as he went about his work, not wanting to simply leave them alone in a strange city. Luckily for him, he was accompanied by Edward Hatch, who could take the children when Holmes was busy. Hatch also functioned as an intermediary between Holmes and Miss Williams, ensuring that money made its proper trip and also that Holmes did not interact much with his onetime mistress. As Holmes parenthetically informs his readers, Hatch "claimed he was married"[10] to Miss Williams.

This simple statement—one which Holmes passes on with an air of disbelief—complicates the situation further in ways that Holmes does not explore. Part of Holmes' argument is that many who thought they saw him in and around the various rental properties, accompanied by assorted children, in fact saw Hatch, meaning that the men in fact looked quite similar and could be mistaken for each other. Holmes had in essence set Miss Williams up as having been rejected by one man only to take up with one who could easily be mistaken for his twin. Hatch is, in many ways, a replacement for Holmes, both considering the newspaper headlines and taking Minnie William's love life into account. Although Holmes had since married, his autobiography presents him as delicately negotiating his tour of northern cities not just with the Pitezels and Georgiana Yoke, but also with his former mistress' new lover. The fact that Holmes continues to refer to Minnie as Miss Williams and not Mrs. Hatch indicates his feeling on the legality of their relationship—a hypocritical stance, if his readers believe what the newspapers were printing about Holmes.

Further, because of the complicated emotional situation, Holmes was prevented from meeting with Miss Williams himself and thus ensuring that she was doing all she wrote in her letters and what Hatch passed on. Miss Williams also had no desire to cross paths with Holmes' wife, which meant that she rarely occupied the same city as the rest of the group. According to this version of events, Howard had personally chosen to leave his sisters and had ended up in Buffalo with Miss Williams while the others were in Canada—at least, according to what Hatch had passed on to Holmes. When various members of the group assembled in Toronto, Hatch "stated that the boy Howard was well, and that he had wanted to come to Toronto with him, but he had thought it best for

Five. Holmes, Pitezel and Hatch

him to wait and accompany Miss Williams if she came."[11] It would seem that, although Holmes was negotiating his own complicated scheme, he was not the only man lying about the location of members of the Pitezel family.

In his autobiography, Holmes makes sure to indicate that he had to piece much of this information together after the fact, including information gathered from the inquest into Alice and Nellie's deaths. He blocks out his time in Toronto in order to show that he would not have been able to have been the one to kill them, especially since some of that time had been spent buying them fruit and toys—again, showing how he cares for the children through the exchange of money. He also argues that the girls had "been in Hatch's care more than with me while in Toronto,"[12] allowing him even less of an opportunity to rent a house and take the girls there in order to kill them. In fact, Holmes recalls the last time he saw the girls and how they had changed into warmer clothes for their trip to meet Miss Williams and their brother, after which Miss Williams would take all three children to London with her. Holmes points out that he bought the girls those warmer clothes and gave Alice a silver brooch to pass on to Miss Williams so that Hatch would not see him giving his former mistress a present. Alice was also given money to hide in her dress and a telegram she should send from Niagara if Miss Williams was not there to meet them.

The brilliance of the telegram is that its presence makes it seem as though Holmes was truly concerned about the girls, even if he did not accompany them on their train journey. Even Hatch only went with them part of the way, later telling Holmes that the conductor took charge of them when Hatch alighted. If Miss Williams met the girls at the station, then Holmes would receive no telegram and could assume that all had gone well. The telegram was meant to inform him if something had gone awry, but this would only happen if the girls did indeed arrive in Niagara and if Alice was able to send it. Clearly Holmes had been thinking that nothing worse would happen to them than to have Miss Williams arrive late or mistake the time of the train and he, personally, would never harm the children—Nellie even kissed him goodbye on the platform, a gesture meant to show that the children felt fondly about him, as well. The lack of receiving his own telegram also relieves Holmes of responsibility in that it allowed him to assume that all three Pitezel children were now safely with Miss Williams and on their way to London, so he did not need to worry about them, even if he also did not inform their mother of what was happening.

At this point in his narrative Holmes moves on chronologically to the visit with his parents and then his own arrest. He does not explain what had happened to the children or Hatch's role in it, likely for two reasons. First, at that point in his narrative Holmes was not aware that anything had happened to the children—he was guilty of disfiguring their father's corpse and running an insurance scam, but Holmes did not harm the children. Secondly, he picks up the threads of Hatch's crimes in his prison diary, published as an appendix to *Holmes' Own Story* and ostensibly written before he penned this opening autobiography. In his diary Holmes will puzzle out exactly how Hatch managed to murder the Pitezel children, but, for the moment, he still believes Hatch to have been an ally.

There was also a moment in Toronto in which Holmes' interactions with Hatch parallel those he had with Pitezel. Hatch invited Holmes to spend the evening with him but Holmes, telling Hatch of what had happened to Nannie Williams, refused, explaining that, since his marriage, he had been doing his best to live cleanly. This part is a bit unclear since he does not indicate outright what he and Hatch would have gotten up to during that evening. It could be that Hatch had proposed activities that would be offensive to upright married man—in spite of his own claim to having married Miss Williams—or Holmes may have simply not wanted to spend the night away from his own wife, in case she made the same assumption that Minnie had. Likely it was the second, since Holmes later reconsidered his response to Hatch and realized that "inasmuch as he had helped me so during the preceding weeks, it seemed like ill-treatment toward him"[13] and, if Hatch renewed the request, Holmes would take him up on it.

This statement has two elements to unpack. First, since Holmes refused the first invitation because it reminded him of the situation with the Williams sisters, he inadvertently indicates his fear that Georgiana might react in the same way Minnie did. Minnie thought that her own sister had been sleeping with the man she called her husband and then, in a single impulsive act, killed Nannie. Granted, Georgiana would not be able to make the assumption that her absent husband was with her sister, but the comparison still speaks poorly of the woman Holmes claims time and again as his dutiful wife. Minnie's actions are, according to Holmes, forgivable because of her own mental instability which caused her to respond so violently in the first place. Does Holmes believe that his wife might snap in the same way if she suspected he was cheating on her, even though Georgiana has shown no such tendencies toward mania or depression?

It is meant to be an indication of Holmes' own character in that he has not only learned from his past, but he cannot relieve himself of the guilt of Nannie's death. Pitezel's death is not a matter of concern, but Holmes feels responsibility for Nannie's fate because he sees himself as the indirect cause. Now, in the present day of writing this autobiography, this guilt should transfer in the readers' minds to the Pitezel children: although Holmes did not murder them, he indirectly allowed them to be killed, and this will also weigh heavily on his mind. The man currently in prison is suffering both from these wrongful accusations and from the fact that, if not for him, the children would still be alive today. Unfortunately, this statement also draws parallels between Georgiana and Minnie that do not present Holmes' wife—or his opinion of her—in a favorable light.

Secondly, Holmes has recently undergone a situation in which one of his male friends was so despondent that he took his own life. While Holmes had managed to prevent this on at least one previous occasion, he had apparently overlooked the signs this time around, since Pitezel had not seemed so upset as to be seriously considering suicide again. Once more Holmes presents himself as having learned from his past, since he recognizes that he was perhaps a bit short with Hatch and that his own actions might influence the emotions and actions of his companions. Here Holmes again shows his readers that he is indeed capable of learning from the past in order to prevent tragedy from striking yet again.

Holmes' relationship with Hatch is certainly nothing like his relationship with Pitezel. Pitezel was a friend and confidant, someone with a family Holmes helped—and is continuing to help—support, who worked for Holmes for many years and in varying capacities. The loss of Pitezel, as Holmes mentions multiple times, was devastating for Holmes and certainly would not have been in his plans, a fact that

Holmes feels bears repeating. Hatch, however, was a newcomer to his schemes, and the man who claimed to have married Holmes' former lover. On the one hand it would seem that Holmes might not have minded if Hatch had gone on to feel so neglected and depressed, but on the other, he makes it a point to say that he would have been sure to have paid more attention to Hatch should this melancholy continue.

In this account Holmes is aware of his possible mistreatment of Hatch in a way he was not with Pitezel or even the remaining members of the Pitezel family. He was willing to continue lying to Carrie and having her believe that her husband was not really dead and that she would meet him soon, and his descriptions of the children emphasize how much fun they were having in the various cities on different adventures with either him or Hatch. Holmes' concern for others' emotional well-being centers on his wife and Hatch, and no others. Everyone else receives money or gifts as a sign of his attentiveness, but Hatch is worthy of attention to his emotions and thus of Holmes' time. At this point in the narrative Holmes' concern and consideration may be seen as a reflection of what he has learned from his previous male friendship, although later Holmes will accuse Hatch of murdering the children. He directs his own empathy, therefore, on two figures in his narrative: the woman who cannot testify against him if she is proven to be his wife, and the man who committed the child murders in which he himself is the suspect.

Nearly a century later Harold Schechter makes his own connection about the character of Edward Hatch when he observes that Hatch is Holmes' "own version of Robert Louis Stevenson's Edward Hyde."[14] Robert Louis Stevenson's novella had first been published in 1886 and suggestions that murderers might indeed possess such a double personality had already been put forward during the Jack the Ripper murders in London in 1888, not in the least because a stage performance of the story had been showing in the West End at the time. Because of his convincing portrayal of the title roles, actor Richard Mansfield was even named a suspect in the Ripper killings, since he had audiences believing that he could indeed change his personality so seamlessly.

Holmes presented readers with a narrative of himself undergoing a single transformation from gullible child to capable, confident, smooth-talking physician. Once he obtained his respectable upper-class status,

Holmes did not want his readers thinking that he was anything but perfectly capable and thoroughly put together. He was not a murderer, and certainly not a bloodthirsty monster utterly removed from propriety and reason. Holmes was writing in an age when a deranged mind was meant to be displayed in a man's body and thus a handsome man in a well-cut suit would be assumed to be good, while a man whose facial features were not symmetrical or pleasing would be more likely to be suspected of being evil. Holmes himself references this belief later in his confession published in April 1896, the subject of part four of this book. The preface to his confession, as well as evidence in his own life, suggest that Holmes' appearance was pleasant and not the least bit off-putting, since he was capable of interacting pleasantly with both men and women, earning their trust before betraying it. In his autobiography, Holmes presents Hatch as being a real man, completely separate from himself.

Accusing another man of having committed the horrible crime of murdering three children is complicated, however, by the argument that Holmes and Hatch looked enough alike to be mistaken for each other by numerous witnesses. Hatch, then, also did not appear to be monstrous on the outside, no matter what Holmes reports his actions or intentions to be. Hatch is therefore able to present himself as an equal to the upstanding, well-spoken, elegant physician in spite of his internal corruption. If this duplicity were possible for Hatch to achieve, then why could the same argument not be made for Holmes himself?

From his first mention of Hatch, Holmes presented his readers with the explanation: Hatch, like Miss Williams, was an actor. She had known him from her time in the theater and thus there is reason to believe that Hatch, like Richard Mansfield, would be able to contort his body and present himself as both good and evil, depending on the needs of the moment and even when one of these faces was false. If Mansfield could give such a convincing stage performance that he could be accused of the brutal murders of several East End prostitutes, then Hatch could be able to transform himself into a respectable gentleman so he could pass unnoticed—or rather, noticed and mistaken to be Holmes himself. Minnie Williams and Edward Hatch, whom Holmes will disclose as masterminding and carrying out the murders of the Pitezel children in his prison diary, are thus presented as being capable of duplicity far above and beyond that of which Holmes himself is capable. They had, in fact, done it for a living.

This is not to say that Holmes was incapable of lying or, to take the lighter view, spinning a story in order to entertain. Much of what Holmes wrote in his autobiography does not stand up to corroboration even if it cannot be proven to be an outright lie, but Holmes' selection of events to be recorded and disseminated to a wider reading audience is also revealing. After the death of Nannie Williams, but before delving into the story of Benjamin Pitezel and his resulting romp from city to city that Inspector Geyer painstakingly followed months later, Holmes chooses to turn the act of defrauding an insurance company using a substitute corpse into a delightful adventure that includes not only an inept police pursuit but a ghost story besides.

Six

Holmes the Storyteller

The position in which Holmes finds himself as he writes his autobiography is no less than grim. He has been in police custody since the previous November, locked away for crimes he did not commit, reading newspapers that accuse him of murdering multiple people, including children. He has been separated from his loving wife and concerned about how all of this is affecting her health and disposition, since he is limited both in the number of visits and the number of letters he may receive. Holmes is, after all, in jail under charges of defrauding an insurance company and waiting to go on trial for the murder of his friend.

It is a grim situation that he outlines in his prison diary and alludes to in his autobiography, but although depression may rise every now and then, Holmes is still able to think positively. As he walks his readers through his past, quickly sloughing off Nannie Williams' death and Minnie Williams' flight to a Wisconsin institution in the wake of having both murdered her sister and having had Holmes break off their relationship, he turns to a lighthearted tale that had happened years before. Although Holmes refused to divulge many details about his time in medical school, save to assure his readers that his degree did not include a course in grave robbing, there is one element from those days that remained with Holmes, both in the headlines and, apparently, within his thoughts: procuring a cadaver in order to run an insurance scam.

This time around, however, Holmes seems to have taken lessons from his previous failed attempt. Considering the difficulty in procuring the proper "material" to enact the scheme with an entire family, he decided to insure a single person and thus required only a single body. And, to protect himself against failure if his partner once again died unexpectedly, and also to be sure that his partner in this scheme would not betray him, Holmes chose perhaps the only victim he could trust with such a scheme—himself.

A Successful Fraud

He presents the incident as a comedy of errors in which the policeman pursuing him is only slightly more inept than Holmes himself. The plan itself is almost self-explanatory, especially since Holmes points out that "some time previous to this I had, while in Minneapolis, insured my life for $20,000 in favor of my wife."[1] Thus it seems that Holmes need only find a dead man who looks enough like him for the substitution to be overlooked and he and his wife will inherit twice what Pitezel's family was meant to receive. But here, even before Holmes has begun the process of finding such a cadaver, he has already made a misstep.

Although his retelling of this incident follows immediately after the disposal of Nannie's body and Minnie's departure to an institution, Holmes discloses that he set out to make his quick thousands in the fall of 1887, nearly eight years previously. Holmes married Georgiana in 1894. Throughout his narrative Holmes has insisted that he has only taken one wife by simply ignoring the presence of the other two women, so this woman who would benefit from the insurance could not refer to a wife he had since divorced in order to marry Georgiana. The entire incident appears to have been invented solely for *Holmes' Own Story*, since it lacks corroboration, and Holmes seems to have confused himself about his own timeline. He also shows a complete lack of concern that anyone reading the tale would search for such a policy in which $20,000 was awarded to Georgiana—or any other supposed wife, for that matter—and would prove the entire thrilling recitation false. As it stands this is a quick slip of Holmes' pen to explain how he would have been able to profit from the scheme when he was the one who was meant to have died and thus could not have collected on his own policy.

It is also the only mention of a wife in the entire scheme. "No person was to be in my confidence,"[2] he writes, and he makes no mention of warning his wife or making other plans to reassure her that he will not, in fact, be dead. There are also no provisions for the identification of the body in order to assure others that it is indeed Holmes, although he goes to great lengths to find a suitable substitute. A contact of Holmes' at an undisclosed medical college helps him on his search, which includes a "gloomy"[3] wait of two weeks to come across a body not only of the right age and general appearance, but also with a cowlick that would mimic Holmes' accurately enough. Since the body had been delivered to the medical college, Holmes was able to take possession of it without arousing suspicion from the dead man's family, who had apparently already surrendered him and did not expect to have a funeral.

Holmes had clearly prepared for this moment since he describes the special trunk he had ordered that would contain the body of a man, presumably in a fetal position, surrounded by ice. The outer part of the trunk was supposed to have been waterproof, although Holmes did express some concern at how roughly the entire setup would be handled as he traveled on a train. Using a train would cause less suspicion than hiring a carriage, and certainly he would have been more anonymous as simply one more passenger with his luggage, but this meant adding in a level of uncertainty to his plan as he surrendered the trunk and simply hoped it would not draw attention to itself by leaking or emitting an extreme odor.

He shows an extreme lack of planning—and his first sheepish admission—when it comes time to transport the body, safely in this trunk, from the medical college to the train station. Although he had been looking for such a body for two weeks, Holmes apparently forgot to make contact with the expressman he trusted, since the man had died "some time previously."[4] As much as Holmes may have put his faith in the other man, they had been out of contact for enough time that the man could die without Holmes realizing. This is just one indication that Holmes is in fact not suited to the elaborate planning necessary to enact such an insurance scam, an argument that would support his claims of innocence when it comes to Pitezel's death. If Holmes were incapable of enacting this, a much simpler, scheme, then it would be impossible for him to have tried to defraud an insurance company years later, having learned just how difficult it would be.

The man he does end up employing to cart the chosen body from the medical college to the train station attempts to blackmail Holmes, threatening to go to the police if Holmes does not pay what he demands.

Holmes delights in his own cleverness when he promises the difference between what he has already handed over and the newly quoted price once they have reached the station. After the trunk was unloaded, Holmes then refused to pay and stated he was of a mind to demand his $5 back. He told the expressman that the dead man had in fact been murdered and, since the expressman had helped load the body into the trunk, Holmes would see him arrested as an accessory if the expressman reported the murder. Holmes then informed the expressman of a familiar proposed fate for the trunk: to be sunk into the lake so that there would be no remaining trace. Although Holmes places this event in his narrative *after* the murder of Nannie Williams, whose body was placed in a trunk and then pushed into a watery grave, he is relating an event that occurred half a dozen years prior to Nannie's death. Apparently Holmes had been well suited to returning to the apartment he had shared with the Williams sisters and learning one of them was dead, since he had already conceived of how he would dispose of an unwanted body.

The narrative placement of his first insurance scam attempt confuses the timeline by being the single instance in which Holmes relates events out of chronological order. According to the timeline Holmes presents, his attempt to fake his own death occurs shortly after the death of his friend from medical school. Earlier, his friend's death led to the decision not to pursue the insurance scam that required three bodies, and Holmes then explained how he had gone to Chicago, his purchase of various properties, and how he had finally had to dispose of his share of the "material" he had acquired for that scam. The friend's death is the only shared element between these two explanations of what happened after, so it is difficult to tell when Holmes is meant to have transported this new body to the train station in order to journey with it to "the timber lands of Michigan."[5] Because these events are separated in the text and Holmes had already surged ahead with his tale of the Williams sisters in 1893, it appears to be difficult for him, much less for his readers, to follow a distinct order of events. This, of course, is a strong indication that at least one of his explanations for what happened after his friend's death is a complete fabrication, if indeed any element of this adventure is factual.

Although the narrative of Holmes' arrival in Chicago was already documented, the tale he offers now is far more exciting. His comedy of errors continues when his trunk attracts attention from a number of others on the train, and he decided that Grand Rapids was far enough for his first leg of the trip so that he might reclaim the trunk and see how to go about fixing or repacking it. In the baggage room in Grand Rapids, Holmes comes across another man examining his trunk and "soon concluded that he was a Secret Service man, and that I had been 'spotted.'"[6] In order to extricate himself from this situation without an arrest—which readers must know Holmes has accomplished, since no record of this event had been printed elsewhere—Holmes had to think on his feet. He writes that he wired himself a message at the hotel supposedly from a man named Harvey, asking Holmes to take his trunk for him, although at this point in time Holmes did not indicate that he had already chosen a hotel since his original plan had been to complete his journey further north. At the hotel he showed the telegram to the clerk and sent someone for the trunk, presumably so the Secret Service man would not see Holmes himself retrieving it. Why he chose to use the name Holmes at the hotel and in the telegram when he could have easily chosen from his wealth of preferred pseudonyms, such as the ones found in guest books from his travels with the Pitezels, is not explained. Perhaps Holmes wished to show his readers that, even when it seemed to not be in his favor, he would still give his true name—or at least the name he had adopted for himself and used most often since his arrival in Chicago. According to his timeline, this ordeal took place in the summer of 1887 and this move had only been recent, but apparently he had already committed strongly to the name.

When the trunk is brought to Holmes' room, he discovers that it is as he had feared: something had gone awry and there was a terrible smell. Holmes argues that this was not a failure of his purpose-built trunk but rather because of something both out of his control and personally offensive to him: he had been "imposed upon"[7] because the body had in fact been dead much longer than they had told him. In this instance Holmes' planning seems to have been perfect, but he was once again foiled by the role others had played in his scheme, and played poorly. After the difficulty of finding a body with a suitable appearance and the threat of blackmail from the expressman, Holmes must now figure out how to make up for the fact that the college attendants had misrepresented how long the man had been a corpse.

Just as he did with the fake telegram, Holmes displays his quick thinking when put in such a difficult situation. He is, after all, quite clever, even if the conclusion at the end of this event will be that he is not in fact clever enough to attempt the same scheme twice. Although there is not much time left in the afternoon, Holmes grasps a number of difficulties about his current situation: he needs to repack the body or otherwise dispose of it, but currently he only has the one trunk which he has already presented to the desk clerk as being Harvey's instead of his own. A traveling man would also have his own belongings, so it would not seem strange for Holmes to return with another trunk, albeit one that looked brand new. That trunk, however, would be carried by the porters, who would find it odd if it were empty. Thus, while Holmes is waiting for the lock to be changed on his newly purchased trunk, he also bought a number of lengths of lead pipe in order to put them in the trunk and add weight.

Just as Holmes' narrative does not clarify how he sent himself a telegram care of a hotel at which he had not previously made mention of booking a room, or how he then arrived at the hotel with that telegram already in hand, he also does not consider the witnesses to this strange series of events. He reports that he made several trips and that the pipes had to be cut in order to fit in the trunk so that, at one end, someone would be cutting the pipes and watching Holmes leave with them, a handful at a time and clearly not prepared for transporting such a large load of odd lengths of pipe; and at the other, the locksmith would watch Holmes walk in with his heavy packages and place them inside his new trunk, again a bundle at a time. This lack of forethought offers Holmes' Secret Service man the opportunity to spot him at his task and Holmes catches sight of him as well, but at this point he notes that he cannot let this stop him.

Although he is being observed, Holmes notes that the night is warm, and he knows that the smell from his purpose-built trunk will soon spread throughout the hotel. He makes sure to purchase both a waterproof hunting bag and a large amount of ice to take back with him to the room, where he had to open the window, ostensibly from the heat instead of from the smell, since this would only have made his predicament worse if it allowed the stench to escape. Then, in spite of his fears about others noticing the odor, the pursuing mysterious stranger, and the late hour, he states simply, "I decided to defer further work until after I had eaten."[8] Apparently neither the anxiety over being followed nor the stench he encountered in his hotel room were enough to affect his appetite. His dinner is only ruined by the fact that, when he enters the dining room, that same man is already at the bar.

After dining, Holmes returns to his room and prepares the ice in the new trunk before opening the old one and contemplating what he sees inside. Indeed, "[t]he sight was disgusting,"[9] as the average reader might have assumed it to be. Cultural opinions of death and the surrounding practices were in the midst of change in the late nineteenth century, shifting from loved ones preparing and displaying their deceased relatives' bodies at home to the practice of employing undertakers who removed the body soon after death and turned these practices into dirty work. Not only had this man been dead for quite some time, long enough for the smell to have escaped the trunk, but he had also been surrendered to the medical college for dissection. He was therefore, in a way, a cast off, since public opinion concerning dismemberment was so negative that even murderers who had done the same to their victims could receive sentences that included clauses preventing them from ending up as medical specimens.

Instead of making this observation and quickly moving on, Holmes continues to ponder the body as he places it in the bathtub on the ice so he can, as he explains, "freeze it hard enough for another day's transportation."[10] He gets lost in contemplating the man's mortal remains and asks himself a number of questions about the man's identity—questions Holmes has no way of answering, unless moved by a divine sort of empathy his readers would likely doubt he possesses. There is no indication of how long Holmes is lost in staring at the dead man and perhaps he himself could not say, since he is interrupted in his reverie when the Secret Service man comes into his hotel room and holds a gun on him.

It appears to Holmes that both the Secret Service man and his associate broke into his room using the window, possibly so that Holmes himself did not try to escape out it if they knocked at the door. Although startled, Holmes is not thrown entirely off his game and notes that the Secret Service man had a "merry little twinkle in his eye"[11] that allowed him to read the man's character at once. Said character is apparently not much better than Holmes' own, since the Secret Service man sent his companion away with strict instructions not to breathe a word of this until told to do so. Holmes mentions in his recollections that he had the money and thus might have some measure of power in this situation, despite having been caught with a dead man in his bathtub, and in his recounting of the tale the Secret Service man wastes no time in beginning negotiations. When he suggests that Holmes will likely hang for this, Holmes counters with the suggestion that the dead man is his brother, rescued from a medical college, and invites the stranger to go into the bathroom and take a closer look at the dead man's features.

The stranger's reaction comes across as comically overblown since, at this suggestion, he not only turns gray but trembles badly enough to drop his gun, which goes off. Showing a cooler head, Holmes grabs the gun and orders the man back out the window, firing the gun again as the other man went—not directing the shot at him, but rather into the air. Once again when in a stressful situation Holmes shows his ability to think on his feet and to use every advantage he can find. Caught up in the cops-and-robbers feel of his narrative, he does not pause to consider how wily and cunning this makes him seem, or how that appearance might affect his readers' opinion of his current situation. In this case Holmes' quick thinking works to his advantage, as he can point at the fleeing figure and convince the others in the hotel that the man was a burglar and Holmes was merely defending himself. The fact that this shows that Holmes can swiftly turn a situation to his advantage with a clever lie is not emphasized, even though it plays a pivotal role in then allowing him the time to once again make a narrow escape. Because Holmes is penning this from prison, clearly he has encountered a situation in which his quick thinking and ability to spin lies has failed him.

Holmes hurries to pack his "dead friend"[12] in the new trunk even though he seems to think that the Secret Service man believed his story about who the corpse is and why Holmes had him in his possession. He does not, however, indicate exactly why turning gray and dropping his gun is enough of an indication that the man believed him, since this series of events happened after Holmes suggested the man take a good long look at the cadaver in order to satisfy himself that they could be brothers. Holmes' assumptions about human nature seem faulty, but the momentum of the story carries him through to the next morning when he boards another train with his new trunk, leaving the old one behind with the reassurance that "Harvey" will soon be by to retrieve it. Holmes further reminds readers of his cleverness by adding that, if the Secret Service man—now called a detective—returned to Holmes' room and found the trunk still there, he would wait around a while for Holmes to return, thus buying him more time.

Unfortunately Holmes does not have long to relax, even though his luck is in and he is able to watch a telegram come in at the Western Union of a station thirty miles from Grand Rapids. This telegram passes on the message that a man with a black trunk should be arrested and detained, failing to provide enough information to distinguish Holmes and his black trunk from any other traveler going about his business that morning with similar baggage. Holmes naturally had a guilty conscience and identified himself as the man being sought in the message straightaway, which necessitated some more quick changes to his plan. Instead of following his ticket all the way to his destination, he has the baggage porter remove his trunk at the next station. Holmes is then faced with having to secure his next move in the middle of a rainstorm.

He believes that the detective from Grand Rapids will be checking every station between that city and Holmes' final destination. Presumably the detective would have gotten Holmes' name from the hotel registry, although there is no indication of how the man could know Holmes' final destination. Holmes had bought his original ticket in Chicago and had the porter buy him one in Grand Rapids, so the teller would not be able to put a face to the ticket, or even to indicate that it was purchased by a likely-looking man with a black trunk. Holmes has not even named his destination nor given any explanation as to why he must go exactly there but, in his next moves, it seems that he must remain faithful to his original plan even though so many other things have gone wrong. Holmes is fixated on reaching his final unnamed destination, as well as holding fast to the idea that this detective also knows where that is and will stop at nothing in order to catch him before he reaches it.

Holmes must, therefore, get himself and his new trunk to a different little town that also has a train station. His desperation is displayed in the fact that he pays many times what a buckboard was worth, since he first believes that the detective is hot on his trail and, secondly, this trunk is failing to do its job just as the first one did. The stench is so bad that, upon reaching the new station, Holmes convinces the conductor to delay the departure of a combination passenger and freight train by half an hour so that he might procure ammonia and some unnamed substances which, when combined, "made a solution that rendered my quiet friend quite acceptable so far as one's olfactory were concerned."[13] First, Holmes refers to the man in the trunk as his "quiet friend" rather than acknowledging that he continues to carry a rotting dead body across the state, and secondly he refuses to name all the ingredients of this cadaver perfume, as though it were a trade secret. Clearly Holmes has no desire to inform his readers of how they might concoct their own batch in order to assist them in committing similar crimes.

Another travesty befalls Holmes when this new train derails not far from the station in an accident that kills the engineer and injures the conductor and two or three passengers. Displaying an uncharacteristic concern for others, as soon as Holmes manages to get out the window of the car in which he was traveling, he goes first not for the baggage compartment but to the injured parties so that he can assist them with his medical training. He does this before even approaching the baggage car to see whether or not his new trunk was still intact, a clear gesture of humanity that, in this case, does not involve any money changing hands. Holmes' physician's training simply asserted itself and drove him to help the people he could before seeing whether or not he was able to salvage his current mission himself.

The trunk survived the derailment in once piece, although—without ever quite explaining how this happened—the first train to follow and offer aid included Holmes' Grand Rapids detective. As clever as the man was to have tracked Holmes and his trunk to this spot, his morals were not pure, since Holmes was able to negotiate the removal of his trunk, unopened, for an amount that he does not disclose, "for that officer still lives."[14] Not only is there honor among thieves, but Holmes seems to have somehow managed to discover the identity of that officer before they parted, perhaps as insurance should the detective wish to talk.

This is the last Holmes saw of his Secret Service man slash detective, and the rest of his tale is quickly summed up. He lived for a while in Northern Michigan, posing as a lumber operator long enough for those around him to recognize him, presumably under the Holmes name, as that seems to be the name for his insurance policy. Holmes managed to keep the body a secret all this time until he decided to disappear and, about a week later, "what was purported to be my dead body was found pinioned to the earth by a fallen tree."[15] Holmes did not rely on eyewitness identification of near-strangers, but also ensured that the body had papers on it to help establish his credentials.

Holmes concludes his tale by saying that "after a great deal of trouble and thrilling escapes from the law's officers, I added the neat little sum of $20,000 to my bank account."[16] It is a thrilling tale, certainly, with a number of near-captures, but in the midst of all the fun he seems to have forgotten first that the insurance policy was made out to his wife and second that he, Holmes, was meant to be dead and thus could not collect on his own policy. There is no explanation for this, and no suggestion that Holmes may have used a fake name in order to collect the money—on a policy which, once again, had been made out in favor of his wife. There is also no mention of whether there was any concern as far as the condition of the body, since the one Holmes had obtained had first been dead longer than he had wished and second had to have been a bit worse for the wear after its long trip north. Since Holmes had been told that the man had died by falling from a freight car, perhaps the injuries mimicked those expected from being crushed by a tree closely enough that no questions arose at the post mortem. Holmes, at least, reports no such difficulties as he ends his tale flush with money and success.

As an aside he adds that, after cleaning this second trunk, he gave it to a friend. Years later Holmes then told the friend all about this hilarious incident, at which point the friend and his wife expressed no disgust and voiced no accusation. Instead, they declared that a great mystery had been solved, since the trunk was known to have mysteriously opened itself after they swore it had been not only shut, but also locked. After this short report Holmes moves on to discussions of Pitezel's insurance policies, leaving this apparently playful scam behind.

"My Quiet Friend"

There are numerous parallels between this comedic account and the situation surrounding Benjamin Pitezel's death, including a large insurance policy that is payable to the man's wife. In each case, the man is in rather desperate need of money, or else he would not attempt to undertake such a scam in the first place. Holmes appears to have spent his windfall rather quickly, considering his account of his life in the years between this scam and Pitezel's death. He had to both continually pursue cons and assure others that he was giving them all the money he had to spare, while Carrie Pitezel was fleeced out of much of the insurance money of the second fraud and ended up with very little which, owing to the continued moving around as she followed Holmes' orders, was soon spent.

The insurance scam surrounding Pitezel, however, is no such laughing matter. He is identified and known to Holmes, who needs not sit contemplating his corpse and asking himself what sort of man he had been or whether he had had a family. Pitezel has not been cast off to become a specimen at a medical college—his body was not surrendered for strangers to do with it as they chose in order to advance scientific knowledge. According to Holmes, Pitezel left him a note explaining exactly what he, a friend, should do to his corpse in order to make his death appear to have been an accident. Pitezel's death was also no accident, at least according to *Holmes' Own Story*, since he took his own life as a result of his depression and his drinking. There is nothing comedic about the end of Pitezel's life.

In recounting his previous successful insurance scam, Holmes' tone is almost playful. He wishes to entertain his audience with the thrill of the chase and his own cunning and derring-do, a tale in which he emerges the victor, if not the hero. During this entertainment, Holmes confesses that he has in fact cheated an insurance company before, although he had not been caught at it and clearly not even suspected of it. What, then, makes this con one that can be told for the purpose of entertaining his audience as opposed to one against which Holmes must defend himself?

First and most obvious is the fact that, during the scam of 1887, no one dies. Holmes is surrounded by less-than-moral men who will provide him with a body, help him get that body in the trunk, transport that body, and ignore the presence of that body all for nominal fees, but the man died because of an accident before he even crosses paths with Holmes. His relatives, if he had any, had already consigned him to being cut open at a medical college which, according to the feeling of the day, was one of the worst ends a man could imagine. Although Holmes may not have treated his quiet friend with utmost respect, he did not dismember the man and, presumably, the body ended up with a proper burial, even if any marker would have stated the wrong name.

The second reason this earlier tale makes for an amusing story is that it follows the fascination of David and Goliath. Holmes in this case is a lone man whose life has not been entirely kind to him and, in spite of his medical degree, a poor man in need of money. This degree means that he has access to avenues not always open to the average man so that he could indeed arrange to take possession of a body that could pass for his own. Goliath comes in the faceless form of the insurance corporation, an industry that itself has a poor reputation of bilking clients and refusing money to those who could use it most. If Holmes manages to scam the insurance company, there is not one person harmed, just the overall feeling of satisfaction that comes when the predator momentarily becomes the prey. It is an amusing story because the loser is a corporation, and one that is determined to be easily able to afford the loss. Thus the scam is really only a minor inconvenience to the loser.

Third, Holmes in this story is an upstanding man who happens to be down on his luck. He has learned the many lessons of childhood—although really, he has learned merely to lie better instead of not to lie at all—and is really only trying to make a good start for himself as a physician in Chicago. He is hapless in his timing and all his plans seem to end up failing, supporting the idea that he is an underdog in this narrative and one worth rooting for. When tragedy strikes in the form of the train crash, Holmes extricates himself from the car and goes immediately to help the wounded, even though he has not looked to see whether or not his trunk has been opened and his plan will soon be foiled.

Fourth, Holmes presents himself as being able to take the various blows to his plan in stride as he continually outwits the man following him. First called a Secret Service man and then presented as a detective, it is this lone man who is the biggest threat to Holmes' success and his insurance payout. Holmes sets himself not only in opposition to the insurance company, but also in opposition to the law that this nameless figure represents. The law in this case is on the side of the company and thus Holmes can continue to position himself as the small, scrappy fighter who has a better future in mind. His intended crime against the insurance company is not so great, and thus readers can cheer for him and feel the suspense when the detective continually follows Holmes' trail. Holmes, like some of the best fictional investigators of his day, can think on his feet and alter his plans just as quickly as his persecutor in order to continually outrun him and, in the end, come to victory.

All of these elements run counter to the narrative of what happened to Pitezel, either in Holmes' own various descriptions or those printed for popular consumption. Pitezel died, and the manner of his death was debated and brought into question. As a result of the events following Pitezel's death, the conflict is not seen as Holmes versus the insurance company, but as Holmes versus the remaining Pitezels: a grieving widow and her children. Compared to their situation, Holmes is more than well enough off and he lists the number of times he has given the Pitezels money or bought them presents to show that he would not need any of the insurance payout even if it were offered to him. Since he himself is not a family member, perhaps there is no way he can intervene when the lawyer takes a large amount of the insurance money away from Carrie, although he does not mention if he tried to come to her aid. And finally, the Holmes recording this account is a man in prison who was outwitted by law enforcement instead of the other way around.

The insurance scam of 1887 can be turned into a comedy because it seems that no one actually gets hurt. Holmes' medical colleague, the expressman, and the detective all end up paid for their roles, even if the expressman did not receive as much as he would have liked. Holmes himself managed the scam and found his account nicely padded with an extra $20,000. Even the man whose cadaver was carted around and displayed as Holmes' own was dead before his part in it began. The only character in the entire ordeal to take a loss was the insurance company, and they apparently did so without a fight.

By the late summer of 1895 when *Holmes' Own Story* was published, the $10,000 lost by Pitezel's insurance company was the least of the public's concern. The cost of Pitezel's death could be read in the deaths of three of his children and in the arrest and eventual release of his wife.

Earlier in the year Holmes had pled guilty to defrauding the insurance company, but it was not merely fraud Holmes had to answer for this time. Now it was murder, but not even a single murder. Holmes had to defend himself against accusations of murder against not only Benjamin Pitezel but also the three children: Alice, Nellie, and Howard.

Seven

Protestations of Innocence

The amount that Holmes is willing to confess in his autobiography is perhaps meant to assure the reader that he is being candid and utterly forthcoming with his recitation of his past. He is clearly willing to relate tales of his previous crimes, including those that had previously been undetected, to show the limits of his criminality. If he were to claim complete innocence and present himself as a man of strict morals, he would have been setting himself up for disbelief and complete dismissal, especially in the face of what the newspapers and others had already been printing. Further, the autobiography of an innocent man would have been far less interesting and would have sold fewer copies. Holmes needed to reach a wide audience in order to both sway public opinion about him and also make the largest profit.

In general terms, Holmes suggests to the reader that he had no desire to undertake any activity that would place him in danger of being arrested, thanks not to his father's penalty for lying about the cows but to his own first capture in St. Louis. Prior to this, Holmes confessed that "I had never been arrested, and I had the same horror of it that I would of being shot"[1]—a fear that might have been mitigated by his first imprisonment since it would, at least, have changed from the unknown to a known entity. Being arrested for selling mortgaged goods, however, was bad enough, and Holmes did not wish to find himself locked up again for running an insurance scam—much less, his readers would have to assume, for murder.

Being imprisoned is, of course, not meant to be a pleasant experience, although Holmes perhaps suffered more than his fellow inmates. For a man who had been used to having the freedom to lie and cheat, with the ability to escape consequences through use of his quick tongue, being surrounded by angry men who had been put away for crimes against people and not just against property could have very well been a terrible shock. Holmes could no longer trust that the men he confronted would be content to keep arguments civil and depend on the court system for justice, while Holmes had previously relied on the fact that none of his deeds were so egregious that those he swindled would think paying for a lawyer would be worth it to them. These men were already behind bars, so they could not incur much worse from the legal system should they lash out against Holmes. Even having a shave in prison is an ordeal, as Holmes realizes that the razor selected for the task could just as easily be used to slit his throat. He pays his fellow prisoner above and beyond the price requested for the privilege of having the sharpest razor used on his face, although preferably not on his throat.

While he does not stress this, the prison environment would be one in which Holmes' medical degree brought him no respect and was indeed nearly worthless. Perhaps for the first time, Holmes found himself as just one man among many, considered no better than the others. He shared a cell with Marion Hedgepeth, a Wild West outlaw with a history of robbery and murder. In spite of the fact that Hedgepeth tipped the police onto the insurance scam Holmes was running with Pitezel, Holmes still shows a fascination with Hedgepeth in his autobiography, mentioning that he seems far too intelligent to be a criminal. If Holmes was impressed by Hedgepeth's demeanor, it suggests not only that Holmes ascribed to the contemporary belief that crime indicated a lack of intelligence, but also that these two men were surrounded by dullards and idiots. Prison would not be a place where a physician would feel at home, nor one where Holmes would wish to draw connections between himself and the other men. He presents himself in his autobiography as intelligent and cunning, and nothing like the common criminal brute.

Although he was not imprisoned for long before being released on bail, Holmes was still present to witness another prisoner being prepared for execution by hanging. "If I had been in need of any warning to deter me from almost immediately placing myself in a similar position," he writes, "I know of no stronger one."[2] Holmes reports on watching the execution, mentioning the slow death of the hanged man as well as observations about the reactions of the crowd, these being far too lighthearted for his assessment of the situation. The fact that they began to fight over the dead man's clothes and pieces of the rope, common souvenirs of the day, cemented this in his mind. Clearly execution was a terrible fate for any person, much less a gentleman physician and sometimes con man like Holmes.

These are all arguments of a general nature outlining why Holmes would not want to be arrested at all, much less for charges so serious as to keep him behind bars for an extended time or during a wait for his own meeting with the noose. This imprisonment occurs in his narrative chronologically before Pitezel proposes that he and Holmes should undertake an insurance scam of their own. In this autobiography Holmes had not already discussed the idea with Hedgepeth while he was incarcerated, and the idea for the scam is Pitezel's and Pitezel's alone. This is where Holmes continues moving beyond the argument that he would undertake no activity whatsoever that would possibly land him in jail to focus specifically on reasons why he would not, and could not, have murdered Benjamin F. Pitezel specifically.

The Suicide of Benjamin Pitezel

Because Holmes had already confessed at his spring trial to defrauding the insurance company, the question of insurance is an important one for him to address. Previously he had recounted the instance in which he took out a policy on his own life that he then wrongly inherited through a previous scheme, although Holmes does not indicate that he specifically chose that earlier policy in order to use it in such a way. It seems that Holmes had secured it and only later decided that obtaining a corpse and faking his own death in order to secure that $20,000 would be his best option to remedy his depleted bank account. In that story, Holmes was more focused on the cat-and-mouse chase between himself and the Grand Rapids detective than arguing the details of insurance and scams.

When Pitezel chose his insurance policy, Holmes remarks that it was not "one I should have chosen, if any fraud had been anticipated at the time."[3] The date of the acquisition of this policy is unclear, although it seems to have been mid to late 1893 and therefore about a year prior to Pitezel's death. Holmes does not choose to clarify why he would not have chosen such a policy if he were plotting to murder Pitezel and defraud the insurance company, and he presents the scenario as Pitezel having selected it himself without any input from Holmes. Unfortunately the tale of Holmes' previous experience with defrauding an insurance company has just ended in his book before this discussion, and in that tale it does not seem that Holmes had chosen his own policy for the purpose of fraud, either. The lack of a well-chosen policy thus does not necessarily exonerate Holmes from choosing to enact insurance fraud after said policy has been put in place. His choice of it, however, may work in his favor while arguing for innocence, since he can advance the proposition that the selection of such a policy automatically negates planning for fraud. However, a lack of such advance planning does not mean that the crime was not committed.

Holmes further presents the policy as the sole concern of Pitezel since, if Holmes wished to murder Pitezel and collect on the policy, he would certainly not have urged Pitezel to let it lapse.[4] Holmes indicates that he had let his own policy lapse, although he also adds that there were other ways in which he had provided for others in case of his death. He does not state whether Pitezel, who had children as well as a wife and whose family was living in much poorer conditions than Holmes and his wife, had taken any other such precautions. It would be entirely understandable for Pitezel to be concerned about his insurance policy if he knew that, without him, there would be no income available for his wife and their five children.

Unfortunately, Pitezel is also not in a good position from which to finance his own insurance payments which, in and of itself, could be a strong argument against his holding on to that insurance in the first place. Because of Pitezel's difficulty in managing money, the only reason he was able to keep up his insurance is because of the funds Holmes provided to him and his family. Once again Holmes' concern for others takes the form of money changing hands, although this emphasis is a double-edged sword. By helping Pitezel make what became the final last-minute payment on his insurance premium, was Holmes being a good friend and looking out for the entire Pitezel family, or false friend ensuring a proper return on his investment? In his autobiography all of the concern for making the payment is placed on Pitezel's shoulders, so not only is the policy not the sort Holmes would have chosen had he plotted to murder his friend, but Holmes is also utterly unconcerned about whether or not the policy lapses. Since the phrase "reverse psychology" had yet to be coined, Holmes did not need to defend himself against any such accusations, either. In the end Pitezel is a grown man who made his own decisions, even if he had to rely on someone else to help him pay for them.

Holmes stresses that Pitezel largely acted on his own in Philadelphia, which included leasing the house in which he set up his patent business and in which his body was found. He also argues that he himself had not gone there more than four times[5] before the day he found Pitezel's body although, as his bad luck would have it, Pitezel had a customer during one of those visits and that man later recognized Holmes at the graveside. Granted, this lack of involvement in Pitezel's life may have indirectly caused his suicide, but even then Holmes feels more or less at peace with the way he treated his friend. Not once during the whole ordeal of discovering Pitezel's body or coming to terms with his death does Holmes feel "the great horror"[6] that engulfed him upon learning of Nannie's murder, since Holmes felt that he had in some way caused Minnie to kill her sister. In the case of Pitezel, however, Holmes is content to blame the man himself and his "pernicious habits,"[7] which were Pitezel's own fault. Any conflict Holmes feels is not caused by Pitezel's suicide, but by the action Holmes himself chose to take afterward. Holmes therefore feels no guilt surrounding Pitezel's death, although he is indeed regretful that he followed his friend's instructions afterward and thus landed himself in prison.

Before explaining his actions, however, Holmes first assures his readers that no physician would have chosen to kill Pitezel in the way Pitezel decided to kill himself if he wished to stage the entire event as an accident.[8] This comes in the middle of a discussion of how Pitezel looked when Holmes found him, including the strange contraption by which Pitezel had caused chloroform to flow not only into his lungs but also into his stomach after death. Holmes carefully describes both this setup and the elements he found in the room with Pitezel and on his person, showing a mind for detail even in the middle of what Holmes describes as a shock. The room itself, up on the third floor of the rented house, was also full of chloroform fumes to the point where Holmes needed to leave it to seek fresh air and a wet towel to press over his face if he went back in.

This retreat is what gave Holmes enough time to read the rest of Pitezel's suicide note, which included Pitezel's instructions for what Holmes should do next. It is thus Pitezel who is giving the orders and directing his friend on what should be done next, even though Holmes is loath to do it. This note, seen only by Holmes and thus uncorroborated, included the instruction that Holmes should "'do enough with me so there won't be any slip-up on the insurance; I shan't feel it.'"[9] This sentence especially encourages Holmes to stop and think the situation through from a logical standpoint.

Pitezel was lifeless with no chance of resuscitation—Holmes himself gives the estimate that Pitezel had been dead somewhere around six hours[10] when he found him—and was currently positioned in such a manner that his death would easily be ruled a suicide. However, if the insurance company deemed his death a suicide, they would not pay, and Carrie and the children would be worse off than they had already been. Instead of living in a shabby apartment on money that Pitezel could spare, or on funds Holmes sent their way, they would be without what little income Pitezel provided them. Further, since Holmes had already promised Pitezel that he would continue to look out for his family and Holmes was a man of his word, it would fall upon him to care for a wife and five children that were not his own. Since Holmes himself was often hard-pressed for funds and had recently been going through a low point, even that supply would be meager. The compassionate thing for him to do would be to cover up his friend's suicide and follow Pitezel's instructions to make sure that Carrie inherited her deserved $10,000. Pitezel had placed himself beyond help, but his family's need would soon be desperate if Holmes refused to act as he was bidden.

Although the end goal—ensuring his suicide appeared to be an accidental death—was the same, Pitezel apparently gave Holmes a number of suggestions for how to stage it. Holmes rejected one of them immediately, claiming to be entirely unable to bring himself to hit Pitezel's dead body, much less hard enough to crush his skull. Clearly Holmes would have been aware that the insurance money could still be realized even if Pitezel's head was thus deformed, since he had previously related the fact that he had effected his own death by crushing the stranger's head underneath a fallen tree and assured identification through the papers in the dead man's pockets. In his earlier escapade Holmes had felt no compunction about doing just what Pitezel suggested, but that involved the body a stranger. Once again Holmes wishes to stress that Pitezel was "far more than an employee,"[11] since it would be much more difficult to find a motive for a man to murder a close friend. By emphasizing this personal relationship, Holmes further argues that he could not have murdered Pitezel.

Holmes is in the house with Pitezel's dead body for quite some time, first in his shock and then as he works to arrange the scene according to Pitezel's wishes. This involves carrying the body down a flight of stairs to where it was later found on the second floor, as well as burning part of Pitezel's body to ensure that the clothes were singed to match the skin that, due to its contact with chloroform, already appeared burned. The amount of time this takes Holmes is not a testament to his feelings for his dead friend but rather an argument of his innocence: had he been guilty of murder, Holmes would have wanted to spend as little time in the house as possible, lest he be caught with the newly dead man and no explanation for his presence. By his own insistence, since there were no witnesses and no one came forward to say he had been to the house that day, Holmes took his time and did not worry about what might become of him if he were discovered in the act. Pitezel was dead and his family needed the money, so Holmes obeyed his dead friend's wishes, stressing that he in fact had no idea whether the suicide clause was even part of Pitezel's insurance, or if the clause were valid in Pennsylvania. He adds parenthetically that he really would have found all of this out had he intended to commit fraud,[12] a reminder to his readers that this was not very well planned and yet, at the same time, a callback to Holmes' earlier insurance fraud in which he claimed exactly the same thing.

Holmes seizes on another known fact in order to emphasize first that Pitezel had planned the fraud himself, and second that Holmes himself could not have done so on his own: Pitezel's pipe was discovered near his body filled and ready for use. Since Holmes did not smoke pipes, he had no idea how he would have gone about preparing one in such a way as to convince others that it had been done by someone who did indeed smoke. By pointing out that he did not fill the pipe, although he did place it where it was found, Holmes hopes to indicate that he did not murder his friend even though he did stage the scene. As he does with other elements of his story that might be too troublesome to explain, Holmes glosses over the fact that it would have been possible for Pitezel to have filled his pipe before being murdered.

For a man who was overcome both with chloroform fumes and emotion upon finding his friend dead in such a way, Holmes still managed to think quickly enough on his feet. Although Pitezel wrote him a suicide note telling him to make the death look like an accident through further mutilation of his corpse, Pitezel's letter offered suggestions only. Holmes had to select the method and then ensure that whatever he did would be convincing to those who found the body afterward. In his autobiography Holmes emphasizes the time all of this took as he recovered from the fact that discovering Pitezel dead in such a way had "unmanned"[13] him, since Pitezel had been his friend and not simply his employee. As he has shown in his recitation of his previous experience with insurance fraud, however, Holmes is able to think on his feet, and the cool, calculating side of him that argues gifts and money prove emotional attachment once again rises to the surface. However shocked he may have been at finding his friend dead of suicide, Holmes was able to act in such a way as to follow Pitezel's wishes and fool the insurance company long enough to ensure that Carrie Pitezel was granted the $10,000.

Caring for the Remaining Pitezels

After having done his part in staging Pitezel's death, Holmes argues that he did his best to support his widow and fatherless children while at the same time faithfully following the instructions left by Pitezel and given to him by Carrie. He is careful in his autobiography to present himself as a man doing what he thinks is right given the conditions set for him, but certainly not a mastermind of any plan, grand or small. Holmes is not even all-powerful in this account, since, even though Pitezel's letter asked him to be sure that all of the insurance money would go to Carrie and not be borrowed away by family members, the Pitezel lawyer relieves her of a large chunk of it and she is left to inform

Holmes of this, clearly upset. Since he was not an immediate family member, and since Carrie did not ask for his help or his presence, there was nothing he could have done in that instance to assist her.

Although she seemed helpless and out of her depth at first, Carrie, thinking that Pitezel is still alive and that Holmes will help the family to reunite, made some decisions of her own and was soon instructing Holmes further. Holmes recounts that it was Carrie's decision that all letters between her and Pitezel should go through Holmes, and that her children should continue to believe their father was dead. If they knew he was alive, she argued, they would tell someone; besides which, "they are young, and will soon get over the worry."[14] If Carrie herself did not seem to be overly distressed in the wake of her husband's death, then the children would pick up on her mood, as well, and feel reassured without having to have the entire situation explained to them. Unfortunately for both Holmes and the Pitezels, he continued to lie to them. Although he himself was aware that the man who had been buried under the pseudonym B.F. Perry was in fact B.F. Pitezel, Carrie believed it was a stranger whose body had been acquired by some unknown means and that she would be reunited with her husband soon enough.

Holmes' involvement in the Pitezel family's affairs continues when he agrees to travel to Philadelphia for the disinterment and identification of "B.F. Perry," although once again this is not presented as having been his idea. Since Carrie was too ill to travel and she needed her eldest daughter, Dessie, to help her care for the baby, fourteen-year-old Alice was selected to make the trip with the family lawyer. Not only does Holmes lament the fact that such a child was forced to look upon the long-dead man's face and determine whether or not he was her father, but he also indicates that he felt his own presence there was unnecessary, since there were "two other physicians present."[15] His use of the word "other" reminds his readers that, whatever else he may be, Holmes has his medical degree, and this statement also indicates his own unwillingness to participate further. Since he knew for a fact that the body was Pitezel's, there was no need for him to worry about a misidentification or to concern himself over whether he would have to look for the agreed-upon identifying marks on a body that had "unmanned" him previously and had decomposed in the meantime.

Perhaps since this encounter was not a surprise, Holmes was able

Seven. Protestations of Innocence

to remain unruffled throughout the ordeal even though he was indeed asked to help make the identification. He reports that he was even the one to excise the identifying marks, including a wart and a scar. Apparently the men tasked with digging up the grave had not thought to bring along any surgical implements and Holmes, in spite of not having prepared to go on a house call or other professional work, had a lancet with him that proved up to the task. Lest his audience believe him to be too cold-hearted, Holmes reported that, after Alice had also identified the body, he made arrangements to have Pitezel buried elsewhere, paid for out of Holmes' own pocket, and he was "well satisfied to be able to perform this final act for my friend."[16]

Readers of *Holmes' Own Story* would have already been aware that Holmes' most recent confession included the fact that it was indeed Pitezel who had died and not a substitute cadaver, but, at the time he purported to have made these arrangements, his actions might have aroused suspicion. In the telling of his autobiography Holmes means it as a reassurance that his caring for Pitezel has continued on until after his friend's death, not only through his staging of the body but also continually with his pocketbook. The insurance company might have been swayed by this extra expense since it would have been an indication that the body really was Pitezel's, because his friend went out of his way in order to care for it. Carrie, however, might have wondered why Holmes would have been so willing to pay for this reburial when she thought that the body in question was not her husband. If she had been informed of this expense, Holmes does not mention it, nor does he complain about the cost even though he, too, was not currently in a situation where his pocketbook was full.

The difficult part of his story to explain is what happened after he left Philadelphia, since this was where Holmes began moving six members of the Pitezel family and his own wife through various cities on an apparently random path. Holmes argues that his wife did not know of the Pitezels, thus keeping her from also having suspicion cast upon her, but he also kept Carrie, her eldest child, and her youngest apart from her three middle children. He continued to lie to Carrie and manipulated her through these various train rides and hotels with the promise that she would be reunited with her husband at any one of them, and even argued that all of this was necessary because he "felt that any move, without regard to expenses, was better than to have Mrs. Pitezel arrested and myself as well."[17] Certainly it would be best for all of her children if Carrie remained at liberty, since her arrest would mean they had neither parent to look out for them, but why should she be kept separate from three of those children?

The initial division occurred when Alice left St. Louis to identify her father's body, since both Carrie and the baby were ill and could not travel. This parting, it seems, was inevitable if Carrie wanted to be sure to receive the insurance money, since it was unlikely that the insurance agents would accept an identification from Holmes alone since he was not a family member. When Nellie and Howard left with Holmes, ostensibly to meet up with Alice and the woman who was looking after her, it was so that Carrie might be able to visit her parents unencumbered by her children. Dessie would, of course, be present in order to continue looking after the baby. But Holmes offers no explanation here for their continued separation. Carrie did not know where three of her children were and would not have been able to meet up with them again on her own, but Holmes does not explain why he did not return them to their mother.

He does clarify that there came a point when he thought it best to keep more from Carrie than he already had been, indicating that he "did not now think it prudent that she should know the probability of trouble arising from the insurance company,"[18] but there is still no explanation for why she could not be with her children while he shielded her from further issues. Holmes wishes to protect her from worries about money as well as the knowledge that her husband is in fact dead and not waiting in the next city to meet her, but he does not ease her concern for her children by reuniting them. Instead, Holmes only reports on their activities and their well-being to Carrie, as he does for his readers.

Alice, Nellie, and Howard had been in the care of Miss Williams, who had been sure to let Holmes know she would prefer to avoid meeting his wife. Hatch, who has told Holmes that he and Miss Williams are in fact married, had helped Holmes not only with the children, but also with organizing Carrie's belongings so that they would not be carting useless items around with them as they went. Even when the children separated, the sisters wishing to go to Chicago to see if they might meet

Seven. Protestations of Innocence

up with old friends and Howard not wanting to join them, the girls went with Hatch and Howard with Miss Williams. Holmes ensured that he did not leave the children alone and uncared for, perhaps locked up in a hotel room with little to do to amuse themselves. Instead, the children were being taken out to see the sights of the different cities and to ride trams, being treated to the sorts of experiences that their family could not normally afford. Holmes frequently bought them sweets, fruit, and toys, and reported that he purchased warmer clothes for them specifically thinking of the transatlantic voyage in their future, since Miss Williams was to take them to England. On the day when Holmes accidentally ran into Carrie in Toronto, he even reported that he was holding some underwear he had purchased for Howard to send to Miss Williams.

These specific mentions of clothing are important for Holmes' continued protestations of innocence. Although the weather was growing colder as fall deepened, he would not have needed to waste the money on warmer clothes for the children if he had intended to murder them, or if he had known that they would soon be murdered. By mentioning these purchases he clearly indicates that he expected the children to meet Miss Williams and take the sea voyage. The—possibly traceable—act of spending money is a concrete indication of his expectations at the time and cannot be written off as hindsight or lies, if they are indeed found to be true. Since newspapers had already reported that Howard had been killed before Holmes and his various parties arrived in Toronto, the fact that he claims to have made a purchase for the boy after his death likewise supports the idea that Holmes did not know what was happening to the children. Why would Holmes waste his money making purchases for children who will not live to use them when it would be a simple enough task to track down the store where records of those transactions could be found? There is naturally no suggestion that a man who would murder children might be so conniving as to buy them treats and things after the fact so as to prove his innocence, since Holmes sets out to simply prove he did not kill them in the first place.

In case those purchases were in and of themselves not enough to convince his readers of his own innocence and good intentions, Holmes describes how, at his final parting from the girls, he made sure to ask them if they were comfortable traveling part of the distance alone.

Hatch, of course, went with them on the first segment of the train between Toronto and Niagara, but Alice and Nellie were meant to meet Miss Williams at the station by themselves. Holmes had given Alice $400, pinned inside her dress for safekeeping until it could be given to Miss Williams, and the telegram she was to send if they were stranded alone at the station, so Holmes assures his readers that the girls were confident they could make the journey just fine on their own. He even "cautioned Nellie about quarreling with Howard"[19]—a senseless admonition had he known the boy was dead or expected the girls to soon be, as well—and accepted a kiss from her before they boarded the train. Having seen them off into the presumably capable hands of Hatch, who had already done so much for the children, and not receiving a telegram to inform him they had run into trouble, Holmes was left to assume that all had gone well and the girls, reunited with their brother and under the supervision of Miss Williams, were on their way toward a bright future.

A Question of Timing

All of the preceding arguments Holmes makes for his innocence, even including those that simply involve spending or giving money, are centered around the idea that he cared so much for the Pitezel family that he could not have killed any of them. Even when he argues that Pitezel was worth far more than $10,000 to him in any given year, the inference is not simply that Pitezel brought in $10,000 worth of business, but was indeed Holmes' friend. Holmes was severely shocked at Pitezel's death and followed his friend's orders out of respect and concern not only for Pitezel, but for his family. He meant to see the Pitezel children schooled under Miss Williams even if he could not reunite Carrie with her husband, as promised, and he had chosen both Hatch and Miss Williams to help him negotiate the difficulties that came with being a wanted man in so many cities. From the start, no matter how unorthodox his methods, Holmes wished to demonstrate that he cared very much for every member of the Pitezel family. Even if he did not display as much emotion as his readers may have wished, he certainly was not the sort of depraved monster who would murder children. For the readers who wished to dismiss out of hand any emotional argument Holmes put forth, he begins to construct a logical argument in favor of his innocence.

At this point, in his autobiography and before the prison diary appendix, Holmes appears to not entirely have concluded that Hatch must have been the one who murdered the children. Holmes is unconvinced that Hatch could have managed it considering the constraints of timing, and, concerning the fact that Alice and Nellie were murdered in Toronto, he muses that it seems to him "hardly possible that he [Hatch] could have found a house at once so well adapted to his purpose as this seems to have been"[20] based on the timeline of when Holmes, Hatch, and the girls arrived in Toronto and the activities during which Holmes was with Hatch. The timeline becomes his key focus because of the sheer number of events that had to have lined up in order for Alice and Nellie to have been murdered within Holmes' own version of the timeline.

Someone—in this case Hatch—would have needed to locate a rather isolated house for rent and secured the keys for it before Alice and Nellie were sent off on the train. The timing is the only place where Holmes finds it difficult to believe that the man he had chosen to help him look after the children could in fact be their murderer. He has no arguments of character to defend Hatch, only stating that he does not think Hatch would have had the time to find the house between caring for the girls and seeing Holmes. Since the girls' bodies were found together buried in the basement, Hatch would have needed access to a spade, as well—a matter upon which Holmes harps greatly, since it seems Hatch was loath to leave behind just such an implement during all their packing, unpacking, and travels, even though the trunk with that spade was not with them in Toronto—and the knowledge that the basement was dirt so that he could indeed dispose of their bodies.

Hatch would also have had to coax the girls to return to Toronto with him and go with him to that house so he could murder them, but Holmes does not address this. Even though he had earlier reported that Alice did not wish to return to St. Louis once having gone to Philadelphia because she had told all her friends that she would not be returning, he does not consider how difficult it might have been to convince the sisters, once on the train to go to Miss Williams and then on an exciting trip to England, to get off the train and turn back. Although Holmes would have known about the difficulty of securing a suitable house in such a short time, he had no personal experience with getting Alice and Nellie off the train and back to Toronto, so he had no reference for how difficult that aspect might have been.

Instead of pursuing how Hatch must have managed it, Holmes returns to the idea that, even if his own character and clear fondness of the Pitezel family will not relieve him of any suspicion concerning the girls' deaths, the timeline will provide him with a solid alibi. "It may be asked how at this late date I can fully remember what occurred ... nearly a year previous to the writing of these pages,"[21] Holmes acknowledges, since an innocent man who believed his charges to be safe would certainly not need to remember every store he visited or every task he undertook surrounding the date of what has later been revealed to him to be their deaths. Luckily enough for Holmes, he was in prison when the newspapers reported that Detective Geyer had discovered the girls' bodies, and this meant he had very little to do but sit and think. Holmes also suggests that a man in his position might be able to force himself to cogitate faster or more accurately simply because his life might depend on the answer.

Since the newspaper coverage of both the search for Alice and Nellie and its aftermath, including the death inquest, was extensive, Holmes was at least helped along with certain elements of his timeline. Carrie spoke of what she had done in Toronto, including how she had crossed paths with Holmes unexpectedly in a department store, and there were reports from hotel managers and the real estate agent who had leased the house. Holmes was able to use this information, which was also readily available to his audience, to help pin down moments in which he was indeed seen. The fact that the real estate agent thought he had caught sight of Holmes was perfectly explicable since it was a photograph of Holmes that was shown around, and Hatch looked quite similar. For that interaction Holmes was not able to rely on pinpointing his movements to that office at that moment, but rather had to recall where he had been while Hatch was negotiating for the house.

Holmes' choice of language in discussing his movements indicates a detachment from the situation, positioning him as an outsider without any personal knowledge of the central event. When making a careful

Seven. Protestations of Innocence

inventory of his whereabouts and actions, which is mostly a list of what he has bought and where, Holmes identifies October 24 as "the day when it is reasonable to suppose the two girls were killed."[22] Here he is careful not to show certainty about something that has not been printed as fact in the newspapers, displaying an attention to detail that had already served to help him avoid implicating himself earlier: the newspapers reported that Pitezel's body was in Chicago instead of in Philadelphia and so, when Holmes first wrote to offer his help in identifying him, he suggested plans based on having Chicago as his destination. In his autobiography Holmes negotiates what the newspapers have said about the case while refraining from confirming what has only been speculated. By indicating that this is only a reasonable supposition of when Alice and Nellie were murdered, Holmes is in effect saying that his readers know just as much about it as he does.

He further emphasizes that he did not see much of the children in Toronto, since they had "been in Hatch's care more than with me,"[23] a statement supported by one given by Carrie Pitezel and printed in the newspapers. It concerned the time that she had run into Holmes by surprise—the encounter during which he reported holding in his hands some underwear for Howard—and, although Carrie insisted that she knew her children must have been in Toronto at the time, they were not with Holmes. In order to cinch the timeline and tighten his alibi Holmes reported going directly from this meeting to the train station where he saw the girls off and left them in Hatch's care. As an added emphasis Holmes indicated that, at the time, he was glad that mother and daughters had not been reunited, lest it ruin his plans and lead to his arrest, but he later naturally regretted the unfortunate circumstance.

Yet even as he argues his own innocence, Holmes also fails to fully implicate Hatch in the murders at this point. He even mentions another logical issue surrounding a spade that Hatch had purchased and refused to leave behind during their travels because it was new and in perfect condition, since the trunk containing that spade would have been accessible to Hatch. Since a neighbor reported a man—presumably Holmes, but possibly Hatch—had borrowed a shovel on that fated afternoon, it would seem that Holmes argues for Hatch's innocence, as well. Logically it would make no sense for a man to ask to borrow a spade and place himself in someone else's mind as having needed an implement on that very day when he had access to one of his own and could have dug the girls' grave without arousing such attention. Holmes' construction of the timeline in his autobiography is meant to show why he himself could not have murdered the girls—the explanation of how Hatch managed it must wait until his prison diary appendix.

It should also be noted that, at this time, Holmes does not construct a similar outline of his movements in Indiana for the most likely time period in which Howard was killed. There seems to be the assumption, held not just by Holmes but by reporters as well, that the murders of the Pitezel family were all enacted by the same person and thus the question is of all or none. If Holmes did not murder Benjamin Pitezel or his daughters, then he most certainly did not murder his son.

Holmes concludes his autobiography by stating that he can best explain his imprisonment by copying directly from the diary he has kept while incarcerated. He indicates that he has not chosen to display the entire contents of that diary, but has specifically chosen entries surrounding his worries about his wife and his daily life in confinement, both of which torture him greatly since he had previously been a loving, devoted husband and a physically active man. It is only here, as the diary entries run to a close, that Holmes presents Hatch as the true murderer and explains how he thinks the mysterious man who looks so much like him managed to get away with such a crime.

Part III

Moyamensing Prison Diary Appendix

Holmes' diary, ostensibly written while he was in Moyamensing, also known as the Philadelphia County Prison, is included—and named—merely as an appendix to *Holmes' Own Story* even though his narrative would not be complete without it. The diary entries do not simply supplement the information provided in his autobiography, but also add to it. Holmes continues to present his wife as a locus of empathy, yes, and protests his innocence, but a large portion of the diary is devoted to outlining how, exactly, Hatch betrayed Holmes and murdered three children. At the end of *Holmes' Own Story*, no such accusations have been leveled. Holmes apparently parted from Hatch soon after Hatch saw the girls off on their way to meet Miss Williams and Howard and, at this time, Holmes was concerned that he had perhaps been treating Hatch poorly, considering all Hatch had done for him. If readers were only presented with the autobiographical text, which wraps up with Holmes' visit to his parents and an account of his own arrest, there would be no explanation for how the children were killed.

It would, of course, have been possible for Holmes to build up an argument of his innocence based on a timeline of his own activities and the lack of unobserved hours in which he could have undertaken the crime, but this would likely have left his readers with a sense of anticlimax. From the printing of the first execution sermon, crime narratives have set out to explain how the crime happened. When the center of authority surrounding these narratives shifted into the secular, the purpose expanded to include an explanation of *why* it happened. These narratives, whether they are trial reports, newspaper articles, or modern true crime books, fulfill the task of crafting a series of events into a story with a beginning, middle, end, and an explanation. Most of these narratives, following the example set by the execution sermon, include the consequences meted out to the guilty party following a trial or an explanation of the subject's acquittal. These retellings of crimes and trials are meant to end with a sense of closure brought about by hardworking members of law enforcement and the justice system.

Holmes is instead attempting to argue an injustice by declaring that the system has currently failed and imprisoned the wrong man while letting the true criminal run free. The fact that it seems no one will believe that Hatch is a real person is yet another blow against the police and detectives who have worked to puzzle out the truth of what happened during the fall of 1894. For Holmes, these men are either too blind or too fixated on him to realize the truth that would be perfectly clear to an outsider who did not approach the situation with the preconceived notion that Holmes, a swindler, must also be Holmes, a murderer.

While *Holmes' Own Story* was clearly written with a wide audience in mind and meant to be sold to and therefore read by large swatches of the American population, the diary is presented without a preface explaining its genesis. Presumably Holmes kept it as a means of passing the time, although he gives no indication that he generally kept a diary. It would seem as though he had not begun one before November 24, 1894, since even a pocket diary consisting of a few lines a day would have helped him organize the dates and locations of his odd journey with Georgiana and the Pitezels. As it was, Holmes continued to insist that he would have to consult with his wife in order to clarify where they stayed and when.

The diary begins with dated entries that have two points of focus: Georgiana and the way Holmes is organizing his time while being locked away. Once again Holmes continually refers to Georgiana as "my wife" and emphasizes her plight in tandem with his own, continuing the theme he began in *Holmes' Own Story* at his arrest. Interwoven are comments with how he spends his days, filling his hours with gentlemanly tasks that, presumably, would not be associated with a murderer.

These shorter entries, prefaced with clear dates, begin to break down until, sometime around mid-July, Holmes leaves them off completely for a long narrative study of what he has deduced must have actually transpired in Irvington and Toronto during the hours when Hatch and the children were out of his sight. There are no indications of how long it took Holmes to write this passage and, since it does not record the contents of his days but instead reflects back on past events, does not match up with the rest of his diary. This is where Holmes finally lays out his interpretation of what happened, answering the question of how the children died, and by whose hand.

This is followed by the most logical aspects of Holmes' argument in which he lists the names of other people he supposedly killed and refutes them one by one. Then he picks apart the use of photographic evidence in Inspector Geyer's quest to find Alice, Nellie, and Howard, once again spelling out his argument logically. The question of motive is addressed in the same way: not as though Holmes must explain it to himself and get it straight in his own mind, but as though presenting his arguments to a jury made not of his peers, but of his readers. Again, these are not diary entries to record the passing of the days or any events that might make one stand out from the others, even though they are included in the appendix clearly labeled "diary." While the earlier pages might pass as the sort of record a man might make when there is little else to do, the illusion falls apart in the second half when Holmes' true motive shines through: he wishes to convince his audience, before his trial even opens, of his innocence, not just in the case of Benjamin Pitezel but also concerning the deaths of his children. Even in his "diary," Holmes writes for the wider world.

Eight

"My Wife"

Finding himself behind bars for the second time in their short marriage, Holmes naturally concerned himself with the condition of his wife. During their jaunts across various states and into Canada he had often reported on her health, indicating when she was ill or when she was well enough to travel. Georgiana, continually referred to as "my wife" instead of by name, seems to be prone to sickness and simply not a healthy woman to start with, although the stress of travel and having her husband arrested for the second time could not have been helping. She was dependent upon Holmes to take care of her since she, unlike the Williams sisters, had not inherited land or other resources to claim as her own.

In his prison diary, Holmes mentions her physical health twice: first, during his opening entry on November 24, 1894, a week after his arrest and once he has been transferred to Philadelphia, where he will remain for the rest of his diary—and indeed, the rest of his days. Holmes' lawyer visited him and informed him that his wife would be able to visit in two days' time, and that "she was no longer seriously ill."[1] This news came as a great comfort to Holmes, who reported that his burden, while not lifted entirely, was certainly lighter for hearing it. Even though Georgiana may still have been sick, she was not doing as poorly as when he had last seen her—and at which time he had explained why he was being arrested.

The fact that this news comes as such a relief also reveals where Holmes' concerns lie. Since he had been insisting on his innocence throughout the book and his initial arrest in Boston was for horse thievery and not for insurance fraud, much less murder, Holmes himself must simply bide his time until the situation is rectified. At this point in time astute readers might note that Holmes had given his first confession, claiming that Pitezel and his children were together somewhere abroad, but that there was as of yet no concern that the children might have been dead. An intelligent and cunning man such as Holmes would have ensured that any diary entry he wrote after his first interview, but before his second confession, would do nothing to contradict what had gone on record at the time, and even if Holmes had constructed his supposed diary after the fact, his initial entries focus much more on prison life and his concerns about his wife than they do on discussing the case against him. Holmes may not have specifically written these pages meaning for them to reach a wider audience, although he must have been aware that they could have been read at any time and it would be unwise to discuss in too much detail the charges brought against him.

Although many of his early entries focus on his wife, Holmes only mentions her physical health once more, at some point in or after mid-July when the entries are no longer dated but instead run together as a longer narrative. With his first trial over and a murder trial looming, Holmes learns from a newspaper report that his wife has been bullied and mistreated by local law enforcement officials, and he writes that he "feared that the threats they made would cause her to worry until she became very ill."[2] Once again his concerns are not for himself, but for Georgiana's health. Holmes' readers need not depend solely on his concerns as fall and his murder trial approach since a person's physical health can be corroborated by an impartial third party in the form of a physician. What Holmes can tell his diary—and his readers—that no one else can would be reports on her mental and emotional health.

"She Has Suffered"

Holmes' discussions of his wife are a balancing act between concern for how she is fairing during his incarceration and how this anxiety is less about Georgiana than it is about Holmes himself. Her first visit to him in Philadelphia occurred on Monday November 26, and his diary entry for the day is devoted solely to this meeting. It occurred at 9:30 a.m. and apparently did not last long, since he lamented even upon first seeing her that they would have to part again after only a few minutes.

It was hardly a private conversation, having taken place in front of prison officials. It thus seems unlikely that husband and wife might have been able to say all they wished to say even if it did not involve the fate of the Pitezel family, although it is also doubtful that Holmes would have wished to record it had she asked him if he were truly guilty of the crimes. As long as his wife believes in his innocence, then his readers are free to, as well.

Humiliation is mentioned twice in this short entry. First, Holmes himself must use all the courage he possesses to "go to her under such humiliating circumstances,"[3] even though in Boston he considered it a privilege to be able to speak to her and personally inform her of what was happening. He even had the chance to look forward to this visit specifically since his lawyer had informed him that she would be visiting. Holmes' previous two entries have spoken of worry and tedium, but nothing about which to be humiliated. Being arrested under false charges is not cause for celebration, but neither does he report feeling ashamed—until his wife comes to visit.

Holmes has thus far presented himself as a man over whom emotions hold little sway. The vast majority of his decisions have been made so that he is the one to benefit. When Minnie Williams told him that she had killed Nannie, Holmes was persuaded to avoid reporting it to the police not because Minnie begged him but because his relationship with her would have been made public. His own reputation would have been ruined. He even resisted all of Carrie Pitezel's pleas to be reunited with her children because he feared not only her arrest, but also his own, if this meant she would stop listening to him and moving on as he ordered. As long as the people in his life could be swayed to do what Holmes decided was best, he did not care what they thought of him or how pitiful they might have appeared to others. Georgiana, though, appears to be different.

He can endure being imprisoned once more well enough as things stand, but it is the thought of being observed by his wife that makes Holmes balk. Humiliation is, after all, an insult to one's pride, and Holmes has always been a proud man. When he related the story of his "first imprisonment" from childhood it was because of a flaw based off of pride: that his family owned the entire herd of cows and he himself was the master of the best one. Even when he was in prison in St. Louis

Holmes managed to project a sense of pride since even his cellmate, the infamous outlaw Marion Hedgepeth, could only be assessed as a "bright mechanic"[4] at best. In St. Louis Holmes still had his intelligence and his position as a physician to set him above the accusations, and he did not mention whether his wife was able to visit him. At that time, however, she had been able to furnish his bail which allowed him to walk free. Holmes' wife cannot come to such a rescue this time.

She holds a power over him so great that the threat of illness or desertion on her part is able to crack Holmes' tough exterior in a way that even threats from law enforcement and the insurance company cannot. Being imprisoned is a minor inconvenience when it interferes with his business dealings, but when Holmes considers what this means to his wife, the humiliation comes to the forefront. He presents himself as having a strong emotional connection with her in an instance when he cannot express it tangibly in the form of money or a gift. He is, in fact, unable to provide for her at all in this moment and must gather himself to be able to even enter her presence when he is thus unmanned.

Their meeting is a brief one in which Georgiana did her best to keep her husband from seeing how much she was suffering. He is able to recognize it all the same, and he terms her struggle "heroic."[5] His brave wife was doing her best not to add to his worries and in doing so shared the anguish instead of relieving it. Knowing that she would have to leave him and endure interactions with others who held their own poor opinions of him wounded Holmes "more ... than any death struggles could ever do."[6] His love for his wife is what allows this image to torture him so much and, though she promised to visit twice a week, he states that he cannot ask her to do so. During such visits the humiliation would be hers since she would be putting herself in the position of at least appearing to be a devoted wife, suffering the taunts and accusations of the general public as she ran the gauntlet into the prison for a short fifteen-minute visit.

It is not his incarceration that troubles Holmes, but the fact that he believes the detectives are pestering his wife and that she might in fact come to harm before this is all over. Being in prison seems to have little effect on Holmes, but being in prison unable to know if she is being seen to makes every day "a living death."[7] All of Holmes' personal suffering is centered upon this one woman.

This was likely meant to inspire pity in his audience who would know that Holmes' imprisonment continued for many months past that November, constantly keeping him apart from his wife. However, at the time of publication, Holmes had retracted his original confession and thus there were a number of areas in which he could have expressed concern instead of solely over Georgiana. The well-being of a woman whose husband has been falsely imprisoned for crimes he did not commit is a very different concern than the well-being of a woman whose husband has likely murdered four members of a family, one of them his good friend and the other three children. The emotional concern Holmes shows for Georgiana takes on a very different light when he may be discussing a woman he has deceived frequently in order to commit crimes far worse than fraud. His readers might in fact be less concerned for Georgiana since, if her husband has been imprisoned, it means that she is safe from his murderous intentions. Carrie Pitezel, for example, had suffered far more since her losses were permanent and Holmes had already admitted to manipulating her, but his concern is focused entirely around his wife.

His One Concern

Holmes tells his readers that his wife remains devoted to him, not just through the twice-weekly visits she is willing to undertake but also through her letters and even small gifts. On one occasion in March she brought him flowers and spoke "so strongly"[8] of their married life that he could not bring himself to continue to look at them, even though they must have been the sole bright spot in his cell. Through her letters, her gifts, and such conversations, Georgiana is presented to readers as still being his devoted, loving wife very much in spite of the efforts of detectives and other law enforcement officials to turn her against Holmes. This both shows the detectives in a negative light, in contrast to the amount of positive press various others had received for tracking down Holmes and the children's bodies, and strengthens Holmes' claims to Georgiana, since she has endured not only his imprisonment but these strong negative pressures and yet still remains faithful and loyal to him. Holmes variably uses words such as annoyance,[9] humiliation,[10] intimidation,[11] and threat[12] to describe the way his wife has been treated in an attempt to turn her against him while he, powerless, sits in prison with only limited methods of contacting her.

Holmes himself wishes to do all he can to spare his wife from enduring even more of this sort of treatment, going so far as to declare "I would rather serve a longer term of imprisonment than thus humiliate her"[13] by having her called as a witness at his trial. This, then, is the closest Holmes comes to touching upon his real reason for concern about his wife: his impending trial for the murder of Benjamin Pitezel. Should Georgiana take the stand in any capacity, she would not be able to provide him with an alibi for Pitezel's—or his children's—murder. Since a man's wife is not allowed to testify against him without his consent, Holmes should still be able to prevent such a fate from befalling Georgiana. However, the newspapers had already discovered that she was not the only woman to have been known as, or thought herself to be, Holmes' legal wife. Robert Corbitt had already printed interviews with Myrta Holmes in which she discussed how her husband's temperament and love of children made the charges against him patently ridiculous. Holmes had chosen not to mention Myrta in his autobiography, but the fact that she has been represented as his wife is a threat that could turn devoted Georgiana against him.

His wife seems to be Holmes' only redeeming feature, and his diary indicates that he is well aware of it. His concerns center on how she is being treated not only by the detectives but also by reporters, since some of the intimidation efforts were not related to him directly but ones he had read about in the daily newspapers. In order to combat the accusations that he has taken more than one wife, Holmes must show his dedication to Georgiana and how much the separation from her has been affecting him, especially when he must hear and read such negative things from others. Georgiana herself refrains from complaining to her husband when she visits, leading to such emotional conversations about their past life together that he could not even bear to look at her gift of flowers afterward. He had, after all, been the one to rob them of that previously happy life.

Holmes shows at least this much self-awareness when he declares that he felt anger "towards myself that for the sake of business gains I had ever allowed myself to enter into the petty transactions that had been the cause of all her troubles."[14] He is willing to take responsibility for putting Georgiana in this position, although Holmes could not have predicted the actions of others or known that the detectives would have been so cruel to her. Holmes is, after all, responsible for the actions that led to his arrest, although those actions, to him, are "petty." It was merely an insurance fraud and a crime he had already succeeded in perpetrating once before. What Holmes apparently fails to see is how his earlier fraud differs from his current situation and makes his predicament all the more precarious. This lack of appreciation of the semantics once again throws Holmes' argument out of alignment since he cannot see how detectives might wish to gain insight from the bigamous wife of a murderer in order to support their case, and why they would feel comfortable continuing to seek her assistance when they would, for example, not pester Carrie Pitezel to the same extent. The minutiae are lost to Holmes who feels a responsibility to Georgiana and is affected by her current situation far more than he seems to be by Carrie's.

Georgiana's suffering is her husband's suffering. When Holmes reports on her condition, whether it be physical or emotional, he more often than not adds how this current update affects him. When she is no longer ill, his load is lighter. When she is suffering, he suffers. When he reads that she has spoken to detectives he determines that it must have been through threats and intimidation, and he writes passionately on her behalf. It is not only torture to be separated form Georgiana while he sits in prison, but also to read in the papers and see in her face how the situation is negatively affecting her. As a dutiful wife, she does not speak of such things, but he—devoted husband—interprets them all the same.

Georgiana's commitment to him is by necessity secretive and hidden. He has, after all, been arrested, and even though he is innocent of all but the insurance fraud, Holmes knows that she has not been treated kindly by likely anyone but himself. Were she to publicly declare devotion to him, reactions would be far worse. As it is, Holmes notes how difficult his wife currently finds her situation, although he does what little he can to assist her. For example, Holmes indicated that, "until the world at large ceased to look upon me as a murderer[,] I should not in the presence of the others greet her as was my usual custom."[15] Presumably this greeting would have been just as tender and obvious as the flowers she had given him previously, or the way in which she spoke of their past life together.

Although the words Georgiana would have spoken to him would have been in front of witnesses and thus likewise observable, Holmes represents her devotion as being more invisible to outside observers, who have likely overlooked it completely. He notes that, in spite of everything, she continued to wear both her wedding and engagement rings as an outward sign of her commitment. Although others may have noted that she continued to present Holmes with small gifts, only he himself could understand the deeper meaning she meant to impart to him. The newspapers, of course, could choose to print what they wished, especially since journalists would likely not know the secret messages passing back and forth between husband and wife, and Holmes himself staunchly declared that "until she tells me that such is not the case I shall hold to the belief that she is yet loyal to me."[16] Her loyalty could greatly boost his image, since a man who could command the heart of such a lovely young woman of her class in spite of all outside efforts to convince her to betray him could hardly be seen as a murderer. Further, as long as Georgiana is loyal and believes herself to be Holmes' only wife, she might help convince others in court that this is true and thus not be accessible as a witness for the prosecution.

It would almost seem that, were Holmes truly upset at his wife's continued suffering at his expense, he would find a way to release her from it. Although he mentions that it tortures him to see her coming in twice weekly for their short visits, he does not take a stand and tell her to stay away for her own health and sanity. Nor does he reject the flowers, gifts, and letters she continues to give him, even when he is concerned about his own income and business transactions, much less where his wife is being housed and fed. Holmes' mention of his business matters includes having his lawyer travel to settle up on his own behalf, although he also grumbles that the insurance company has been making such things difficult. Although Holmes' accommodation and meals are being provided by taxpayers, Georgiana must do the best she can, and yet she continues to spend money on what many might argue are frivolities. Even though Georgiana's appearance and demeanor cause Holmes himself to suffer, and he knows that it is his connection to her that is causing her such grief, he cannot bring himself to suggest that she change her actions in any way.

Toward the end of his entries Holmes fixates on another man as though he is the only source of Georgiana's suffering: the district attorney. It is for Holmes perhaps a preview of what his murder trial will entail, centered upon the idea that Georgiana has suffered so much already and could not possibly be asked to endure more. Whatever thin means of emotional support Holmes has attempted to provide for his wife, the district attorney has no interest in tending to these, and likely every interest in destroying them.

First, Holmes points out that the district attorney's office told the press that, at a time when he met with Georgiana, she "shrank from me as though in fear."[17] Holmes does not phrase this as an accusation, but rather as a semi-helpless observation that, if Georgina did indeed react in such a way, Holmes himself did not see it. With everything else he has noticed when it comes to Georgiana—presumably that the papers did not print, since no one else was that observant and Holmes would not have gone to the reporters himself—it would be odd indeed if he did not notice his wife possibly flinch away from him. Holmes has apparently been bracing himself for such subtle signs since the moment of his arrest and his desire to tell Georgina himself, as well as to see her, would be to help him judge her true reaction to the situation rather than relying on what the newspapers had to say. Holmes presents himself as a man clinging to hope—the merest thread, perhaps, but one that would certainly be dashed if he thought Georgiana feared him. She had, after all, worn her rings to that very same meeting. Lest Holmes wonder if this information had been leaked and was not part of the district attorney's overall plan, he reports that, when he asked about providing for Georgiana, the district attorney himself told Holmes that "he did not consider it part of my business at the present time to either know or care for her welfare."[18]

Holmes had asked for the meeting between himself, the district attorney, and his wife to, as he put it, attempt to piece together where Howard's body might be found. The diary entries have lost their dates at this point, but it seems safe to assume that he would have proposed this meeting after Alice and Nellie's bodies had been found, since their whereabouts are not an item of discussion. It would seem that Holmes, shocked by the discovery of the girls since he would have continued to assume all three children were with Miss Williams in London, chose action and an attempt to help ease Carrie Pitezel's pain as he wished to assist with the investigation—albeit in a way that still centered on his own innocence. Georgiana's presence would have helped him make the argument that he did not have enough time in Toronto to have killed the girls, and thus he also would not have murdered their brother. A meeting between the three of them in order to have such a discussion would have not only allowed Georgiana go come to his defense, but also given the district attorney the chance to see exactly how poorly off Holmes' wife was, while at the same time marking Holmes as a helpful prisoner. Unfortunately, none of these aims was realized and Holmes, claiming he saw how much of a toll this had taken on his wife, quickly brought their discussion to a close.

It is his last mention of Georgina in the prison diary, since Holmes moves on to address how Hatch could indeed have had enough time in Toronto to murder the Pitezel girls, and from there to other segmented arguments about his own innocence. Even in his conclusion he does not refer back to his wife specifically, including her in the category of "those who have looked up to and honored me in the past"[19] if she is indeed a part of this group at all. For as much as Georgiana's suffering tortures Holmes he is, in the end, concerned with his own life—and death—first and foremost.

Suffering and Humiliation

As good-looking and charming as Holmes knew himself to be in his life prior to being arrested in Boston, he is at least aware of the fact that this has changed. He can no longer simply talk himself out of a questionable situation or even rely on his class or schooling to help positively affect the way others interact with him. Previously he was a smooth-talking, well-dressed conman with a confidence born of continued successes. Even his arrest in St. Louis did not alter his basic character. In person and one-on-one, Holmes had still been capable of talking his way around almost any situation. Unfortunately for Holmes, however, after his arrest his reputation spread much further to the point where, even if he had been free to do so, he would not have been able to speak with each and every individual whose opinion of him might matter. Those who would file into the jury box in Philadelphia were not the only men he needed to convince of his innocence, since the Pitezel children's bodies had been found in two other cities, one of them not even in the United States. The only way to reach such a wide audience in a short amount of time was through a written document.

Good speakers are not always good writers since a conversation with someone allows the speaker to judge the reaction of his audience and change tactics if his current approach is not yielding the desired results. If a joke falls flat or a strong opinion is not shared, the speaker can work to save himself in the audience's eyes and still aim to convince them of his end goal. In his autobiography and continued in this prison diary appendix, Holmes' intent is to convince his audience that there is at least a reasonable doubt of his guilt, if not outright proof of his innocence. His audience, who have likely devoured all news of Holmes and his crime if they were willing to then pay twenty-five cents for a copy of *Holmes' Own Story*, would be more willing to listen to him if they could relate to and understand him as a fellow human being and not some inhuman monster.

Georgiana plays this crucial role within Holmes' prison diary. As a man arrested first on suspicion of insurance fraud and then slowly suspected of multiple murders, there seems to be little about Holmes to inspire a stance of pity or empathy from which his audience might reconsider the question of his guilt. The general public has been reading articles that refer to Holmes as a deranged monster and not as a human being—not an unusual approach in true crime accounts that followed execution sermons—and there is no need for empathy between people and monsters. Monsters fall outside the morals of men and thus their actions might be examined and possibly even admired, but only within the scope of monstrosity. In order to consider Holmes as a man, and a possibly innocent man, he must be examined via the lens of humanity, but a cold-hearted con man is not likely to be treated much better than a monster.

Thus Holmes invokes his wife as the human face of his suffering. Georgiana is innocent both of the illegal activities that were taking place around her and of any knowledge of them. The fact that her husband has been wrongly imprisoned causes her grief and difficulty in her daily life, and Holmes' readers are meant to wish there was something they could do to spare her. An acquittal at his next trial would certainly be a step in the right direction, even though he would have to continue to serve his term for fraud, but at least Georgiana would be comforted by the fact that the jury did not find her husband guilty of being a murderer.

This is a difficult rhetorical move to make, however, since the focus of all emotion centers on Georgiana and the fact that her misery is causing her husband to suffer. Since Holmes has already admitted to breaking laws and is under suspicion for multiple counts of murder, his readers might argue that, considering he sits in jail, Holmes has every right to be tormented. They might further argue that Georgiana's situation is entirely Holmes' fault, and that he is the one prolonging her ordeal by refusing to tell her to stop coming to see him or to break off her involvement with him. If Georgiana is Holmes' legal wife, then the amount of devotion she shows to him during his imprisonment is immaterial, since she would not be able to testify against him in court. Holmes takes pains to center Georgiana not only in his diary but in the segments he chooses to publish for public consumption, displaying her suffering to an audience who would likely not have read about it otherwise, considering the preferred newspaper narrative. Although Georgiana has chosen not to speak to the press herself and has done her best to keep her struggles from her husband, he decided to publish them for the wider world without any comment as to whether or not she consented to it.

It would be understandable for Holmes to keep track of his wife's situation in his diary if it were a real locus of concern, but the fact that he has chosen to make her private suffering public is another matter entirely. A devoted husband might indeed record the emotional and mental anguish of his wife as a means of attempting to deal with it personally and perhaps to find a way to ease her situation, but publishing those musings without mention as to her permission or foreknowledge just adds to the impression that Holmes is only writing about Georgiana in order to bring the focus—and the sympathy—back onto himself. Her suffering becomes his, but she only suffers in the first place because of his activities that landed him in prison and his following inaction concerning releasing her from her current continued misery. In his diary Holmes seems to perhaps even encourage her suffering because of what it means to him to be able to write about it in such a way. He does not appear to write in order to protect Georgiana, even though the fact that she is the only person on the face of the earth who could hurt him means that any harm caused to her would wound him as well. Holmes has spoken to the district attorney concerning her care, although he only mentions this after he has been imprisoned for half a year. Holmes further does not indicate that he has attempted to stop the newspapers from hounding his wife and, although he complains about her treatment at the hands of the detectives, complaining seems to be as far as he goes. When it comes to words, Holmes has plenty to say about his poor wife, but as far as action is concerned, he finds himself stymied by the district attorney when he attempts any sort of assistance at all.

Georgiana's apparent centrality to the Prison Diary Appendix is meant to mark her as a person of importance in Holmes' life, both as a means of encouraging empathy in the reader and as an argument to prevent her from being called to testify against him in court. His constant repetition of "my wife" does not, in fact, bring Georgiana to center stage but is a tool for once again focusing the conversation, and the concern, on Holmes himself. In his diary, which is ostensibly about his day-to-day life and thoughts while in prison, Holmes spends little time on himself directly, using his words to center someone else, or another issue, as a roundabout way of bringing the conversation back to him. In the case of his wife, Holmes presents her as deserving of pity so that he might gain that reaction from his audience by association, likely because his discussions of himself and his current situation are not well suited to inspiring empathy in and of themselves.

Nine

Life Behind Bars

Most diaries are written in order to keep track of daily events in its author's life, and, at first, this seems to be the purpose of Holmes' prison diary. He begins it a week after his arrest in Boston, once he has already been relocated to Philadelphia, and at first the diary opens every entry with a notation of the date. These fall by the wayside quickly enough, with a single entry, undated, standing in for all the events of February and a more narrative tone emerging through June and July in which dates are mentioned in passing, but no longer as headings. The tone of the diary changes to be more like that of the autobiography as Holmes records his thoughts and musings concerning not current events, but how Hatch and Miss Williams must have enacted the murders almost a year before.

Most of Holmes' descriptions of prison life come in entries marked from November 24 through November 30, when the situation is new to him and daily life might indeed be something worth noting. However, his existence as a prisoner is not the focus of this diary—Holmes spends more time discussing his wife and aspects of the case than he does day-to-day events and developments. What Holmes does mention about his current living situation can be divided into three categories: the disagreeable, the surprisingly amenable, and his own marks of character.

Hardships

Prison is, after all, not meant to be an enjoyable experience as it aims to remove questionable or criminal persons from general society so that they cannot continue to commit their crimes. It is indeed meant as a punishment in and of itself—a fact that Holmes does not seem to grasp within his diary. Earlier, when describing his incarceration in St. Louis or the time in his childhood when his father locked him in a room, he demonstrated more fear and shame not only about the situation itself, but the fact that he had done something to cause it in the first place. Since Holmes spent November 1894 insisting that Benjamin Pitezel was alive and in possession of his children, having already confessed to insurance fraud, this current situation seems to him to be entirely unfair and undeserved. It was, after all, Pitezel's idea in the first place, and Holmes merely went along to help out his friend.

For this good deed Holmes has been locked away in "practically a place of solitary confinement."[1] Prisons in the nineteenth century were generally divided as far as their approach to prisoners. The Auburn System, also known as the New York system, held that prisoners should work in groups during the day and return to solitary cells at night, all of this in silence. Prisoners were meant to move in lockstep and were not safe from beatings or whippings. The separate or "Pennsylvania System" was developed at Eastern State Penitentiary in Philadelphia, which opened in 1829 and removed any social aspect from life behind bars. Prisoners were alone in their cells and often unable to socialize even during time in the yard or in the chapel, thanks to the way the prison and its grounds had been designed. The separate system was meant to mimic monastic life so that, instead of doing labor that might help them find jobs upon release, prisoners were forced to meditate on their past actions and thus hopefully emerge as changed men. Moyamensing Prison was not constructed to fulfill the role of a separate system.

In his previous stay in prison, Holmes had been able to interact with other prisoners in a situation that did not, in fact, work out in his favor. In St. Louis Holmes had struck up conversations with Marion Hedgepeth who, of course, then reported his following insurance scam to the chief of police. If Holmes found himself alone in Moyamensing with no one to speak to but prison employees, it may have in fact been a situation that played in his favor. Without anyone to brag to or show off for, he would thus be disinclined to discuss his current situation with others. Aside from his visitors, all Holmes has is his diary to confide in, although it would be difficult to find the same satisfaction in bragging to its pages as he would in speaking to another man who could indeed be impressed.

While solitary confinement is considered a higher form of punishment for prisoners in prisons that allow for both solitary and general population confinement, it can also be used to protect certain prisoners. If a prisoner is deemed to be a threat to himself, placing him in solitary confinement makes it easier for officers to both keep him under suicide watch and make sure that he would not have access to items that he could use to harm himself. Prisoners may also be put in solitary confinement when it is thought that other prisoners might be a threat to them, often based on the sort of crime a prisoner has been accused of committing. Therefore, if he were placed in a form of solitary confinement, Holmes would have been unable to once again overshare to a fellow prisoner who may have become his undoing; carefully overseen so that he could not commit suicide before justice had been carried out; and protected from the other men in the prison who, if they were anything like those he met in St. Louis, according to the belief of the day would have been of a lower class, intellectually inferior, and therefore more likely to resort to physical violence.

Holmes' isolation—and lack of a ready audience—is further emphasized when he laments that "I must restrict all of my correspondence to one letter a week."[2] He had been allowed to write more than that during his first week or so in Moyamensing Prison in order to settle his business affairs, but now Holmes' communication with the outside world is restricted to what his readers might assume is the normal amount allowed to prisoners. Since Holmes also reports in the same entry that he seems to have lost at least twenty pounds and is only now adjusting to his bed made of straw, it is understandable that this new restriction would irritate him further. Although Holmes is allowed to see his wife twice a week—and indeed just saw her that morning, bearing up as well as could be expected—his verbal communication is otherwise limited to employees of the prison or the criminal justice system. He is also well aware that there will always be at least a keeper present when he speaks to his wife and that all of his mail will be read.

Where Holmes suffers, then, is not just through the trials and woes of his wife but through the fact that he has no ready audience. The only communication that might possibly go unread by prison officials would be his own diary, and even that is not a certainty. When he speaks, he knows there is an outsider listening and when he writes it must be with the same awareness, especially since he apparently does so in plain English without the use of a code. Holmes' confessions to the police have, after all, involved discussions of ciphers, and he even shares one with the police with the intent of contacting Miss Williams and urging her to reveal her location and the safety of the Pitezel children. All that Holmes writes or says will be scrutinized, but not by the audiences of his choosing.

So much of Holmes' life has been spent interacting with and manipulating other people. Even when he found himself in a bind, generally as a result of his own schemes, Holmes thrived on the challenge of emerging from the encounter unscathed. When his autobiography told of the chase surrounding his successful insurance scam, Holmes was not ashamed or even rueful—he was flush with success and the opportunity to finally share this story with a wider audience. The cat-and-mouse game with the Grand Rapids detective was thrilling in and of itself, but for Holmes the retelling of the event, casting himself as the plucky underdog, is at minimum just as satisfactory. He thrives on interaction with others, especially in cases where he can emerge feeling superior, and so life in prison is arduous not just because he is limited in the amount of time he can spend with his wife, but in the amount of time he can spend with anyone.

In his next entry on December 3, three days after he has been informed that his letter writing is restricted, Holmes reports that he has "commenced to write a careful and truthful account of all matters pertaining to"[3] his case. This is perhaps why the frequency of diary entries drops off in spite of the fact that his letter-writing privileges have been restricted: at the same time that he continues to write in this document, he is also penning the foregoing autobiography, *Holmes' Own Story*. Readers who are able to keep the timeline straight will also recall that, on December 2, Holmes asked to give his second confession in which he admitted that the body identified as Pitezel's was not in fact an imposter but his own friend, who had committed suicide. Since Pitezel was now no longer alive to care for his children, this was where Holmes introduced the idea of Minnie Williams as being the one currently in possession of the children.

It is difficult to say whether or not Holmes had intended this to be his story all along. His second confession was necessitated by the fact

Nine. Life Behind Bars

that others were all too willing to once again dig up the body that may or may not have been Pitezel's in order to go through with another round of identification. If this were to happen before Holmes had changed his story, he would have been proven a liar—assuming, of course, that an identification could be made months after the burial, when Holmes and Alice had such difficulty the first time. If Holmes stuck by his initial story that the children were with their father, his proven death would have caused concern for them much sooner than it arose. By admitting that Pitezel was dead and placing the children with Minnie Williams, who had her own reasons for going into hiding and staying out of sight, Holmes was able to prolong the onset of suspicion that something may have happened to the children, after all. In December 1894 the main focus was on Benjamin Pitezel, and Holmes needed to construct a new story to allow for his death.

The figure of Edward Hatch, who looks so much like Holmes as to be mistaken for him, was not introduced until later. Indeed, Hatch's first appearance in the diary is a mention made on June 18, 1895, which, although late in the timeline of Holmes' confession, still occurs almost a month before newspapers reported the discovery of Alice and Nellie's bodies in Toronto. It can be assumed, therefore, that in December 1894 Holmes had not constructed his tale in full, since he had allowed for the disappearance of the children but had not taken pains to present detectives with the real criminal mastermind. Perhaps his time in near-solitary confinement did him some good, after all, since it allowed him the chance to develop his entire narrative line of defense. He even had the foresight to name Hatch before the children's bodies were discovered so that it did not seem to be a hastily changed story made by an overly desperate man who could not, in fact, prove his innocence. Holmes the entertainer had taken the time to construct his story and deemed it the best time—or perhaps the second or third best, considering his first two confessions—to tell it.

The fact that this isolation grated on Holmes was not lost on the prosecution. As summer rolled on and the district attorney threatened Holmes, it was solely with a loss of connections to the outside world: no letters, no visits, and no reading of newspapers to discover whether he was still being written about, and how. They did not come for any of the other privileges Holmes wrote about in his diary, going unerringly for the aspects that Holmes valued the most: his ability to be the center of focus in any room or conversation. Since he had his diary and his autobiography, however, along with the desire to be released from prison as soon as possible, Holmes did not give in to such threats, and the only further confession he made was in his writing, to be published for his own benefit.

Interacting with others and having an audience was, however, something of a double-edged sword for Holmes. As a man who had gone to medical school and who considered himself more intelligent than many, if not all, the people he met, being a prisoner—even a famous one—was damaging to his image. "The great humiliation of feeling that I am a prisoner is killing me far more than any other discomforts I have to endure,"[4] he lamented in a rare moment of self-pity. When Holmes writes of prison his tone overall is of a man who must suffer with dignity and in general silence, lest he stoop to such base emotions as would be expected of a murderer. Most of his pity and anguish are directed at his wife and the poor treatment she has been receiving in his absence. Even though prison is meant to be a hardship, Holmes does his best to present himself as being above all of the petty sufferings, as though to admit difficulty would also be to admit guilt.

Amenities

Even from his first diary entry, Holmes is looking for the positive elements in his situation. In spite of his near solitary confinement, he writes that he has been given cocoa which is a "most healthful drink"[5] for a man in such a situation. The use of the world "healthful" serves as a reminder that Holmes is himself a physician and thus speaks from a place of educated knowledge. He is not simply declaring it because the drink made him feel better, but because he, with his medical degree, is able to acknowledge that the prison is managing to do something right by him. Although they have imprisoned him and removed the chance for social interaction, they do not seem to wish to make matters worse for Holmes by giving him something unhealthy in the bargain.

The food also passes muster. In prison a week, Holmes already knows that there is "not a great variety,"[6] although he receives plenty to satisfy himself and notes that the food is properly cooked and he has no concerns about the cleanliness of what is given to him. The fact that he later mentions having lost twenty pounds runs counter to his description of the food. Perhaps it is too bland and repetitive to encourage him to eat properly, or perhaps Holmes decided that a drastic physical change would better represent his internal turmoil and anguish. Being in prison would give him little chance to walk and thus he would have little to do aside from sitting and writing between visits from his wife, his lawyer, or the district attorney. Gaining weight, or maintaining the heathy physique he possessed when he was arrested, might cause reporters to suggest that Holmes is not only happy but thriving in prison, which would not bode well for a man proclaiming wrongful arrest. Prison might not be as terrible as Holmes had once feared but a man insisting upon his innocence should not be shown to be overly complacent as to his current predicament.

In spite of the fact that Holmes has been limited to one letter a week outside of his business affairs, there are other ways in which he seems to be more privileged than punished. Holmes observes, for example, that "unsentenced prisoners are allowed to receive eatables,"[7] perhaps as a counter to the weight loss they might suffer when dining solely on prison food. If his wife sends him packages containing food, then this is another sign of her support for Holmes and a concession that a man of his standing would not find prison meals up to his usual expectations.

Holmes is likewise grateful that he has been allowed to wear his own clothes instead of "the convict garb."[8] This is a visual means of setting him apart from the jailed masses and allows Holmes to wear the suits to which he was accustomed. These suits would, of course, reflect his personal style and wealth, although it is difficult to imagine that they would fit properly when they had been tailored for a man who was twenty pounds heavier at the time of purchase. After Holmes went on trial for insurance fraud in the spring of 1895 and pled guilty, he was no longer an unsentenced prisoner and was therefore not eligible to receive care packages that contained food. His weight and appetite are no longer on his mind by the end of his diary entries, though, since he concerns himself more and more with the details surrounding his case that point to his innocence.

Aside from his healthful drinks, sufficient amounts of food, and the permission to wear his own clothes, Holmes was granted one freedom that greatly affected how his confession and his case developed: access to any newspaper or periodical he wished. This not only allowed Holmes to keep track of his public image as he wrote his autobiography and prepared his diary excerpts for publication, but also gave him an undesirable edge over the police as the full extent of the case unfolded. Detective Geyer's account of his search for the children in Toronto included the fact that he relied heavily on the newspapers to spread the word about what he was doing so that he would not repeatedly have to explain his search to real estate agents. This involvement with the press meant daily updates in the headlines, including the news that the girls' bodies had been found. Unfortunately this news had reached Moyamensing Prison before the detectives could, since Holmes had heard the commotion of reporters and asked to see the morning paper. His access to news had not been restricted and thus, before anyone could arrive and hope to catch him off guard in an interview with the revelation that Alice and Nellie had been murdered and their bodies found, Holmes was able to read of the events himself and prepare for just such an interview.

It did not give Holmes much time to compose himself, but then, Holmes had already demonstrated a talent for thinking on his feet and acting in such a way as to protect himself. Luckily enough he had already introduced the mysterious Mr. Hatch at the beginning of Geyer's search. It is possible that Holmes' response to the news of the girls' deaths would have been the same with or without the advanced warning, since he had already established the foundation of the narrative of his innocence. All the same, the detectives lamented the loss of the element of surprise, and no restrictions were made on Holmes' access to the papers. Although it was threatened, Holmes does not report that he ever made a request for written material that was refused. Holmes, like the men who would potentially be chosen as his jurors that fall and the reading public beyond, was able to follow the developments in the papers.

All of this makes Holmes' imprisonment seem rather dignified since he could sit down with the morning or evening paper, wearing his usual clothes and having been fed a hearty enough meal, much like he may have done while he was free. It even seems that he saw little enough of his wife before his arrest in Boston, considering how often he reported her ill or how much time he spent with others, such as members of the Pitezel family. In prison Holmes needed not even bother to stir himself for church, since someone ensured that a door was open enough for Holmes to hear the service from his cell. Even his indignance at being suspected of murders he did not commit hardly taints the atmosphere since, while he allows himself to express hardship at his wife's situation, Holmes does his best to avoid sinking into self-pity. While his readers might share his emotions on the first, it was unlikely that they would be willing to endure page after page of the second, so Holmes' attempt to make the best of his situation may have been a good rhetorical choice. He might be in prison and have confessed to insurance fraud, but Holmes is still a gentleman.

Proof of Character

Simply because he has been imprisoned with the lower classes and common criminals does not mean that Holmes must act like one. He writes letters to continue to tend to his business affairs, takes the paper so that he may stay informed of events in the outside world, and keeps a diary, all hallmarks of literacy. Since intelligence and class have long been considered signs of good character, Holmes would naturally seek to cultivate his image in both aspects. Gentlemen do not murder others, much less children.

In his fourth diary entry, on the day after Holmes has been visited by his wife for the first time since he was moved to Philadelphia, Holmes reports that he met with his lawyer. This, he observes, is the only time when someone is allowed "to visit my room and converse with me alone."[9] The discussion between the two men did not center on Holmes' predicament or his case, however, but rather on how "to furnish bail for Mrs. Pitezel, who must be set at liberty at all hazards."[10] Holmes has been reassured that the two Pitezel children whose whereabouts are known are in Philadelphia and being well cared for, and he had letters sent to Miss Williams, presumably to ensure that the other three would also be quickly located. If all five were together, and Miss Williams had already been revealed to have murdered her sister, it would be unlikely that

Minnie would either accompany the middle set to America in the first place or that she would remain free to watch over them. The eldest daughter was still in charge of the baby, but, if Alice, Nellie, and Howard returned, they would need their mother.

The mention of bail for Mrs. Pitezel—another example of showing care with the exchange of money—turns Holmes to his own predicament. Having been arrested for insurance fraud he could indeed pay bail, but he has been assured he will be arrested again for murder if he were to do so, and murderers are not given the luxury of bail. Mrs. Pitezel has only been charged—and will only be charged—with insurance fraud, since she admitted to knowing of the scheme before it was enacted. Even though she did not know the location of her husband or three of her children, in November 1894 Carrie was still treated as a criminal instead of as a victim. Even Detective Geyer insisted that Carrie, knowing about the plan in advance, should have stopped her husband from moving ahead with it before it could even be begun.

At this point Holmes had not changed his story to indicate that Pitezel is in fact dead. His first confession was the only one he had given as of November 27, 1894, in which he stated that Pitezel was abroad somewhere with his children. Miss Williams, being a former teacher, may indeed have been with them, but Holmes' first confession did not indicate this. In fact, his first confession does not implicate Minnie Williams at all, and the only record of his attempting to contact Minnie is through the letter sent to the district attorney in May 1895 long after he had changed his story to say that yes, the children were in fact with her in London and not with their father possibly in South America. In his diary, however, Holmes indicates that he mailed letters to Miss Williams far in advance of that May, and indeed before he had even mentioned her name in connection with his current situation.

When *Holmes' Own Story* with the Moyamensing prison diary appendix was published, this latter version was the story being reported and debated. Holmes' readers would have known about his second confession and the details that had grown up around it and, even if they had not, they would have read about it in his autobiography before reaching these diary entries. In an entry where Holmes was informing readers of his concern for the Pitezel family, it therefore makes sense that he would have written to Minnie Williams in an attempt to receive a response that would soothe Mrs. Pitezel as Holmes worked to pay her bail and have her released. Since Holmes had not yet implicated Minnie Williams in the events of the fall of 1894, however, the mention of the letters at this time seems to be a mistake.

Granted, Holmes does not indicate outright what those letters might say, or whether or not they indeed had anything to do with the Pitezel children, although his next sentence mentions the two that are indeed in Philadelphia. Since the plural is given and other discussions indicate that he has only been allowed to send multiple letters if they relate to business affairs, they might indeed be business letters and meant to help him secure the necessary money needed for Carrie's bail. Still, with the associations he had given Minnie Williams since then, it seems that Holmes meant this mention to be a reference to the children. Readers at the time of publication would know that the children had since been discovered to be dead and thus such a small comment on Holmes' part turns into an indication of innocence, since Holmes did not know where the children were after he had entrusted them to Miss Williams' care.

At this point in time he makes no mention of attempting to contact an Edward Hatch, or even that he last saw the children in Hatch's care instead of Miss Williams.' Even though Hatch represented himself to Holmes as having been married to Miss Williams, all attempts at communications are addressed to Minnie herself and not to her supposed husband. In spite of the fact that Holmes admitted feeling uncomfortable about personally giving Minnie presents or money without using one of the girls to deliver them because of this stated relationship, all concern for angering Hatch apparently goes out the window even though, on November 27, no one suspected that Holmes would need to argue his innocence in three cases of child murder. Mentioning Miss Williams so early on and then choosing to include that part of the diary entry in his published book either indicates ignorance as well as innocence, or suggests that Holmes worked to plant these ideas as though they had occurred to him long before they were entirely necessary, confusing his own various timelines in the process.

Even if his readers did not catch the confusion, they would have known that Carrie Pitezel remained locked up for over half a year before she was released. However long Holmes and his attorney were in discussion that November day, it came to nothing. The time they devoted to discussing Carrie's predicament would have detracted from the time that Shoemaker could have focused on his own client's case, a sacrifice readers should note. Holmes was putting Carrie above himself in his concerns—or at least including such an event in his published diary. There is no corroboration that this conversation indeed took place, although it certainly presents Holmes in a kinder light than many of his reported activities.

In order to continue to separate himself from the other prisoners and continue to emphasize his superiority of class and mind, Holmes also makes for himself "a methodical plan for my daily life while in prison, to which I shall hereafter rigidly adhere."[11] This plan is laid out in his journal on January 1 as both a New Year's resolution and a method of helping him through the long, dark, solitary days—a complaint, but also a proactive approach to his current situation in order to counter the numbing effects of prison.

The way Holmes structures his day makes it seem as though he himself chooses when to wake up, take his meals—he lists four times for these—and what those meals may include, since he declares he will eat no more meat while so closely confined. Between rising at 6:30 and going to bed at 9 p.m. with the goal of forcing himself to sleep through the entire night, Holmes declares that he shall take a daily sponge bath; exercise; read the daily paper; keep up on his studies, including medical works, stenography, French, and German; and fill any remaining time with more reading from the prison library. It makes for a demanding schedule with no time to simply sit idle, and demonstrates Holmes' desire to let neither his mind nor his body wither while he is imprisoned.

While in jail in St. Louis Holmes reported reading *Les Miserables* and now in Philadelphia he turns to such works as *Trilby* and some poetry, of which he quotes a few lines in his diary. Classics and poetry are not the entertainment of the unwashed masses, after all, and further demonstrate not only a well-educated but a well-bred mind. If prison is meant for beasts and brings out the monstrous in even the best of men, Holmes is fighting this handily and retaining his image, at least to himself, of a gentleman. He is a man who has been given this utterly unfair hardship of being imprisoned and suspected of more than the petty crimes to which he had already confessed, and yet he was bearing up admirably.

A Stiff Upper Lip

Based on his diary's account of it, life in Moyamensing Prison for Holmes really was not such a trial. His treatment—being allowed to wear his own clothes, read what he chose, write as many business-related letters as necessary, and make his own schedule—seems more as though Holmes had gone on a relaxing vacation of his own volition. Overall the life of the imprisoned physician is really not so terrible. He suffers when he hears and sees how his wife has suffered but otherwise must not tax himself with matters of day-to-day living. Holmes need not even worry about gathering funds for bail since it would merely be a monetary loss and another charge, this one of murder.

When Holmes suffers it is because his audience has been limited. The only person with whom he can be assured of having a truly private conversation is his lawyer, a man who must work with Holmes in order to defend him against all allegations and therefore likely not enough of a challenge for Holmes, whose usual discussions with men over legal issues were adversarial. His wife's twice weekly visits occur in the presence of at least one employee of the prison, and Holmes can neither alienate her nor set her free because he needs the figure of a devoted and loving wife in order to make the argument that there must be something redeeming about his own character. Holmes is allowed to speak with the district attorney and Detective Geyer, but those are tricky conversations in which he must be careful of what he says, since Holmes no longer has the opportunity of adopting another pseudonym and disappearing to another city.

Trapped in both the prison and the statements he has already made, Holmes must search for an outlet for all of this energy. Although his diary declared he would set out to tell the true story and determine what had happened the past fall in an entry dated December 3, Holmes' New Year's timetable for his days does not include time devoted to the writing of that account. His careful plan to keep himself occupied while in prison centers around reading and the taking in of other peoples' words, but not the writing of his own, be it in the form of his diary, his autobiography, or letters either business or personal. The most important activity of his prison life—Holmes' construction of his own story and therefore his defense of his innocence—is left out of his plans.

Holmes clearly wrote his autobiography to be read by the general public and composed it as a manuscript to be published and therefore seen. The imagined audience for *Holmes' Own Story* existed as a collection of people whose opinions of him might matter, either because they were men who would find themselves in the jury box come October or because they might be in positions to sway public opinion at large through new headlines or articles. Holmes' prison diary begins as a personal diary might, with him recording daily events as a means of keeping track or passing the time, but, as the dated headings for each entry break down, so, too, does this illusion. In late June Holmes writes the phrase "I do not need to state to any intelligent reader"[12] in what is ostensibly a diary entry written for no reader except himself. This declaration, though, signals that Holmes is not his sole imagined audience. Instead of being a tool for him to record his days and maintain a semblance of normalcy, his diary, too, was meant to convince others of his innocence.

When the practice of dating each entry finally falls through, Holmes delves into a long narrative account of what he has pieced together of the previous fall. While keeping his second confession intact, Holmes works to reconcile the facts that had afterward come to light, adding to the bare outline of his second confession in order to present readers with what he purports to be a complete account. Here, presented as part of his diary and named a mere appendix to his story, Holmes finally points an accusing finger at the man he purports to be the real murderer.

Ten

Hatch, Miss Williams and the Children

In late June, after having attempted to communicate with Miss Williams twice, Holmes' diary reports that he met with Detective Frank Geyer before the detective's search for the Pitezel children. Holmes records earnestly that he "made a most honest endeavor to place him in possession of all the facts"[1] so that Geyer—whose name Holmes misspells as "Guyer"—might have every advantage in his search for Alice, Nellie, and Howard. Although Holmes had long since given up on securing bail for Mrs. Pitezel, noted in an entry from December 3 of the previous year, he still positions himself as trying to do the best he can for the poor family, despite his own current predicament. By late June Holmes had already pled guilty in his first trial and been sentenced for insurance fraud, but the question of the death of Benjamin Pitezel—as well as the fate of three of his children—still hung over him.

Holmes even goes so far as to say that, without the information he shared with the detective, Geyer's "search would have been a failure"[2]—a clear indication that the text was not being written in diary format by that point in the narrative. While foreshadowing may be a tool used often in fiction, it cannot be applied to real life unless the text has been composed after the fact. While Holmes was writing about a meeting with Geyer that took place at some point in June, the suggestion that Geyer's search would have been fruitless without Holmes' help could only have been written after the girls' bodies were found. Even if Holmes had prior knowledge of where the girls were killed and buried—a proposition that, at the time, he would have dismissed due to the fact that his current explanation centered on Hatch being the murderer—he could not have known that Geyer would indeed find them at all. The format of diary entries, which had been kept up neatly—if increasingly sporadically—for months, breaks down.

The last date Holmes' "diary" mentioned is that of July 16, 1895—a memorable date indeed as this was the morning the newspapers revealed that Alice and Nellie's bodies had been found. Holmes reports his initial reaction as one of disbelief: "[f]or the moment it seemed so impossible"[3] that he thought it must have been a preemptive declaration based on thin evidence, much the same way that many of the headlines surrounding his "Murder Castle" were later retracted in smaller, more out-of-the way articles. Holmes adds that his shock was so complete that, even when he was taken to the assistant district attorney for questioning, it took him a long time to realize how the new headline related to him and to perceptions of his case.

The girls' deaths, unlike their father's, equaled that of Nannie Williams in Holmes' mind even before he realized that others would also blame him for their deaths, albeit in a much more direct way. Holmes meant it in a manner that would have paralleled his treatment of Pitezel around the time of his death: just as Holmes left Pitezel to his own devices, he left the girls in the care of someone else and, once again, his absence allowed for a death to take place—this time a double murder instead of suicide. It is this shock of learning not only of the girls' deaths but that he was being accused of killing both them and Howard that leads Holmes' diary to the narrative of what, he presumes, must have happened.

"It Could Have Been No One Else"

After being taken back to his cell, having argued that he certainly would not have murdered Howard and attempted to get rid of his body in a furnace because of the smell such a method produces, Holmes spent the next two days carefully examining what he knew in order to determine how Hatch would have managed it. Holmes does not question that Hatch was the murderer or even suggest that Miss Williams might have laid a hand on the children. Instead, he immediately focuses in on the figure of Edward Hatch and starts to puzzle out how, exactly, the other man did it.

Ten. Hatch, Miss Williams and the Children

Holmes' first question is one of motive. Murdering children is, he reasons, both risky and monstrous, and thus a man would need a good reason to embark upon such an endeavor. Presumably because Holmes knew the man he does not even suggest that the reason might be madness, or perhaps he thinks that such a motive would not be explicable in the first place because of the care that went into hiding the girls' bodies. Even the $400 Holmes had given Alice to pin inside her dress is quickly dismissed as being too "small"[4] of a sum to interest Hatch. Indeed, since the insurance frauds already mentioned in *Holmes' Own Story* yielded ten and twenty thousand dollars without the need for murder to obtain it, the question of killing two girls for only $400 does seem ridiculous. This does not mean, however, that Holmes' deduced motive makes any more sense than robbery.

Holmes chooses to blame Miss Williams.

His reasoning is complicated. First, he suggests that Minnie would like to at some point blame the murder of Nannie on Holmes himself, in order to clear her own name. It seems that she—or Holmes, or perhaps both of them—believes that Holmes was with the Pitezel children at the time of Nannie's murder, and thus they form his alibi. Were the children to be removed, his alibi would collapse and he would not be able to defend himself against the accusation. The fact that Holmes and Miss Williams were meant to have snuck Nannie's body away in a trunk and sunk it deep in the lake where it had yet to be found does not seem to have occurred to either Minnie or Holmes. Nannie's death was kept such a secret that, at best, the police may have been able to determine the last time anyone but Holmes or her sister saw her, but the exact date of her death would have been in question. Even if Holmes *had* been with the children at the time Minnie knew she had murdered her sister, such an alibi would not be broad enough to cover all possible times at which Nannie could have died. Further, Holmes himself made no indication that he had seen the Pitezel children at all on the day he had come back to the apartment to find Minnie in such a state.

His second line of thought, and the one Holmes seizes on as being more likely, is that the murder of the Pitezel children was directed by Minnie because she was still hurt by Holmes' dissolution of their relationship and jealous of his wife. Miss Williams' goal, then, seems to be to ruin Holmes and therefore his marriage. The fact that she chooses to do so by murdering children—or rather, having someone murder them following her orders—makes her even more monstrous than a woman who would murder her own sister accidentally and in hot blood. By the fall of 1894 Minnie had been parted from Holmes for over a year and had known about his marriage for months. Further, she seemed to have found a replacement for him in the form of Hatch, who claimed to be married to her. Holmes' own insistence on continuing to call Minnie "Miss Williams" instead of "Mrs. Hatch" indicates his personal opinion of the legality of such a relationship. Miss Williams might still be seething about how Holmes left her, but he also in turn seems to be unable to let her go completely.

Holmes had previously indicated that Miss Williams had been reluctant to come forward because she had murdered her sister, but the difference between Nannie Williams' death and those of the Pitezel children is great. The way Holmes described it, an already unstable Minnie had returned home to hear from her sister that Holmes had been with her all night and, upon seeing Holmes' bed had not been slept in, dealt Nannie a single blow. Nannie's death was neither premeditated nor enacted in cold blood. Minnie is presented as having hit her sister without thinking first that it would actually kill her, and second, how it would affect her and Holmes' lives. It was a single act in the heat of the moment.

If Minnie Williams had orchestrated the deaths of the Pitezel children, however, then it was a case of cold, calculated murder. She was not striking out at the person who had angered her, the way she hit Nannie when she thought Nannie had slept with Holmes, but at others who were only even tangentially related to the man who had snubbed her. They were Holmes' business partner's children, and the only reason they could be used against him was because he had willingly taken charge of the three of them in the wake of their father's death. To add to Minnie's derangement, she chose to have children murdered in order to forward her own agenda, and she asked her new lover or husband—who looked very much like her old lover—to kill them. Had Freud coined the term "psychoanalysis" prior to 1896, Holmes could have expounded upon the motive he ascribed to Minnie Williams in much more detail. Instead, he merely mentions this reasoning in order to move on to the real subject of this section of his diary: Hatch.

Ten. Hatch, Miss Williams and the Children

Gathering Evidence

Edward Hatch, according to Holmes, was merely acting on the orders of his purported wife. When Holmes and Hatch first met up in Cincinnati shortly after Pitezel's death—Holmes does not mention why they had done this, or what he might have hoped to use the other man for—Holmes was convinced that Hatch had no plans for the Pitezel children. This, at least, makes sense, as he and Miss Williams could not have planned for the insurance scam they knew nothing about, or for Pitezel to have committed suicide and thus been unable to help Holmes with the children in some way. Minnie William's plan for her belated revenge against the man who had helped cover up her sister's murder and then left her was only developed when Holmes and Hatch parted for a few days. Upon reflection, Holmes concludes that Hatch must have gone to see Miss Williams instead of to Chicago, as he had told Holmes. Hatch must have spoken with Minnie because of all the small changes that Holmes noticed when they came back together.

Hatch both took more interest in the children and spent less time with Holmes, choosing to book his own private room at a hotel that was not where the children stayed. His reasoning there, according to Holmes, was that, since Holmes was being watched—possibly by another Secret Service man like the one who had latched on to him in Grand Rapids—"it was unsafe for any of us to be at a hotel."[5] Since Holmes had begun moving his wife around with the other groups, as well, it seems unlikely that he and Hatch would have shared a room even to cut the expense, and when Holmes discussed traveling alone with the children he made it clear that they always had separate bedrooms. Hatch's insistence on his own room thus only seems suspicious in hindsight, as was his continued desire to hang on to a spade he had purchased in spite of how difficult it was to continue packing such an implement in the trunk for each move.

Even though Holmes reports him as paying more attention to the children, this does not mean that Hatch in fact cares about them. As presented, this seems to prove nearly the opposite. Holmes reports Hatch expressed an "almost querulous objection to my buying a jacket in Detroit for one of the girls,"[6] in spite of the fact that the children's clothes were in very poor condition and not suited to the increasing chill of the fall. This might have been passed off as being part of the same frugal streak that would not let Hatch part with a spade he had paid for in spite of the impracticality of continuing to carry it along, but denying a child a jacket comes across as less thrifty than cruel. It also seems to be an attempt to deny Holmes the act of caring for the children, since refusing to buy an item that would serve Alice or Nellie's well-being is also a refusal to allow Holmes to spend his money on them and to once again show his concern for someone through a dollar value. What may have been interpreted as unnecessary thrift in the moment takes on a much more sinister connotation after the fact, since Hatch's frugality centered not around questions of budgeting and how much would be left after the purchase, but on the fact that the girls would not be around long enough to make such a purchase worth the cost.

Also suspicious in hindsight was the fact that Hatch had gone to a barbershop to have his beard shaved off. Holmes himself sported a mustache and, since he and Hatch already looked so similar, this decision was not made because Hatch had grown tired of his facial hair but because he wished to be all the more easily mistaken for Holmes. This was necessary since it was not enough that the children should go missing—or turn up murdered—while having been under Holmes' care. Hatch, and therefore presumably Miss Williams, wanted it to appear as though Holmes himself had murdered them. Holmes does not come out and say this directly, presumably since it is another aspect that he should not have to tell the intelligent reader. Hatch and Miss Williams' scheme to frame him for the Pitezel murders is largely ignored as Holmes sets out to prove *how* Hatch managed those murders in the first place.

To be fair, Holmes does not find it difficult now to ascribe Hatch the time to enact the plan. While earlier he made it clear that neither he nor Hatch could have readily been able to rent the house in Toronto and convince the girls to return to it, the addition of motive seems to erase all of Holmes' hesitation at accusing his companion of three murders. Since he has puzzled out for himself that Miss Williams would have wanted the children dead in order to put Holmes in his current predicament, Holmes accepts that Hatch would have had the necessary drive and determination to pull it off.

It is Hatch's suggestion that separates the children and here Holmes indicates that Howard was with Hatch the last time Holmes saw the boy.

He had already mentioned that Alice and Nellie had been with Hatch after Holmes had himself disembarked the train and now, with this entry, reveals that such was the fate of all three Pitezels. Although Mrs. Pitezel could only be sure that she had sent Nellie and Howard off with Holmes, and that Holmes had told her he also had Alice in his care, Holmes himself is able to extend the timeline to say that the children were last seen with Hatch and not with him. Unfortunately for Holmes, he is the only one who can say this—and, it has been challenged, the only man who can confirm that Edward Hatch does, in fact, exist.

The district attorney once again becomes the focus of Holmes' ire, this time not because of his treatment of Georgiana Yoke but because he, along with Holmes' own lawyer, "branded my statements concerning Hatch as untrue, and said that he was a mythical person, asking me to name anyone who had ever seen him."[7] Holmes immediately lists a number of people who had indeed seen Hatch, from a representative of the insurance company, to the barber who shaved Hatch's beard, to the proprietors of the places where Hatch and the children had boarded, to others who had stayed there at the same time. More specifically he names both his wife and Mrs. Pitezel as being able to attest to Hatch's existence since they, unlike a number of other witnesses Holmes dismisses, would have been able to recognize the man as Hatch and not as Holmes. It is Hatch's fault, Holmes indicates, that rumors have spread about how he knew and visited Miss Williams in Denver as early as 1888, since witnesses mistook one for the other, and so much of the case against him thus falls apart.

Holmes does not admit that he has done himself no favors in offering various pseudonyms in his travels and business deals, or acknowledge that Hatch and Holmes are names that are indeed quite similar and could be easily confused. According to his autobiography he has gone by Holmes since arriving in Chicago, but he does not mention any other names he might have used, even though Geyer tracked various pseudonyms through the hotel registries on his quest to find the Pitezel children. Holmes' pseudonyms, like his first two wives, are very carefully not mentioned.

Formerly of the Stage

Even as Holmes ignores the inconvenient elements of his story, he also seems to overlook the importance of actually laying out a full explanation of Hatch's nefarious plan. Holmes never specifically says that Hatch shaved his beard in order to look like Holmes. In fact, it takes him until page 241 to even brush against the idea that those who may have been shown his photograph and recalled having seen him may in fact have seen Hatch. During a round of interrogation, Holmes is asked about a meeting that had taken place in Toronto. Holmes was apparently observed having a discussion with a "light young man"[8] near the house where the girls were murdered but, of course, Holmes had neither rented nor been in that house. According to his diary, Holmes immediately knew not only that the man in question had been Hatch, but also the identity of that young man in spite of the fact that he, personally, had not been present during that meeting. Holmes writes that he held his tongue at the time of the interview since, of course, there were doubts as to whether or not Hatch actually existed, although this silence does not end up supporting his case.

Holmes does not in fact bluntly state that the man was Hatch. Neither does he point out to his readers that, since Hatch looked so much like him, it would be easy to mistake one for the other. Perhaps he felt that to do so would be to invite the opposite argument—that such sightings by strangers could not be proven to have been of one man or the other, and thus would not in fact be proof of Holmes' innocence. Holmes had mentioned in his autobiography that Miss Williams had met Hatch when they both worked in the theater, and presumably his readers should remember this and extrapolate that Hatch would not only have looked like Holmes, but done his best to adopt Holmes' mannerisms, as well. Hatch was not even alone in this endeavor, but could rely on the advice and suggestions of Miss Williams in order to ensure that his presentation was accurate.

Although both Miss Williams' and Hatch's pasts as actors were previously referenced in Holmes' explanation as to how they had originally met, it is only after this meeting in Toronto is mentioned that Holmes expounds on the extent of Minnie's talent. Holmes recalls an encounter from the spring of 1893 reminiscent of a Sherlock Holmes story in which he passed by a "jauntily dressed young man"[9] on his way to his office. Holmes only noticed the lad because he was smoking, and asked him to quit it. Apparently Miss Williams had made use of her theater costume, makeup, and acting skills so skillfully that she had fooled him completely. Holmes even recounts that he allowed her to join him on two business trips when she was "costumed in this manner."[10] Minnie Williams, then, apparently made for a very convincing young man, and this occurred two decades prior to the famous case in which Dr. Crippen and his mistress fled across the Atlantic with Ethel Neave disguised as a—less convincing—lad. This even ties in to the suggestion that one of the Pitezel girls had, at one time, been disguised as a boy in order to allay any suspicions caused by two sisters and a brother traveling together.

The theme of women attired as men, then, plays a central role in Holmes' explanation of all that had happened to the Pitezel family, but even Miss Williams' extraordinary talent to that end is only mentioned at this late date. Even though Holmes insisted that Miss Williams had the children and had taken them abroad, emphasizing that she would be difficult to find due to the fact that he had revealed her to be a murderess and informing the detectives that their only means of communication was through encrypted notes published in the newspaper, he failed to mention that Miss Williams might not be going about as a Miss, after all. Holmes had earlier passed on the suggestion that one of the girls may have been disguised as a boy, but he had made no such mention about Miss Williams, in spite of her apparent skill.

The problem that Holmes apparently fails to see as he constructs his more elaborate explanation for what happened is that, had he honestly been in possession of the information that Hatch looked like his twin and Miss Williams made a very convincing man, he should have informed the detectives of this from the time of his arrest. He could gain nothing by withholding it and would in fact have been better off had he given up the names of Edward Hatch and Minnie Williams from the beginning. Granted, during his first confession Holmes insisted that Benjamin Pitezel was in fact still alive, but even during his second confession he did not make such a complete statement as he does here in his prison diary more than six months after his arrest. Although Holmes may have felt a desire to protect Miss Williams since he felt responsible for the death of her sister, he did not in fact believe that she had actually married Hatch and thus his aversion to even mentioning the existence of the other man is questionable.

Holmes himself does not offer an explanation as to why he had not previously told the detectives the entire story as he has laid it out for publication, although he once again hints at an element of his story that seems important enough to have been stated outright. After Alice and Nellie's bodies were discovered, Holmes says that he told the assistant district attorney that he believed Howard's body would be found in Detroit. It was, of course, guesswork, since Holmes himself had not murdered any of the children and had been working off much of the same evidence that Detective Geyer had found. Holmes, however, had the advantage of knowing all of the places he had stopped with his various groups of hostages and did not find himself facing the same gaps that stumped Geyer in his search. Holmes, that is, would have known of the short stay near Indianapolis, even if he claimed ignorance of a rented house outside of it.

The fact that Howard was not found in Detroit turns into a mark against Holmes and his credibility. "From this I have been characterized ... as an extreme falsifier,"[11] he writes a bit petulantly, arguing that the only falsehood he told authorities and let stand was that the children were in England, which, Holmes points out, he honestly believed. Yes, it is true that his first confession was full of lies, but he told them in order to continue to keep up the illusion he had constructed for Carrie Pitezel and only broke down and told the truth after, he insists, it would have been impossible to continue to save her from it. In other words, although Holmes admits that he did indeed lie to law enforcement at first, he insists that, after his first statement, he has told everything he knew or thought to be the truth. In spite of being a confessed liar and a con man, he is offended by the fact that others treat him as such simply because he, working with very much the same information as Detective Geyer, also reached the same false conclusion as to the location in which Howard was murdered.

Holmes feels he has been mistreated and already judged as guilty by the very men whose job it is to build the state's case against him— an indignance likely shared by many prisoners but one that Holmes presents as a personal affront. Even though he begged the district attorney to be allowed to go to Toronto so that he might be able to collect evidence of his innocence months after the fact, Holmes was, of course, not merely under arrest on suspicion of murder but also convicted of the insurance fraud to which he had pled guilty, and men in such positions are not generally granted freedom in order to act as their own detectives in other murder cases. To Holmes this seems entirely unfair, as though he—a gentleman prisoner—should clearly be allowed to travel abroad, following Detective Geyer's path in order to discover any clues the detective himself may have missed. To Holmes this refusal is an insult against him, and he does not see how his request might be one against Geyer, much less patently ridiculous. Holmes has built up an image of himself as a trustworthy and honest man who happens to have conned others in the past, but whose past should have no bearing on whether or not he should be believed in the present, and it is this version he relates to his readers, who are meant to know him better than the district attorney ever could.

This incident does leave Holmes worried, however. If the district attorney, who had access to all the possible evidence, would not even bring himself to consider all sides of the investigation, "what could I expect from others having a less thorough knowledge of the case?"[12] The jurors who would fill the box at Holmes' trial would not necessarily be as broadminded and well educated as Holmes praises the district attorney of being, and even that intelligent mind could not grasp the importance of allowing Holmes the chance to prove his innocence in Toronto. Not all of the evidence discovered on either side of the case would be admitted into the courtroom, and that, along with the newspaper reports, could very easily shape the opinions of the jurors so that they would already be prejudiced against Holmes. Here, then, in his autobiography and his diary, Holmes is free to tell his side of the story without fear of interruption or cross-examination, although he may have benefited from outside input and suggestions that his arguments could have been clearer. He may even have then explained why he did not reveal sooner that Hatch was for all intents and purposes his double, especially after he had shaved his beard; and that Miss Williams was a talented actress as well as an emotionally unstable murderess and may have put many of her talents to use while in hiding with the Pitezel children.

These elements make for an interesting story, albeit one that seems pieced together after the fact. Holmes does not muse on the way in which Miss Williams has chosen a new lover who looks so much like him—and indeed, who makes a change to his physical appearance to resemble Holmes even more closely. He also does not dwell on Miss Williams' past institutionalizations since reminding his readers of her breakdowns might also cause them to question why Holmes had entrusted her with the children in the first place. It is easy enough to explain that he would not have been seen in her company during these travels because Miss Williams would have wanted to avoid running into Georgiana, and Holmes himself wished to prevent any issues of jealousy on Hatch's part were Holmes and Miss Williams to spend time together, although Holmes offers no such explanation as to why no one reported seeing him with someone who looked enough like him that they could have been brothers.

He also does not clarify why, even though he had named Miss Williams much earlier in his evolving confession, Holmes failed to even mention Hatch's existence. It is not simply the fact that Hatch was traveling around with Holmes and his various other charges, but that Holmes last saw each of the children in Hatch's care that would make naming the other man seem to be of utmost importance. After all, Holmes himself only had Hatch's word that the children had gone on their way to be with Miss Williams, and a man such as Holmes would normally be far too eager to pass off blame if it could in any way be passed. Instead, even when Holmes offers up Minnie Williams and tells of her scandalous history, he almost seems to want to protect Edward Hatch—at least until such time as he can construct a proper story to explain how Hatch first separated the children, and then, with Miss Williams' help, lured the girls back to the house in Toronto where their bodies had been found. Only after Holmes has the entire explanation worked out—and especially once he has emphasized over and over that he himself would not have had enough free time in Toronto in order to enact the murders himself—does he offer Hatch as the real murderer.

Details and Omissions

There is one further incident of interest involving Hatch and the Pitezel children that Holmes notes as suspicious in hindsight. It is also one that parallels one of the few stories he related from his childhood. When Holmes was a boy he sent away for a mail-order watch that, being more flash than substance, soon broke, ostensibly teaching the lad lessons about appearance and value. Holmes recalls another watch in an incident that really should have seemed out of character for Hatch, who had previously argued against spending money on the children when it came to warmer clothing, which could at least be argued to be a necessity.

According to Holmes, he came upon Alice and Howard arguing about who should have an old watch that had once belonged to their father. It was clearly not of monetary value, but certainly of sentimental value and, since there was only one, an object to be fought over. Alice argued that she deserved it, being the oldest one present, while Howard asserted his rightful ownership by dint of being the eldest Pitezel son. The boy also voiced the unsubstantiated claim that his father—absent and unable to confirm or deny it—had promised him the watch. In order to stop the arguing, Holmes took Pitezel's watch and bought each of the two children their own cheap substitute, which apparently satisfied them. Holmes does not mention what then became of Pitezel's watch, and neither does he chastise the children for being bought off so easily and made to forget their quarrel over a sentimental item through its replacement with inexpensive versions.

What he does mention is how he noticed that Nellie was upset by the fact that, even though she had not been fighting for her father's watch, Holmes had not bought her one when he had purchased them for the other two children. Holmes does not specifically connect Nellie's longing to his own childhood desire for a watch, but he does at least notice his own misstep in purchasing watches, and exhibiting care, for two of the three children. Holmes promised Nellie he would buy her a watch of her own, or a small item of her own choosing, "before our journey was ended."[13] Even though he did not think of keeping things equal for the children at the time of his initial watch purchases, Holmes shows his readers that he observed this issue on his own without needing Nellie to say something to him specifically, and that he immediately offered to make things right.

Holmes did not, however, go immediately and purchase another watch for Nellie. This incident occurred in Cincinnati—Holmes marks the timing of the events not by date but by location—and Holmes had still not bought a gift for Nellie by the time they arrived in Detroit. On their fist full day in that city, however, Nellie happily showed Holmes a watch that she said Hatch had given to her. It looked exactly like the two Holmes had purchased for Alice and Howard, although Holmes did not report that he asked Hatch about it at the time. Nor does he indicate that he was suspicious that a man who did not wish to waste money on winter clothing for one of the girls would go out of his way to buy one of them a watch she did not need, taking care to match it to the ones her siblings owned even when Holmes had already promised her an equivalent present. At the time the gesture from Hatch went unremarked, although Holmes writes that he has since concluded that Nellie's new watch was in fact the one that he himself had bought for Howard.

Holmes does not stress the fact that Nellie received this watch in Detroit, or that the spade Hatch later refused to leave behind was purchased in Detroit, even though each of these incidences would help him logically argue that he thought Howard had been killed in Detroit. Detective Geyer even began his search for Howard in Detroit working only off the information he himself could find, since Holmes had not previously reported on the watch even if he had made mention of the spade. It was, in fact, a rather reasonable assumption that Howard had been murdered in Detroit, since no one faulted Geyer for making it or offered him a better answer.

Holmes had likely concluded that informing Geyer—or writing that he had told him—to look somewhere other than Detroit would have made him appear guilty. By telling his readers that he had met with Geyer prior to the detective's search, Holmes makes himself appear to be a concerned, helpful citizen whose current imprisonment is entirely coincidental. He could not report that he had suggested Geyer look elsewhere or even that he had provided Geyer with his entire itinerary because such an argument would not have been supported by the newspapers that followed Geyer's quest. Holmes might be able to tell his readers that he had a private meeting with Geyer without directly contradicting something that had already been written—Geyer's own account, published in 1896, does not mention any such meeting—but claiming to have offered such advice would mean that Geyer had failed to take it. This would also mean insulting the detective who had succeeded in finding the children where so many others had failed and, since Geyer was considered a hero, would have likely been too risky.

It was safer, then, to report that he had suggested Detroit. This made Holmes helpful and also showed how he in fact had no insider

Ten. Hatch, Miss Williams and the Children 171

knowledge that would have directed him otherwise, since Holmes was himself innocent of the murders and Hatch took care to hide them from him. Howard had simply gone with Hatch in order to meet up with Miss Williams, and the fact that Holmes was made out to be a liar after his attempt to help is yet another injustice enacted against him. By this point Holmes has the right to be indignant and upset with the way he has been treated since, as he has now laid bare, he has done nothing wrong. His current predicament has come about because Miss Williams has finally enacted her revenge against him for ending their relationship after the murder of her sister. Since he is now being accused of multiple murders, Holmes has every right to his tone of wounded indignation.

Even if he is not the one against whom the most wrong has been committed, Holmes is the one who is still enduring that wrong. Pitezel was already dead by his own hand, and his children were murdered, but nothing Holmes could do or say would bring them back. Even Carrie Pitezel had been released from prison by the time *Holmes' Own Story* was published. The real villains—Hatch and Minnie Williams—were still free, since Holmes himself was suffering the consequences for their actions.

And, in some cases, for his own inaction. Even when Holmes, as he put it, stopped shielding Carrie Pitezel from the truth, he did not in fact tell everything in his second confession. That confession centered around the question of whether or not the man buried as B.F. Perry was in fact Benjamin Pitezel, and how he had died, but mentioned nothing of the children or what had become of them. Carrie Pitezel had already spoken to the police and told them that she thought she might be reunited with the children now that she had been taken into custody, and she told them that she had last seen Nellie and Howard going off with Holmes, but there is no record that Holmes was asked anything more about them, and he certainly did not volunteer it. His diary mentions letters to Miss Williams in early December, but the newspaper ad, purportedly chosen because Holmes would not necessarily have Miss Williams' address, is not run for months. Hatch is not named for months and, when he is described, it is only a vague reference to the fact that someone who thought he had seen Holmes had in fact seen Hatch. If Holmes had honestly thought any of this information would help, he should have mentioned it and clearly laid out the events of the past few months much earlier, speaking it to the detectives who might be able to do something about the children's safety rather than writing it in a book that was only concerned with one life: his own.

Holmes deals with these issues the same way he approaches the fact that Georgiana Yoke was not his only wife: he ignores them. Although he is upset with the district attorney, among others, for not believing his tales, not once does Holmes lament that he should have revealed some key piece of information sooner in order to clear his own name. He avoids the suggestion that any information should have been given sooner or in a different format as though not giving voice to the thought means that readers will not think of it themselves. Indeed, Holmes explains his "theory" as to how and why Edward Hatch and Minnie Williams orchestrated the deaths of the Pitezel children as though he must simply lay it out for others to save them the strain. It would be clear to anyone who would accept the premise of Hatch's existence, and, if the detectives have failed to substantiate Holmes' tale, it is because they have stubbornly refused to admit to something that should be perfectly clear. The blame, of course, never lies with Holmes himself.

At the end of his diary Holmes changes tactics to focus purely on the logical arguments of why he, personally, could not have committed the murders and why, even if the stubborn detectives refuse to believe in the possibility of Hatch and his visual similarity to Holmes, Holmes himself could not have murdered the Pitezel children. He not only protests his innocence based on timelines and timing, but because he cannot personally find a motive that would explain why he would want to kill the children in the first place. Giving up on trying to continue to convince his readers of Hatch's existence, lest they prove to be as stubborn and unmoved as the district attorney, Holmes once again focuses on arguments of logic.

Eleven

Evidence and Motive

The appendix to *Holmes' Own Story* is labeled *The Moyamensing Diary* even though that section does not maintain the diary structure throughout. While a diary is a personal document meant for a man to record his daily life in a manner that would likely not be read by outsiders, Holmes' prison diary veers away from this structure. First it loses the dated format, although the writing retains a narrative structure that involves the relation of events of his past, including statements of cause and effect. Holmes may no longer be his only intended audience, since this narrative passage is written to be read by others, but he still attempts to construct a reasonable account of the past, generally following chronological order. This writing mimics more closely his autobiography than those early diary entries, but even this narrative structure eventually breaks down completely.

At the end of his diary Holmes has three sections separated by headings printed in capital letters. This style of heading appears at only one other place in the book, marking the start of his Moyamensing Prison Diary. That heading served to divide his autobiography, written specifically for publication, and the diary entries ostensibly chosen to be made public out of a larger possible handwritten selection of personal entries. This division is meant to show readers where they have been allowed a glimpse into private prison life and to make it clear that, from that point on, the writing happened as Holmes experienced the events, taking time at the end of the day to record what had happened since dawn. What Holmes entered in his diary was written close to the experience, thereby increasing the chances that he had recorded them accurately. Even the fact that he had initially penned the words for himself and no other eyes is meant to invite the reader in for a closer look at the man accused of such horrible crimes, since people will put things in their diaries that they would not speak out loud. Granted, the entries have been specifically chosen for publication and thus may have been edited, but the stark heading between *Holmes' Own Story* and the prison diary is still meant to make this distinction clear.

By the three headings at the end of the book, the dated diary entries have been left behind for a more narrative approach, which breaks off at the first of these new headings. Although not advertised as no longer being a part of Holmes' diary, their form and purpose separate them all the same. At the end of his diary, Holmes attempts to carefully and logically lay out the reasons why the suspicions against him cannot be true, and he could not have been the man to murder Alice, Nellie, and Howard Pitezel based solely on solid fact without having to factor his character into the discussion.

Photographs

When Detective Frank Geyer set out to discover where, exactly, Holmes had traveled with the three missing Pitezel children, he brought along photographs to assist him in his questioning. Other detectives had already tried before him to trace Holmes' movements and failed, and Geyer was making his own attempt more than six months after Holmes and the children would have been in the various cities and boarding houses. He showed the photographs to real estate agents and hotel desk clerks, unable to ask them if a Dr. Holmes had rented a house or paid for rooms because Holmes and his various charges were known to have used different names from guest book to guest book. Geyer was therefore entirely dependent upon the accuracy of the memories of the people he spoke to during his search.

Geyer later reported that, while in Toronto, he and a local detective spent a tiring day going from one real estate agent to another, always having to repeat their story. They had to explain that they were looking for a man who may or may not have had any of these children with him, adding that he likely told the agent he was looking for a house to rent for his recently widowed sister. If the person they were talking to had actually worked in the span of days during which Holmes may have rented a house, Geyer at least did not have to wait for the proper person to be found. The real estate agents were curious, so there were questions to be answered before the detectives learned that there was no record of such a man on such a mission during the given time period and left to begin all over again at the next agent.

This time-consuming process was what inspired Geyer to first speak to the press. He was able to tell the story once—and only once— more to reporters who printed it for wider consumption. This meant that, when Geyer again went out to consult with real estate agents, they had already checked their records and were able to tell him much more quickly whether a man answering Holmes' description had been in. Geyer himself still carried the photographs, since newspapers at the time could not replicate them in an effective manner. In order to print pictures, photographs would be turned into etchings that could easily be mass produced. Indeed, the images in *Holmes' Own Story* are all etchings, many of them taken from photographs of, for example, Benjamin Pitezel. Thus those who had identified Holmes based on an image from a newspaper would have been doing so because of an etching of a photograph of his face before being able to see the photograph itself.

At the end of his book, Holmes even goes so far as to reference a study he says took place in 1883 in which ten students were tested. They had watched two sign writers at work and were afterward presented with two photos and asked to choose which man was one of the sign writers. Even though neither photo was of the men who had been at work, Holmes reported that all ten students immediately identified one of the photos as being the man sought.

Another group of ten students, presumably having witnessed the same event, was given a layout of forty photographs and apparently told that one of the sign painters was present. Of these ten, only one identified the proper photo and, Holmes crows, "none looked for or found more than one,"[1] even though both sign painters were present. The students presumably stopped looking after making a single identification. He does not, however, record the exact wording used in asking the students to perform their identification, although Holmes' own representation of the test indicates that they would have been told that one man was present.

In reference to his own case, however, Holmes is very much concerned with how the witnesses were introduced to his photograph. He lists three instances of witnesses who would be willing to swear they had seen Holmes, the children, Miss Williams, or "a man answering my description of Hatch"[2]—who must, after all, closely resemble Holmes himself—on dates when they had not in fact been anywhere near the cities those witnesses occupied. Holmes hastens to assure his readers that he does not believe these witnesses, as well as others specifically in Toronto, were purposefully offering misidentifications, but rather that, when his photo had been presented to them, the wording of the detectives was such that they had "been led to understand that no other decision was possible."[3] It was the leading questions from the law enforcement officials, then, and not their own memories, that made these witnesses conclude that the man they recalled seeing the previous fall had been Holmes.

Here, though, at a time when such an emphasis seems of utmost importance, Holmes does not remind his readers that he and Hatch were so similar in appearance as to be mistaken for one another. He does not reflect that, having shaved his beard, Hatch had ensured that such confusion would be all the easier, or that Hatch and Miss Williams would have incorporated this similarity into their planning. In his argument about misidentification Holmes does not once say that the witnesses who claim to have seen Holmes in cities where Hatch was in fact present likely agreed that the man in the photograph was the one they had seen simply because there was no photograph of Hatch and no others of similar men for comparison. It is as though Holmes completely forgets that his former mistress' new husband, who happens to have been the one to carry out Miss Williams' plan for revenge, looks startlingly like him.

Holmes concludes his section on photographic evidence with a single sentence story in which, when he was taken for identification by twenty or thirty witnesses, the detective accompanying him identified him as "Mr. Holmes" within their hearing. Apparently he thinks very highly of his readers indeed since he does not explain why this occurrence would be either amusing or an example of incompetence. True, detectives had entered American fiction in 1841 with Edgar Allan Poe's story "The Murders in the Rue Morgue," but the existence of C. Auguste Dupin—and, in 1887, Sherlock Holmes—does not mean that Holmes' readers would understand the way an identification is meant to work or how the thoughtless detective was leading the witnesses.

He does not indicate where he was when this identification occurred, though it was likely in Philadelphia since Holmes had been arrested in Boston and moved shortly thereafter. Holmes also does not provide information on who those twenty or thirty witnesses were. Since he has avoided mentioning his use of fake names since moving to Chicago and calling himself Henry Howard Holmes instead of Herman Webster Mudgett, being identified as Holmes in front of those witnesses looks very leading indeed. However, considering the number of pseudonyms Holmes was known to have given during his various travels and ventures, it is entirely possible that the identification, if it happened, was meant to confirm that the man standing in front of them was the one they had seen or known by some other name. This section of the prison diary appendix simply does not provide enough information either to support Holmes' indignation or to clarify the situation enough so that critical readers could feel confident in any conclusions they might reach.

It is interesting to note that, at this point, Holmes has the detective identifying him as "Mr." instead of using his professional title. Holmes was certainly representing himself as having a medical degree when he came to Chicago, although the signature reproduced on the cover page of *Holmes' Own Story* identifies him as H.W. Mudgett M.D. or H.H. Holmes, no title included. Although the medical degree would have been awarded to him under the name of Mudgett, Holmes clearly continued to represent himself as a physician even after he adopted the pseudonym. Harold Schechter even presents an amusing exchange at Holmes' 1895 fall trial in which Holmes asked for documents and Judge Arnold responded by asking if he was a physician. "For a moment Holmes seemed slightly taken aback," Schechter reports, "as though startled that the judge would be ignorant of such a well-publicized fact."[4] This reaction seems more in line with the sort of man who would write his autobiography and choose selections from his prison diary to be published as evidence of his innocence, relying heavily on his character and the fact that his class and education separate him from the rest of the criminals in the prison. By reporting that he had been called Mr. Holmes and had not corrected the detective, Holmes presents himself as just another man, albeit one being brought in for identification purposes.

When Holmes begins to discuss photographic evidence, he does so in general terms without pointing out exactly how it relates directly to his case. He begins with the description of the various experiments involving two groups of students watching sign writers at work, demonstrating that witness identification using photographs was faulty. The witnesses were either led to make a false identification ten times out of ten or, when the true photographs were present, picked the wrong one nine times out of ten. Holmes then goes on to mention witnesses who said they had seen him, Miss Williams, the Pitezel children, and a man who looked like Hatch on days and in cities when he, personally, knew them to be elsewhere. Finally he relates the story of being brought in front of a group of witnesses and being named within earshot of them.

This all seems to be relentlessly logical. Holmes relies on a study in which he played no role, reminds his readers that no one person can be in two places at the same time, and presents an instance in which a detective's incompetence could influence the responses from the witnesses. What Holmes lacks here is the level of detail that would solidly connect these arguments to his case. He does not name the authors of the study or provide the information as to where, exactly, he had read about it or where it may have taken place. His own declarations that he knew where Miss Williams and Hatch were on any given day fall flat because he is the only one who could be said to have seen them there, although it appears to be lucky for Holmes that there are indeed witnesses willing to testify to Minnie Williams' and Hatch's actual existence. As for the final mention of his own identification, Holmes does not tell his readers the purpose of it or the exact question the witnesses were asked, since it may have been a question of whether or not he was the man they had seen and not whether this man in front of them was in fact Mr. Holmes.

By mentioning these aspects as briefly as he does, Holmes leaves himself open to more questions and potentially even weakens his case. Were this written solely as his own personal diary it might be seen as the act of a man sorting out the facts in his own head and only noting them briefly enough to be remembered, but the premise of the Moyamensing Prison Diary appendix is that Holmes specifically chose which sections should be printed. True, it is presented as though his diary were merely transcribed and thus he might feel it to be false representation if he expanded on any of these thoughts for the public eye, but Holmes had already composed his autobiography for that express purpose. If he had wanted to provide more information surrounding the legitimacy of photographic identification he could have done so outside of the diary appendix, in more detail that would have helped his case.

It is possible that Holmes, as close as he is to his own case, simply believes that his readers will be intelligent enough to make the mental leaps and close in the gaps of what he has consigned to the page. His time in prison has been time to think, and he has done nothing but live and breathe his own defense for months. It may be that he sees the connections with perfect clarity and it does not occur to him that his readers might not, or that they might not be able to follow such a long paragraph as it jumps from point to point. It is possible that he is also only seeking to provide enough information to create reasonable doubt, since that is all that is necessary within an American court room. Or, of course, Holmes may have falsified all of that information in order to instill doubt in his readers through apparently logical arguments instead of through emotional appeals where he generally equates his care for others with the amount of money he is willing to spend on them. Having apparently given enough information in order to have various witness identifications dismissed, Holmes moves on to apply this logic to the question of *why* he would have committed the murders currently attributed to him.

A Lack of Motive

In the late nineteenth century, motive was still a new question to be pondered. Between the decline of the execution sermon and the rise of the adversarial trial, guilt became a prospect to be debated and the reason for committing crimes was no longer easily traceable to the concept of original sin. It was no longer a case of community members seeking closure surrounding one of their own who had committed a sin, but a more complicated and widespread desire to see trials unfold in distant cities by means of the mass media. Headlines sought to report not only the horror of the crimes themselves, but of the legal resolution through trials, sentencing, and execution. Although Holmes had already confessed to the insurance scam and had given his reasons for going through with the wishes Pitezel had left behind in his suicide note, they struggled to find an explanation for his actions afterward: the strange journey across the country and the murder of three children.

Holmes lists a number of possible motives and then dismisses them quickly: avarice, temper, and appetence fall by the wayside because Holmes argues he was more likely to give money than keep it, he was not easily angered, and he was of the wrong age for appetence to be seriously considered. He uses more space to dismiss the accusation that he had involved all of his supposed victims in a scheme and then murdered them to keep them silent, but this motive, too, is rejected on the grounds that none of the Pitezels had been involved in any criminal acts. As for insanity, Holmes says that multiple medical experts would testify against it, although his own reasoned autobiography and diary would also stand as argument. He clearly understands that murder is frowned upon and the crimes of which he stands accused, if not entirely why people might still fixate on him as a criminal. There is also no indication that Holmes took leave of his senses at any point in which he was observed, and thus madness, as well as legal insanity, cannot be argued.

Having dispensed with apparently all motives of which he might be accused, Holmes spends some time discussing what he calls "the three more important cases"[5]: Nannie Williams, Benjamin Pitezel, and the rest of the Pitezel family. The only motive he refutes in these specific examples is that of money. Nannie herself had none. Holmes includes a table of payments surrounding a piece of property in order to support this argument and show that he was not in a position to gain anything from these specific people. When it comes to Pitezel, Holmes repeats that Pitezel was worth more to him than the insurance claim. Once again the question of property arises, and once again Holmes receives nothing, since no papers had been signed over to him. As for the remaining Pitezels, three dead and three rumored to have been lucky to survive Holmes' attempt on their lives, he once again states that any possible monetary gain would not be worth their murders and reminds his readers how well he had cared for them over the years, recounting how much money he had given the Pitezels that would have come to nothing had he simply murdered them. Here the argument is that he would not have murdered them because he would have gained nothing from their deaths, and not that Holmes would not have murdered anyone because he is himself a decent man.

Aside from the motive of insanity in which Holmes declares that many physicians will agree on his state of mind, the readers must take his counterarguments on his word alone. It is true that Holmes has made mention in these pages of any number of times he had given money to others or spent it on them, especially concerning the Pitezels, and that he had often been short on cash, but Holmes does not provide supporting evidence to the claim that he was poor because he gave his money to his friends instead of mishandling it. Readers also only have Holmes' statement that he has no violent temper, since it would be possible that anyone who knew otherwise would have been dead and unable to tell of it. Even the list of payments meant to show Holmes' upright character and lack of cause is open for question in spite of Holmes' insistence that evidence does in fact exist.

Holmes sets about addressing his possible motives carefully and deliberately, listing each before arguing against it. In this way he limits the number of motives that could be suggested, likely taking those most often mentioned in the newspapers and not attempting to come up with any variations, lest they be seized upon as being more probable. He treats every suggestion as laughable and deserving of only a minor mention even though, with the evidence against him being circumstantial, it would help his case to carefully dismantle any possible motive with details that could be referenced elsewhere. Instead Holmes dismisses them quickly as though they are not worthy of his time, even though detectives and the district attorney's office have been working steadily to build up the case against him, motive included. It is as though he is dealing with the utmost idiots and can complete his argument by gesturing to them and shrugging them off without needing to say a word in his own defense—an approach that his lawyers would carry through to his trial that fall, arguing that the prosecution had failed to make a case against Holmes in the alleged murder of Benjamin Pitezel.

Although Holmes may have used such a strategy before his arrest, this time he cannot walk away from the situation and remove himself from possible reprisal by traveling somewhere else. Since this is a written document and not a verbal conversation, he likewise cannot judge his audience's reaction in order to determine whether he should continue to clarify or if they have already agreed with him. Yet again Holmes makes the decision to refrain from explaining himself in detail to readers whom he deems intelligent enough to make the connections on their own, leaving them with more thoughts of money as representations of emotion instead of an impression of Holmes as a decent, moral man.

The Murder Castle

In his lifetime Holmes was only faced with a single murder charge in a courtroom, although the newspapers were more than willing to attribute other strange disappearances to him. This practice was so common then that, today, Holmes is known as the White City devil who lured young women to his Murder Castle when they came to Chicago to see the World's Fair. His title of "America's first serial killer" goes hand in hand with his name and the fascination rests with his "Murder Castle." The fact that he was hanged for a single murder, or that he killed three children and their bones were found in other cities, is overshadowed by the estimates of a vast number of supposed victims who were murdered by Holmes on Sixty-Third Street.

Serial murder is a numbers game, and more realistic estimates of Holmes' victims do not carry the same impact as suggestions that he murdered hundreds during the Columbian Exposition. The fact that twentieth-century America saw Ted Bundy confess to thirty-six murders—while hinting at many more—and Gary Ridgway, the Green River Killer, confessed to far more in the beginning of the twenty-first century means murdering four Pitezels and a couple of mistresses makes Holmes look weak and uninteresting in comparison. The fascination with Holmes that continues more than a century after his death rests on the mystery of the Murder Castle.

In 1895, however, Holmes has very little to say about it. His main concern is on his upcoming trial for the murder of Benjamin Pitezel and, as an extension, his role in the deaths of Alice, Nellie, and Howard Pitezel. The mistresses he was accused of murdering, like the two women he married prior to meeting Georgiana Yoke, go largely unmentioned. The exception, Julia Connor, is named in his autobiography where Holmes defends her against accusations of infidelity and loose living. He needs not to counter any accusations of murder since he writes that she has taken her daughter away to live secretly and in safety, presumably out of reach of Julia's husband. The only mistress Holmes confesses to taking is Minnie Williams, and this is a necessary admission since it forms the basis of her motive for orchestrating the murder of the Pitezel children.

Holmes does, however, report an incident in which a lawyer from Fort Worth gains an interview with Holmes and brings up the "Chicago victims"[6] as a point of discussion. In fact, Holmes reports that this man—Mr. Cops by name—presumes to tell him how he believes Holmes did it. This involves Holmes, smooth and charming as ever, convincing woman after woman to step inside the bank vault he had installed for the express purpose of suffocating them. Mr. Cops even mentions the story of the footprint having been found etched inside the vault's door. After a question from Holmes, he adds that he believes the last of the Chicago murders took place in July 1893, identifying his choice of final victim when he admits that, should Minnie Williams in fact turn up alive, this date would of necessity have to be changed. Being from Fort Worth, Mr. Cops knows that Miss Williams had not been in contact with any of her friends from Texas since about that date, although he clearly remains skeptical that Minnie would have gone into hiding because she had murdered her sister. Still, he allows that this scenario would also explain her long silence, perhaps as a means of keeping Holmes in a good and talkative mood—or perhaps as Holmes' means of recording the logic behind his current inability to receive an answer from Miss Williams.

Having established that Mr. Cops' evidence proves that the final Chicago murder must have occurred no later than July 1893, Holmes informs the attorney that the vault he supposedly used to murder his victims was not in fact purchased until November of that year. This transaction was completed after a fire in the building had destroyed a number of valuable letters and papers that would have been protected by such a vault, which was then not installed until December 1893. The fire was newsworthy enough that Mr. Cops or any of Holmes' readers would have been able to find a record of it, and Holmes gave enough information regarding the purchase of the vault that it, too, should be traceable and provable. All of this should easily establish a timeline that calls into question any and all stories involving that safe as an implement of murder.

Faced with such logical evidence, Mr. Cops is also then forced to admit that, back in Fort Worth, Holmes had received a letter from Miss Williams in London. Since he was so sure that Holmes must have murdered Minnie Williams, Mr. Cops humbly admits to Holmes that he "supposed it to be a clever forgery sent there by you to mislead those who found it."[7] Holmes immediately adds that there are other letters from Miss Williams and directs Cops not only to his Denver agent in charge of forwarding such mail, but also to a number of people in Fort Worth who knew Minnie Williams' handwriting and could confirm that it was not, in fact, a forgery.

Holmes does not reveal the name of the person Mr. Cops should consult, writing it only as "Mr. ----- and others,"[8] nor does he divulge the content of those letters. Presumably this means that they had nothing to do with his present predicament, although it seems difficult to believe that letters Minnie Williams wrote to Holmes during 1895 would not have mentioned either the current schooling and whereabouts of the Pitezel children or Holmes' incarceration, especially since Holmes made it clear that Miss Williams, like Pitezel and himself, was conversant in using cipher for delicate information. If she were really writing to him, it makes no sense for Holmes to have kept these letters a secret and not presented them to his lawyer or to the district attorney. Since he had already provided them with the code they had agreed upon to alert her in the newspaper, if Minnie Williams had used it in her letters the district attorney could have translated them himself and not needed to rely on Holmes' interpretation. Further, it would have helped Holmes' case if it could have been proven beyond reasonable doubt that Miss Williams had indeed written those letters—a difficult prospect considering the early state of graphology in the late nineteenth century. It would not have been an easy point to prove even if Holmes had produced the letters but, since no physical evidence was forthcoming, this mention seems to hinder his cause rather than help it.

Holmes dates this discussion with Mr. Cops as having taken place on August 15, 1895. According to his diary he had attempted at least twice to communicate with Miss Williams since his incarceration the previous November. Although proving that she was still alive would not necessarily lead to the conclusion that Edward Hatch did in fact exist, it would have been an important step in support of Holmes' version of events. According to the reasoning in his diary, Edward Hatch personally had no reason to murder the Pitezel children but, since he presented himself as being married to Minnie Williams, it meant he was the husband of someone who did indeed have a reason. Hatch acted on orders from Miss Williams and so, if Holmes were in possession of letters written by her that were clearly sent after the time she had disappeared, he should have produced them. Those letters would have been much more helpful had they been sent since his incarceration and if they had mentioned Alice, Nellie, and Howard, but any proof that Minnie Williams had not been murdered by Holmes in July 1893 would have worked in his favor. Instead, Holmes does not produce these letters for his lawyer, and he does not mention whether or not Mr. Cops consulted with Mr. ----- and the others. Holmes did not report this conversation in order to offer up incontrovertible proof.

Mr. Cops does not exist in Holmes' narrative in order to hand physical evidence over to the district attorney. His purpose is instead in the conversation he holds with Holmes: a calm and reasonable exchange of information in which Cops is able to express his doubt and inform Holmes of what he would need in order to conclude that Holmes must be innocent. Mr. Cops tells Holmes that, if the information Holmes provided about the safe is true, then he must abandon his case. Since Mr. Cops is not brought up again, it must be assumed that he was satisfied as to the dates Holmes had provided of purchase and installation of the safe.

In so many of his other reported conversations, Holmes found himself going over the same ground again and again simply because the others involved would not listen to him or pause to consider that he might be telling the truth. The district attorney, for example, refused to even entertain the idea that Hatch might have existed and thus every attempt Holmes made to explain the situation was foiled. Mr. Cops, on the other hand, was open to the idea not only that the reports of the Chicago murders might be faulty, including whatever evidence he himself said he had collected, but also the idea that Minnie Williams might indeed still be alive. This attorney therefore shows a large measure of intelligence and humility when he concedes that Holmes, and not his own information, must be correct.

At the same time, though, Mr. Cops is not merely trusting what Holmes tells him. He had approached their conversation already having seen a letter purportedly from Miss Williams. Even though Mr. Cops suspected it was a forgery he at least had some measure of evidence that would already have allowed him to consider multiple possibilities. Since Holmes also provided the information that the safe in which Minnie Williams was supposed to have been killed was not in his possession until months after her supposed death, the possibility that the letters are real becomes more feasible. In spite of the fact that Mr. Cops is not as conversant with the case as the district attorney, he possesses a more open mind and thus his interview with Holmes comes across as an intelligent discussion between two polite gentlemen who concern themselves with the facts instead of one man bullheadedly pursuing his suspicions without being willing to listen to what the other has to say. Mr. Cops is set forth as an example of the men Holmes would like to see in the jury box at his trial: willing to set aside what they have heard or seen thus far in order to methodically work their way through the facts.

The extent to which Holmes feels he has been made a scapegoat immediately follows his suggestion of where Mr. Cops should seek corroboration that the letter from Miss Williams was not a forgery. Without breaking into a new paragraph, Holmes relates hearing of the fire that burned down his Castle in Chicago on August 19 and reports that he was thankful he was unquestionably imprisoned during it, since this meant he could not be blamed. Indeed, whenever Holmes heard "of any loss of life, strange disappearances or other misdemeanors not easily accounted for, throughout the United States—anywhere in the world in fact"[9] he found himself likewise grateful for the alibi of being a prisoner, lest he be accused of having committed the crime he read about in the morning paper.

On the one hand it seems as though Holmes may have veered into self-pity or perhaps even petulance, but he follows this observation with a section entitled "Other Disappearances." These are apparently other cases of which he knows himself to have been accused of foul play, and he wishes to dismiss all such accusations quickly and firmly. In a few short pages he lists a dozen names, most of them with little accompanying detail aside from the fact that he did not know anyone by that name or the argument that certain people are known to currently be alive. Miss Cigrand—Holmes gives no first name—occupies the most space as Holmes acknowledges that she worked for him and gives a longer explanation of her disappearance, ending with the observation that she will likely write to him to tell him her married name and where she is before he is "made to suffer for her disappearance."[10] She is the only one in this list that he admits to knowing who is currently unaccounted for, meaning that eleven names have been attached to his in accusations that are baseless either because they are false or because the people in question cannot in fact be connected to him.

With his habits of traveling and changing his name it is not difficult to see why Holmes would be an easy target for newspapers looking to continue printing scandalous headlines. He could certainly be accused of having a hand in the disappearance of any young woman who went to Chicago for the Columbian Exposition and did not return home to her family, since he was proven to have been in the city at the time, even if the excavation of his Murder Castle did not, in the end, support such a high number of victims. Holmes was known to have been in other cities since he both offered up his journeys as alibis against other murder accusations and was carefully tracked during his travels with the Pitezel family, and thus any disappearances around those times could also easily have made headlines. Since Holmes was going to be put on trial for one murder, it did not seem to be such a stretch of the imagination that he could have killed more people.

Holmes' quick dismissal of his involvement with eleven of the names stands in sharp contrast to his more expansive treatment of Miss Cigrand. Although some of the eleven have been mentioned in other documents in connection to Holmes, it is possible that he also simply made up some names in order to make it appear as though the deck were being stacked against him. The problem is that Miss Cigrand stands out against the brief dismissals, possibly because there were clear records of her having worked for him, and of her family's confusion as to why she would have suddenly gone away and stopped writing to them. Holmes' explanation is that she married and did not wish to write to her family until she could send them monetary support but, at the time *Holmes' Own Story* was published, she would have been refusing to write to them for nearly three years. Even the fact that Holmes does not know her current last name is suspicious since he was supposed to have last seen her over a year after her marriage.

Once again Holmes' attempt at arguing his innocence is poorly executed. The story of Miss Cigrand is placed in the middle of the others, standing out against the one or two sentences with which the other names are dismissed. Only his discussion of Miss Anna Betz carries the same feeling of over-explanation. Although she only merits a single sentence, it is a long one in which Holmes protests that he did not kill her—accidentally or otherwise—while performing an "illegal operation" at the behest of an unnamed man whose actions presumably necessitated Miss Betz's need for the abortion. In this case Holmes also feels the need to clarify that his debt to that same unnamed man was canceled through means of a check and, apparently, not through illegal services. Although Holmes will confess to defrauding an insurance company for $20,000, he indignantly draws the line at performing an abortion for $2,500, especially since he was meant to have botched it.

It is the contrast between simple, outright dismissals and the more complex discussions that turns Holmes' litany of strange disappearances that have been hung on his name into an awkward, lopsided discussion. Even his explanation of Miss Cigrand need not be so many paragraphs. Had he simply admitted to having employed her before she moved on in order to marry her husband, Miss Cigrand's story would not stand out and draw as much attention. It is the amount of detail in the discussions of Miss Cigrand and Miss Bentz that carry with them the air of protesting too much. If Holmes had been speaking instead of writing and choosing what elements should be published, he would not have had the chance to edit such an outpouring, but the fact that the manuscript was written meant that he would have been able to shorten those entries before passing them on to be printed. Instead of giving his readers a quick litany of unjust charges against him that overwhelm with repetition, Holmes has instead pointed them toward specific instances to ponder further.

Holmes' Final Plea

Holmes ends his book with a Moyamensing Diary Conclusion that serves to cap both his autobiography and its appendix by stressing what he deems to be important points. First, he reminds his readers that he

Eleven. Evidence and Motive

is "but a very ordinary man, even below the average in physical strength and mental ability."[11] The man who has worked so hard to distinguish himself from his fellow prisoners now wishes his readers to imagine himself as being one of them, perhaps even inferior to them. Just as he presented the detective as calling him Mr. Holmes instead of Dr. Holmes, this conclusion begins with a sense of humility. After all of Holmes' accounts showcasing how clever he must have been in order to hide Nannie's murder, escape a secret service man in order to defraud an insurance company for $20,000, and turn Pitezel's suicide into an apparent accident, he stops trying to separate himself from the masses and instead attempts to make himself one of them. Holmes is no longer the clever underdog but just another man, incapable of committing the crimes that have been attributed to him in spite of those he has admitted to carrying out.

Once he has established his absolute normalcy, Holmes adds that his readers should review the statement he made at the time of his arrest and consider how well that statement has held up in the light of all of the new information that had been gathered. Holmes argues that the creation of such a story would have been even more difficult than committing the crimes, indicating that he provided many details at moments where it would have been too great a risk to tell falsehoods since he had no idea how the case would unfold. This is all wrapped up in one long, complicated sentence that moves from his humble presentation of himself, to the argument of timing, and ends with a plea to allow him the chance to at least disprove the charges against him. Holmes, still humble at the end of the sentence, urges his readers to find him guilty if the charges can indeed be proven although, in this moment, it is clear he does not believe any of them have been. He quite reasonably asks his readers to suspend their judgment until his trial when he and his lawyers will presumably provide the evidence to clear his name.

In the second sentence of his conclusion, not quite so long as the first, Holmes turns the tables to once again strike out at the detectives who have put him in prison. Even though his book is finished, there is no such neat ending to the case, since "there is also the work of bringing to justice those for whose wrongdoings I am to-day suffering."[12] After all, if Holmes' story is true, Edward Hatch and Minnie Williams must be brought to justice for the murder of the Pitezel children, and yet they retain their freedom to the extent that their current location is completely unknown. This is not, however, meant solely to bring justice to the children and comfort to Carrie Pitezel who could at least know that those truly responsible for her children's deaths have answered for it, and not for Holmes himself—who declares that he, personally, is unconcerned if he hangs since he has not cared to live since the day he learned of the discovery of Alice's and Nellie's bodies. Instead he closes with the thought that his own life must be spared so that "those who have looked up to and honored"[13] him in the past may continue to do so without having to know that he was hanged as a murderer.

The amount of ground covered in these two sentences is staggering. He begins humbly—more humbly than he has presented himself in his autobiography—but ends with concern for his reputation. It is not a fear that the true murderers of children will get away with such a crime because he himself was charged with it by men who metaphorically wore blinders and refused to consider that anyone else may have had a hand in it, but that he himself will be wrongly executed for it. For all the concern he showed at the start of his diary, Holmes does not even mention his wife or what his death would then mean for her in more ways than merely marking her as the widow of a murderer. She is simply one of the people in his past who has looked up to him, lumped together with all the rest if she is said to be present at all.

Holmes does not even name Hatch and Miss Williams at the end. If this were the only section to be read, it would seem that he has no idea who could have murdered the children and that an investigation would be needed to name them and not simply to find them. He does not take the opportunity to proclaim their guilt once and for all at the end of his book, where readers would be likely to remember this declaration. In once again arguing his innocence Holmes fails to make a case for their guilt, where he could reemphasize their motive in contrast to his continual dismissal of motives attributed to him and once again stress the similarity between his appearance and that of Hatch. Holmes fails to see the importance of such points and how they could form the backbone of his case, perhaps because it would mean centering Hatch and Miss Williams instead of himself. Since he is able to finally tell his side of the story to a distant reading public who can neither interrupt him for clarification nor derail his thoughts, Holmes retains the focus on himself even as he belatedly attempts humility in his final plea.

PART IV

Holmes Confesses 27 Murders

The publication of *Holmes' Own Story* marks the last time Holmes actually argued his innocence. His trial in October 1895 was notable for a number of reasons: it was the first time a judge in Philadelphia wore full robes to a trial; Holmes's lawyers at one point left him to conduct his own trial and then returned within a matter of days as though nothing had happened; and they did not mount a defense of Holmes' innocence. Although it was highly anticipated that Holmes would take the stand in his own defense, instead his lawyers William A. Shoemaker and Samuel Rotan stood on the argument that the prosecution had not presented ample evidence and that the jury should be dismissed. Judge Arnold did not dismiss the case and in fact instructed the jury on the meaning of "circumstantial evidence" for over an hour before sending them off for their deliberations.

There are many similarities between Holmes' trial in 1895 and the first murder trial of Ted Bundy in 1979. Bundy, who had been a law student, chose to act as his own lawyer. Because of this he demanded extra privileges, including a typewriter in his cell and more time in the library in order to prepare his case. Nearly a century previously, Holmes had made the same requests, although he himself had not been trained as a barrister. Whereas Bundy entered into his trial with the full understanding that his team was for support only and that he himself would be acting as lawyer, Holmes' lawyers repeatedly requested to be released from their duty because Holmes had made it clear he did not want or need them. Judge Arnold eventually allowed that Holmes' lawyers could indeed leave, so long as they knew the consequences of their actions in doing so.

Holmes' behavior as his own barrister was alternately impressive and a joke. At times it seemed that his cross-examination elicited important pieces of information, but in other matters he hammered away at victims in order to prove points that, like elements in *Holmes' Own Story*, were ultimately useless. In one example he interrogated Eugene Smith over Smith's comment that he had seen Pitezel and Holmes go up to the second floor of the patent shop together, harping on the fact that Smith did not see where the men actually went. However, the staircase in question only led up to the second floor. Holmes had harangued a witness for the prosecution over his word choice when the end result in fact made Holmes look foolish. He had spent so much time attempting to discredit Smith that he ended up making himself a laughingstock when the point he was after ended up being moot.

The strain of acting as his own lawyer quickly showed, and Shoemaker and Rotan returned soon enough to finish out the trial—but not as had been anticipated. The defense's refusal to make an argument for Holmes' innocence was likely based on the fact that the prosecution had no direct evidence against Holmes. In Bundy's case, there was a single clue that pointed directly to him: a bite mark on one of the women he had killed that matched his own teeth. For Holmes, there was nothing: no witnesses who had seen the murder enacted and no direct link between him and Pitezel's death.

Because the trial in Philadelphia was for Benjamin Pitezel's death, no evidence from any other case was allowed. Even though the prosecution had gathered many witnesses and evidence from elsewhere, connected to cases in Toronto, Indianapolis, and Chicago, none of it could be admitted. Among this evidence was a box of Howard's charred bones, which had been prepared as evidence much in the same way the dental plate supposedly belonging to Dr. George Parkman had been displayed to the jury at the trial of George Webster in 1850. Judge Arnold upheld the law when he declared that no man may be convicted of a crime based on evidence that he had committed other crimes—in this case murder, although Holmes himself, in his autobiography and at his earlier trial, had already admitted to defrauding insurance companies. The October trial concerned the death of Benjamin Pitezel and Benjamin Pitezel alone.

Judge Arnold also had to make the point that the jury members could not be dismissed solely for having read about the Holmes case in the newspaper. He declared that, as they were now in a more enlightened, modern age, it would be enough for jurors to declare that they would make their decision based solely on the evidence presented to them in court, and not on what they had already seen or heard. Potential jurors were not asked if they had read *Holmes' Own Story*, although the prosecution was likely not overly worried that the book would have influenced them in some way. One man who claimed to have read nothing about the case, however, was dismissed, since it was deemed impossible for anyone in Philadelphia to have managed to escape a single mention of Holmes' notoriety.[1] The men who made up Holmes' jury were already very much aware of the case that was to be put before them.

Of the various witnesses who were called to testify against Holmes in the murder of Benjamin Pitezel, Georgiana Yoke was the most contested. She asked to be called Miss Yoke instead of Mrs. Howard, the name she had gone by since her marriage to Holmes, which was a clear indication of her own thoughts on the legality of such a union. Holmes, who had otherwise been composed or perhaps even overly cold and arrogant during his trial, broke down when she took the witness box, and newspapers were divided over whether this was an act or an honest display of emotion. Unfortunately for the defendant, the jurors were presented with letters in which he had referred to Myrta Holmes as "my wife."[2] There had been no divorce between Dr. and Mrs. Holmes—just as Holmes had not divorced his first wife before marrying Myrta—and thus his marriage to Georgiana was not legal. Her testimony against him was therefore allowed to stand.

Holmes' emotional reaction to Georgiana's presence stood in stark contrast to the stony façade he had erected during Carrie Pitezel's testimony, and this distinction likely worked against him. It did, however, continue the themes set forth in *Holmes' Own Story* in which he reported that his suffering was caused solely by the misery of his wife. Even Holmes' lawyers added to the unease, questioning Carrie about Holmes' treatment of her and her family so belligerently that their attempt to discredit her "not only failed miserably, but seemed heartless."[3] Even when Holmes allowed his lawyers to act in his stead, their attempts to help their client did not always strike the proper emotional chord, which also follows the figure of Holmes as presented in *Holmes' Own Story*.

Holmes himself caught the attention of many spectators both inside the courtroom and out. Daily newspapers printed updates on the trial, especially when Holmes was acting as his own lawyer, and reporters and adoring young female fans alike crowded the courtroom on the day when it was expected that Holmes would testify. Unfortunately for the eager audience, no one testified for the defense. Spectators and readers were left with the closing arguments and Judge Arnold's instructions to the jury, which later revealed that their decision had been made immediately although they had chosen to take the time to eat dinner before revealing their sentence. Holmes was found guilty of the murder of Benjamin F. Pitezel.

That night Holmes composed a formal statement which ran in the papers the following day. He once again protested his innocence and put forth the statement that, by the time a new trial date was set, "I shall have had time, at least, to prepare my defense and to refute the web of false contortions spun by the ambitious lawyers who have prosecuted and persecuted me."[4] What Holmes fails to acknowledge is how he and his lawyers had indeed been given the chance to tell his side of the events and had instead decided to risk Holmes' life on the gamble that the prosecution's case was not strong enough to convince the jury. Even though *Holmes' Own Story* had been published and had clearly laid out an alternate version of what had happened on the day Pitezel died—and even though Holmes had published this book not only for the money it would bring in but also in order to sway public opinion about himself—he made no use of this argument in court. In spite of the fact that it seems as though he had already laid out his defense and arguments against the case constructed by the district attorney before his trial even began, Holmes takes to the newspaper after he was found guilty in order to argue that such a thing must still be done.

In this short statement he does not argue that his own lawyers failed him, or that he failed himself during the time when he was acting as his own barrister. The main point of concern comes in that he was unable to argue against the case the prosecution had presented, even though he had not made any such statements during the trial. Holmes did not protest when his lawyers chose not to present his case, and the prosecution even allowed Rotan to make his closing argument second in spite of the usual trial structure, giving them no chance for rebuttal. While the district attorney laid out the circumstantial evidence surrounding Pitezel's murder, Rotan's closing argument attempted to pick apart that story just enough to instill reasonable doubt about his client's guilt. Because he and Shoemaker had not made a case, Rotan could not present an alternative to the story that would explain the circumstances without turning Holmes into a murderer.

What Holmes *does* argue is that he has never murdered anyone—a statement that, only a few short months later, he himself contradicted twenty-seven times over.

Twelve

The Transformation from Innocent to Confessor

On April 12, 1896, *The Philadelphia Inquirer* devoted two and a half pages to what it deemed "The Most Awful Story of Modern Times Told by the Fiend in Human Shape."[1] In a story that took up all of the front page before continuing on pages eight and nine, Holmes, now less than a month away from his execution, confessed to twenty-seven murders and six more attempts. It was a story that had the *Inquirer* advertising the contents two days in advance and resulted in a flurry of follow-up activity. Indeed, some of those Holmes named as his murder victims came forward in the following weeks to indicate that they were not, in fact, actually dead.

It should be of little shock to learn that his concern for the truth continued to remain in the background while the desire for attention and monetary compensation remained central to his priorities. Such a confession—coming shortly before his execution—would be extremely valuable to a newspaper and give a large boost in sales, especially if they advertised the publication in advance and Holmes included a handwritten denial of any previous statements—both of which occurred. Other newspapers, lacking the publishing rights and wishing to print their own story more quickly than the time it would take to purchase and typeset the *Inquirer*'s story, simply wrote their own. Adam Selzer reports that it was the *North American*'s bootlegged version of the confession that included the now-famous sentiment "I was born with the devil in me,"[2] frequently printed as having been said or penned by Holmes himself.

Although Holmes freely admits to being "the most detestable criminal of modern times,"[3] he does not in fact blame his actions on the devil. There is no overarching motive ascribed to all twenty-seven murders, although reasoning is provided on a case by case basis for most of them. As accomplished as he presents himself when it comes to murder, Holmes is still very much just a man as opposed to possessed by a supernatural beast, and then one driven mostly by the promise of money. The question of motivation is addressed only tangentially as Holmes makes no effort to discover why he might have been driven to become the Greatest Criminal in History and instead focuses on recounting a litany of deaths.

While his reasons for committing the murders remain murky, Holmes does indicate a number of factors that contributed to his writing of this confession. These all center around the marvelous work of the detectives and lawyers who have conspired to put him in prison—men of whom Holmes earlier had little good to say. In *Holmes' Own Story* and during his trial, the detectives and prosecuting attorney refused to listen to his explanation of what had actually happened in Toronto and the other cities in the fall of 1894, and they were stubbornly, uncomprehendingly blind to any course of events that meant Holmes was innocent. Now, in the spring of 1896, Holmes admits that "it would be useless to longer say I am not guilty"[4] not only of the crimes against the Pitezel family, but of so many others besides.

He has chosen, however, not to confess to a member of the law enforcement but instead to a member of the press. While the confession itself may appear to be a change of heart, the manner in which it is expressed still follows the characteristics already displayed in *Holmes' Own Story*. Had he honestly wished to see justice done, Holmes would have made his confession in private to the detectives so that various deaths and disappearances might at last be explained and for the express purpose of bringing closure to the friends and families of the victims. Had he wished to allow psychologists the chance to better understand or explain the aberration that made him commit these murders, he could have also done so on an individual basis without giving interviews to anyone who was not law enforcement or trained in medicine. Even if Holmes had simply wanted to unburden himself before his execution, it could have been done privately in a room with only a handful of people in a confession that resulted in a transcription not meant for public consumption.

The timing of this confession is also an element to be considered. It was not a gallows speech, made to the people who had crowded in to witness his death and only to be published after the sentence had been carried out. It was also not a last-minute attempt to gain a stay of execution like his letter to Carrie Pitezel, sent on May 1, 1896, and offering a large amount of money if only she would petition on his behalf to give him the time to convert a land deed into cash. Certainly a man hoping to have his life spared would not have confessed to further murders, and one hoping a slew of confessions would allow him more time to keep confessing would not have given his victim count such a pat number and listed as many names and details as he could remember. A man hoping to delay his execution would threaten the public with the idea that he had committed many crimes not yet discovered and that only he could reveal them, given time. Instead Holmes assigned his victims a pat number and appeared to confess to everything. He even showed no indication that it would be a comfort to loved ones to know for sure what had happened to the people in question. Holmes wrote, as always, for his audience, and far enough in advance of his execution that he would be able to fully appreciate the reaction to what he had written.

Holmes does not, of course, explain his reasons in this manner. He instead chooses to praise the men who worked so tirelessly to build the case against him, including Detective Geyer, without whom the Pitezel children's bodies would not have been found. Holmes indicates that the men demonstrated "marvelous skill"[5] in their work to track him down. Although Holmes was intelligent, the men who captured him and gathered enough circumstantial evidence to lead to his execution had to, of necessity, be smarter. In spite of the fact that Holmes is only a man himself and not a devil or a monster, he is still a unique criminal, and the law enforcement of the age had to rally in order to meet the challenges he set for them. Because they did indeed complete this task, Holmes seems to feel that it would be almost impolite to leave those men wondering if their conclusions were indeed true.

Even as he makes what he claims to be a full and accurate confession to his crimes, Holmes admits that he has limited himself only to the cases for which he has already been investigated. This is not because he has no desire to talk about other possible murders, but because admitting to them would mean that the detectives had fallen short in their persecution of him and had failed in some way after all. Any readers who continued to search for victims to attribute to Holmes would thus not be slighting the confessed murderer but insulting the men who had caught him. After all, Holmes writes, he did not pen this confession in order to cast doubt upon the detectives or discredit their work. He merely wished to demonstrate how skillfully those men tended to their jobs and give them closure in knowing that yes, he had indeed committed the crimes of which they had suspected him.

Holmes' praise of those who put him behind bars is not, however, a simple acknowledgment of the fact that they did indeed properly piece together the evidence against him in order to secure a death sentence. Any kind words about the intellect or perseverance of the detectives who finally caught up with Holmes or of Detective Geyer, who succeeded in finding the bodies of the Pitezel children when so many before him had failed, attest to the intelligence and skillfulness of the criminal himself. Had it been an easily provable and straightforward case, then Holmes himself would have been nothing more than an everyday criminal hardly worth the headlines or attention.

Harold Schechter points out that a newspaper reporter who had visited Holmes at the end of October had already come to the conclusion that the prisoner had a "desperate 'ambition to be great in some way—and his models of greatness, if one may judge from his talk, are old-time villains of high degree.'"[6] Although on the surface it seems Holmes' cons and crimes centered around money, they also involved other people: men Holmes could outwit, and audiences who would respond properly to his stories of how he had outwitted the others. In his autobiography Holmes presented himself as capable in many situations that would cause others stress and might force them to break down in some way, but whether he was helping his mistress hide the body of her sister before ending their affair, or frantically on the run to escape a secret service agent while clinging to a rotting body stored in a trunk, Holmes kept a cool head and managed to navigate a difficult situation without being arrested.

The truth of these stories did not matter to Holmes and, indeed, his confession in the *Inquirer* offers an entirely different narrative of Nannie's death. What was important to him was the chance to tell others of these adventures and to give himself a starring role. Even though this confession situates Holmes as a murderer, it also makes him a new kind of murderer and Holmes still retains his position in the spotlight. Holmes promises his readers a "true & accurate"[7] recitation of his crimes and presents them with columns upon columns of text describing deaths that have one element in common: Holmes himself. Without Holmes, they would be a string of unconnected events instead of a story with a narrative throughline.

And yet the story itself would not exist if Holmes had refused to tell it. Once he was convicted of murdering Benjamin Pitezel, public assumption was that he murdered Howard, and then Alice and Nellie Pitezel as well, even though Holmes was never brought to trial for those cases. He was kept imprisoned in Philadelphia since he had already been given the death sentence and his appeal had been refused. Because of this, Holmes had nothing to lose by confessing to any manner of crimes, since he could of course only be hanged once.

He tells his readers that he has been moved to confess because he feels it is his duty to confirm the work of the marvelous men who had tracked him down and uncovered his final crimes. According to Holmes it would, in fact, be "the height of folly"[8] to allow himself to be executed without confirming the accuracy of their deductions and giving the men the praise that is their due. When he limits himself only to confessing what they have accused him of, it is because clearly these intelligent men must have tracked down every last possible murder that could have been attached to Holmes' name—and not, of course, because he wishes to keep anything a secret or feel superior at having committed a murder so stealthy that not even the greatest minds of the day could trace it. He even assures his readers that they owe a vast debt to those men for having caught him and put him somewhere from which he could not harm anyone else.

This both chides any reader who may have continued to ascribe to Holmes' prior opinion of the detectives and prosecution, and reads as a mild threat. Whereas earlier Holmes had protested his innocence and demanded that he should be released at once, Holmes now declares that they have placed him "beyond the power of committing other, and perhaps, if possible, more horrible wrongs."[9] If Holmes had regained his freedom, it seems, he would have continued his murderous pastime, and the world owes the detectives many thanks for the lives they have saved by continuing to search for evidence to prove Holmes' guilt. Thus, as a token of his own gratitude, Holmes steels himself to reveal the extent of his crimes.

Difficult and Distasteful Details

In direct contrast to *Holmes' Own Story*, which was presented as his own idea, Holmes was urged to write this confession. His autobiography may have been an easier narrative to pen, perhaps even made all the more appealing by the pressure from his lawyers and friends not to write it, but his confession was apparently torture. The previous tradition of the execution sermon would have allowed him to tell his crimes to others, either well-meaning fellow villagers or the local ministers, and it would have been a minister's job to transmit them into writing in the form of his execution sermon. Had Holmes confessed to these crimes a century earlier, it is likely that he would neither have written them down nor had the chance to read them. The execution sermon, however, had since gone out of style, along with the practice of naming every small sin that had led up to the one meriting a death sentence, and thus Holmes' confession focuses solely on the crime of murder.

Before he delves in to this recitation, however, Holmes hesitates. He boldly states that he is not embarking upon this literary mission in order to parade himself in front of the public for the sole purpose of gaining notoriety, and that, while he commits to writing clearly and in detail about the crimes, he will not endeavor to make himself more appealing in the retelling than he is in real life. This is a commitment of the penitent prisoner—intelligent, yes, but not more so than those who caught him—to remain humble, and an insistence that he is not undertaking this written confession for his own delight. It is, however, something that must be done, although he does not clarify how his respect for the detectives and the prosecution has led him to publish his words in a newspaper. Even if he wished to make it widely known that he had indeed confessed and that he believed those men to be such fine, upstanding examples of humanity, Holmes would not have needed to follow up these declarations with the amount of detail he thus goes on to provide for anyone who wishes to purchase a copy.

In his continued capitulation to the leading legal and scientific thought of the day, Holmes even offers up the observation that, since his imprisonment, he has detected odd physical changes in his body. Even though the etching at the bottom of the front page of the *Enquirer* shows a well-dressed man at a writing desk, labeled "Holmes writing his confession," that looks just as normal as the etched portrait labeled "Herman Mudgett, alias H.H. Holmes" on the same page, Holmes reports that his physical features have altered drastically. "To-day I have every attribute of a degenerate—a moral idiot,"[10] Holmes writes, in spite of the even features presented to his readers through these illustrations. Moral and social degenerates were meant to have been less evolved than their upstanding counterparts, and thus their appearance was said to have reflected this. Holmes, who had committed murder more than two dozen times, should not have been an attractive man in his well-cut suits, but should have instead appeared to be hideous and apelike. This would have served not only to mark him as morally deviant, but to warn the men who had been interested in business deals and the women who may have been enticed by his charms to stay away and avoid him completely.

In the text Holmes insists that his appearance is "rapidly deteriorating"[11] and that he is grateful not to be allowed a mirror in his cell that would remind him of it with every glance. The onset of these symptoms only after the commission of his crimes—and after his trial and death sentence—is worrisome, since it means that he managed to conceal his internal derangement while he committed a string of terrible murders and that his handsome face allowed him to conceal his criminal nature all the longer. It was only the intelligence of the detectives who came after him that allowed them to unmask Holmes and imprison him, thereby revealing the supposedly monstrous visage that had been lying in wait.

The text and the accompanying images disagree in this matter. At his trial Holmes, although clearly suffering from stress, was able to attract any number of young female onlookers who managed to find their way into the courtroom purely by batting their eyes at the guards meant to keep them out. If Holmes' confession is to be believed, in the intervening months his face has undergone a grotesque transformation that would hardly entice such young women but would instead be more apt to send them screaming in the opposite direction. Such deformed visages marked the people who functioned as the attractions in circus freakshows and Holmes' face, had it in fact rivaled theirs as he claimed, would have been a prime candidate for an illustration accompanying the story. The included images, however, show him to be apparently unchanged. Holmes was, in fact, prefacing his confession with an outright lie, as was observed not only by those who visited him before his execution, but those who witnessed the hanging.

In this instance, at least, Holmes was able to construct his tale around the expectations of the day. While late nineteenth-century readers were not equipped with the standard narrative of a serial killer that would inform their reading of Holmes' narrative, they did indeed have conceptions of evil and its manifestations. The Holmes presented in *Holmes' Own Story*—clever, quick-witted, and charming enough to escape the various situations into which he had managed to stick himself—may have aligned himself with the contemporary ideas of a scoundrel or con man, but Holmes in his confession becomes a multiple murderer. It would be difficult to align the same spinner of tall tales of *Holmes' Own Story* with a man who would willingly murder children in cold blood. His tone, like his face, must change in order to assist with the transformation from the wrongly imprisoned to the truly guilty and apparently penitent.

Readers are thus not meant to imagine the same Holmes who sat in his cell, writing both his diary and his autobiography while dressed in his own suit instead of the common prison garb. This is also likely not the same man who would enjoy reading the classics or engaging in daily exercise between his carefully chosen meals so that he might keep both mind and body limber, lest he wither away during his confinement. He is further no longer so concerned with the well-being or current condition of Georgiana Yoke, who had long since retaken her maiden name and was fully known to not have been his legal wife. This Holmes is not a man who retains a spark of hope that the detectives will at last see sense and realize that Edward Hatch did indeed exist, and had himself committed the crimes on behalf of Minnie Williams. No—this new Holmes is hopeless and finds himself with no redeeming features, and no possible redeeming act aside from confessing his crimes so that the detectives' praises might be properly sung.

This Holmes is irredeemable. There is nothing about him to like aside from his willingness to confess, and this willingness is only acceptable because of what it is meant to prove about the work of others. There is also nothing holding him back from confessing everything he has done, in full detail, since he cannot be punished more than by his impending execution. Holmes' declaration that this confession is truthful and tells all, however, is as trustworthy as his claim that his face has finally begun to change and reveal him to be the scoundrel he really is.

Thirteen

Details Revealed and Concealed

The point of this confession—aside from the profits Holmes and the *Inquirer* will make from the copies sold—is for Holmes to finally and completely bare his soul and tell the truth after more than a year of ever-changing lies. He is meant to unburden himself prior to his execution and, through that admission, offer reassurance to the detectives that they are more than up to the task of catching this new form of modern criminal. Readers should likewise feel relieved that, although Holmes managed to murder so many people, he was eventually caught. Since he was also apparently the first of his kind, any information he can offer as to *why* he decided to murder so many people or how he went about it could then be used in the future if more such as Holmes began to surface.

A confession is only as good as it is complete. Sins cannot be absolved unless they have been shared with others, and then only with those who have the power to pardon and assign penance for those sins. In order to thoroughly cleanse his soul and ease his conscience, Holmes would have to reveal all the information surrounding his crimes so that those receiving this information would be able to form as complete a narrative as possible. Holmes wishes to praise the detectives for the work they have done, but a true confession would also then allow law enforcement officials to more properly track down and deal with such criminals in the future.

Since he had already given two confessions and written his autobiography, it is understandable that Holmes' *Inquirer* confession would be approached with skepticism. It, like *Holmes' Own Story*, generated a profit and thus was not written purely out of the goodness of his heart.

Perhaps more enticing to Holmes was the opportunity to once again engage with a wider audience, since the publication of this confession was close to his date of execution but still far enough in advance for him to be able to appreciate the reaction his confession received. Like his autobiography, Holmes specifically wrote this confession to be read and was well aware of the extent of his audience as he was writing it.

A Lack of Information

In spite of his declaration that he will reveal all in his attempt to vindicate the detectives and prosecuting attorneys who built the case against him, Holmes does not, in fact, lay out every single detail of his less famous murders. This may come from a lack of memory, limited space in which to publish all of the details, or simply the fact that such a large listing of murder after murder becomes repetitious and therefore almost boring. Even though Holmes has committed to finally fully speaking the truth, he still ultimately holds himself back.

Early on, for example, Holmes confides that "in each instance when the manner of the disposal of their remains is not otherwise specified, it will be understood that"[1] he sold the remains to someone who goes unnamed. Holmes was unable, it seems, to deal with another previously mentioned anonymous man at an unidentified medical college, from whom he had earlier obtained specimens with which to undertake insurance fraud, but this new man appeared to be more than willing. Holmes reports that he earned between $25 and $45 per corpse that he sold to this unnamed man, who himself was well acquainted with every twist and turn of the Murder Castle and all its secret rooms and passageways, but he does not name his compatriot. If this man had already been persecuted for the purchase and dispersal of such items either still in his possession or sold to museums, it seems that Holmes should have named the man to confirm his story, much in the same way he has undertaken the task of writing this distasteful document in order to confirm the findings of the detectives.

Many of his victims, it seems, were not covered in the newspapers at the time of their disappearance, but Mrs. Julia L. Connor and her daughter, Pearl—victims three and four—had indeed drawn attention.

In this case Holmes decrees that it is unnecessary for him to repeat the details, presumably because some reporter in August of 1895 had already accurately recorded them. There were many articles about Julia and Pearl, and Holmes tells his readers to take their pick. He does admit that Julia died "to a certain extent due to a criminal operation,"[2] thereby admitting to having attempted to perform an abortion on her and likely also conceding that he had been the cause of her pregnancy.

In this account, however, Holmes mentions that he was once again not alone in his guilt. He references a man and a woman—again, without naming them—who were responsible not only for Julia's operation but for Pearl's subsequent poisoning. These people were apparently more soft-hearted than Holmes and only agreed to the girl's murder on his insistence, although they had wished to remove Pearl "to place the child in the care of their aged parents."[3] Holmes apparently argued that Pearl would remember her mother's death and that therefore it would be better to kill the girl rather than run the risk of having her talk about what may or may not have happened. This is Holmes' first confessed murder of a child and is reported purely factually.

The trend of the unnamed confederates continues with the murder of Charles Cole, whom Holmes apparently lured to Chicago and distracted while another man struck him over the head. Although it was this man who in fact murdered Cole, having hit him so hard with this single blow that his skull was crushed and therefore of no use to the unnamed man who purchased Cole's body, Holmes does not name either. Even when Holmes argues that, although this was the man's first murder, he went on to commit even more crimes that made him rival Holmes himself, the name is not printed. This dreadful man, possibly "more heartless and bloodthirsty"[4] than Holmes himself, is apparently still enjoying his freedom while Holmes, the greatest criminal of the age, refuses to disclose his identity.

The man and woman Holmes implicates in Pearl's death might be allowed to go unnamed because of the situation he presented. It seems to have been a one-time occurrence in which they might have contemplated death, although even then they were instrumental in arranging for Julia Connor's illegal surgery and wished to have Pearl adopted. In neither case does Holmes show that they, personally, were expecting or planning for the outcome to be murder. He was the one to perform the surgery and thus was the cause of Julia's death, and he admits that he was also the one to suggest that Pearl should be murdered instead of taken away. Their actions were greatly influenced by Holmes, and he does not report that either of them continued with such homicidal tendencies after the mother's and daughter's deaths were covered up.

The man who murdered Charles Cole, in actuality reducing the number of victims Holmes can claim by one, is a different story. Although Holmes clearly meant for Cole to be murdered, he himself did not strike the blow, and the man who did apparently only then discovered that he had an appetite for murder and wished to continue. It is unclear whether this man is the same one who is mentioned assisting with a later murder, since Holmes makes it seem as though the two of them worked together on a number of murders, because he does not offer to reveal the man's name. He simply declares that he believes this man is still in Chicago and still committing murders.

If this is the case, then either the detectives who have been seeking this anonymous confederate are not as skillful as those who pursued Holmes, or the unnamed man is more intelligent or luckier than Holmes. If Holmes is now confessing to twenty-seven murders and he claims that this other man is more heartless and bloodthirsty than he himself, then it seems that the capture and identification of this other man would be even more newsworthy and would rename Holmes as only the second-greatest criminal of the age. As it reads, Holmes' reporting of the existence of this mystery man seems to be a threat: although he himself has been caught, there are indeed others out there who are still at liberty and will, one day, dethrone him from his position of dubious honor.

Holmes also reports that he had some assistance during his eighteenth murder, that of a young man named Rogers. This time Holmes writes that he would gladly give the name of the man who had helped him scam Rogers and had used his skill as a forger to ensure that the pair emerged from the ordeal with money to show for it. This man, though, does not seem to possess the same attraction to murder as Holmes' previously mentioned associate, since once again Holmes is the one to force the decision to murder Rogers rather than to release him with a promise to not speak of what had happened.

It seems that, in this case as well as in the murder of Pearl Connor,

Holmes specifically wished to manipulate his companions into being the ones to agree upon death as the next logical step. It was perhaps not enough to torture his victims but was important to Holmes to inflict mental strain on his compatriots, as well. He writes that he insisted Pearl should be murdered but that it was not done until the couple acquiesced, and in the case of Rogers Holmes writes that he forced his associate's hand and, by pretending that he would release the imprisoned Rogers and thus threatening his associate with being arrested, caused the other man to suggest that Rogers should be killed. Presumably the man who killed Cole would not have hesitated at the thought of also killing Rogers.

But it is his associate in the case of Rogers that Holmes offers to name. The bloodthirsty compatriot who continues to kill receives no such attention, but Holmes presents himself as more than willing to identify the man he had to force around to the idea of murder. Unfortunately, Holmes informs his readers, since he himself is a confessed criminal guilty of myriad crimes, he cannot accuse another man on his own unsubstantiated word. Whether Holmes had, in private, spoken the name to detectives who might then undertake the responsibility of finding evidence to support his claim is not mentioned. He seems content to simply introduce these mysterious figures and assign them a measure of guilt in the murders he claims in his confession without apparently feeling any responsibility to then name them and prevent them from killing again without him.

The lack of information continues when Holmes declines a discussion of the safe in which he murdered many of his victims, since "sufficient has already been printed"[5] about it. Once again his readers must hope that whichever version of the story they read happens to have been the correct one since the safe, like the tale of the murder of Julia and Peal Connor, was also quite popular during the time when the Murder Castle was explored. The news was sensational enough that Holmes felt moved to attempt to correct it by publishing *Holmes' Own Story* and, although his confession is a retraction to his prior claims of innocence, it does not in fact clarify which of those sensational headlines were in fact true and which had only been published for the express purpose of selling more papers. Where his previous publication seemed to indicate annoyance at the amount that had been printed and read about him, since he had to work that much harder to fight against it, his confession seems to have given up entirely in some cases and almost wearily dismisses any and all discussion of elements that, less than a year previously, Holmes had set out to wholeheartedly disprove.

He even seems to tire of his own recitation of death when he breaks his chronological presentation to include the murder of Miss Gertrude Connor as fifteenth, directly after that of Miss Anna Betts, simply because it "is so similar to the last that a description of one suffices for both."[6] Miss Connor's passing therefore merits a single sentence and nothing more. She functions only as yet another death Holmes can add to his total as a means of separating himself from men who have killed fewer than twenty-seven people.

Even when it comes to Holmes' lifestyle and smaller crimes he admits that he "can add little to what the detectives have already pointed out."[7] They have become the experts on Holmes' life apparently even beyond Holmes himself. He does not reference *Holmes' Own Story* or attempt to fill in possible gaps that the detectives have left, once again relying on the newspapers to have taken what the detectives learned and to have already properly conveyed it to the masses. It is almost as though Holmes surrenders to the popular narrative out of exhaustion—at least where it seems more exciting than any information he himself could offer.

These instances in which Holmes refuses to add detail are thus separated into two distinct categories. The first involves Holmes taking a step back from the narrative when it is information that his readers should already know from their perusal of other sources. This often comes across as an admission that, unlike what he had argued in *Holmes' Own Story*, the detectives, prosecution, and many reporters indeed got Holmes' story correct and now he need only bow his head in submission, although he does so without indicating which of the previous versions of events is the truthful one. This is a Holmes who has lost some of his feistiness and has given up the fight. Whatever the detectives say about him at this point is right, and he will neither argue nor offer further explanation.

The second way Holmes conceals detail surrounds his accomplices. Although they have not been alleged to have existed before, save for the suspicion that he knew someone who would be able to take care of the corpses he was producing at surprising speed, Holmes first introduces the idea that he did in fact have people helping him with various murders and then refuses to say any more about them. His brief confessions of these specific crimes implicate others in the deaths. In two cases—those of the Connors and Rogers—Holmes indicates that he manipulated these nameless others to do his bidding. This suggests that they, too, might be considered his victims since presumably the couple who agreed to Pearl's death and the man who was forced to suggest Rogers' murder would have been wracked with guilt afterward. Holmes does not offer to name the couple but does indeed indicate he would have named the other man if not for the recommendation of his lawyers, so it seems all the more confusing: why mention these various accomplices at all if he refuses to give any more information that would lead to identifying them? Why risk sharing the spotlight with others, especially when it came to the man who willingly murdered Connor Cole with such force that his whole skull was destroyed?

It seems that Holmes, like the serial killers who followed in the nineteenth and twentieth centuries, had come to the conclusion that a full and complete confession would not in fact be in his best interest. If he told everything and soothed all fears, there would be no benefit in continuing to keep him alive. Nearly a century later Ted Bundy attempted to have his execution stayed once more by confessing to crimes that he had not previously spoken of, hoping that the thought of giving his victims' families closure would be reason enough to keep him alive so that he could keep talking. Holmes does not indicate that he had murdered more than these twenty-seven—although he had been accused of making full use of his Murder Castle—but these vague references to various accomplices suggest that Holmes does know more than he is telling, and that he would need further temptation in order to reveal the information he has withheld, including his accomplices' identities. After all, if Holmes hints that he knows the name of a man who is in fact even a more devious criminal than he is, what else has he kept to himself that would be of interest to detectives, lawyers, psychiatrists, and the world in general?

Explaining Murder

One aspect that Holmes does at various times illuminate for his readers is the question of motive. In order to understand him as a person and a criminal—and especially as a new sort of criminal—the question of *why* he committed these murders is just as important as details of *how* they were enacted. Understanding his motive not only allows for speculation about his mental condition, but also grants others insights into how they might protect themselves from falling victim to a similar criminal. If Holmes lists his reasons for committing murders as something that would presumably be under the control of his victims, others—men and women alike—can take care to ensure that they, personally, do not flaunt these traits in front of men that might turn out to be like Holmes.

In a move that directly contradicts his protestations of innocence at the end of the Moyamensing prison diary, money plays a large role in many of these murders. Holmes' first victim, Dr. Robert Leacock, was in possession of a lucrative life insurance policy. His second, like many others, was then sold by Holmes in order to make money off of his corpse. Victim number five, named only as Rogers, was chosen because Holmes learned he was in possession of a large sum of money. A failed triple murder was attempted because of the money that Holmes would have been given upon the delivery of the bodies; his sixteenth victim, Miss Kate Durkee, owned valuable real estate; and the seventeenth, Mr. Warner, was also in possession of large sums of money. All of these murders were attempted or enacted so that Holmes might make a monetary profit.

This motive is, perhaps, understandable. If Holmes had no money and was looking for a way to quickly make some, he might have decided to rob a bank—an endeavor which may also have ended up with murder attached to it—but, considering his background as a physician and his knowledge of the difficulty of getting medical and anatomical specimens, this other, more gruesome method of income clearly presented itself. It is reassuring, however, that a man would need certain connections in order to continue disposing of bodies in such a way, since few would be acquainted with someone willing to receive and process so many without alerting authorities or asking too many questions.

It is also a reassuring motive in that readers can prevent themselves from becoming such victims simply by not bragging to others of their financial status. If Holmes had not known of the insurance claims, real estate, or monetary holdings of others, he would not have thought to murder the victims he listed. Then again, the three nameless women

Thirteen. Details Revealed and Concealed

who managed to escape with their lives only because Holmes overreached by attempting to murder all three at once were selected not because of the money they currently possessed, but because of the money Holmes would receive upon handing over their corpses. Without such a man to dispose of the bodies, at least, Holmes would not have been able to make a profit off of their deaths. Whether or not the men and women reading this confession would be fully reassured of their safety, it is certainly a cautionary tale about bragging of one's wealth.

Robert Latimer, victim number thirteen, was selected not because of money in his pocket but rather because of knowledge he possessed about "certain insurance work"[8] Holmes had undertaken. There is a particular logic to this, as well, if not a generally accepted morality. Since Latimer possessed information he could have used against Holmes, and Holmes no longer had any use for him, he decided that Latimer should die and therefore no longer be a threat.

Similarly Holmes recounts the deaths of "Mrs. Sarah Cook, her child and Niece."[9] The two women stumbled upon Holmes as he was dealing with his previous victim. Since he felt that he could not properly explain the situation in his favor, no matter how much time he was given, Holmes decided on action over words and murdered them. The "child" mentioned and counted among his victims was unborn, since Mrs. Cook was pregnant. This is an inconsistency in Holmes' account since, although he admits that Julia Connor died during a certain illegal surgery, he does not count the aborted baby as one of his victims even though he would have set out purposefully to remove it from its mother's womb. If Holmes counts Mrs. Cook's fetus as a life, it seems he should have counted Julia Connor's, as well.

These murders, like Latimer's, were committed in the vein of self-preservation. Had Holmes not committed earlier crimes for them to stumble upon, they would not have been threats against him. Holmes had clearly made it a practice of introducing other men to his insurance scams, the most famous being Benjamin Pitezel, but the fact that two women could accidentally come upon him while he was dealing with the body of a victim is almost laughable as a display of the arch fiend's ineptitude. Not only would they had to have been exploring his Murder Castle and all its secrets, but Holmes would not have been cautious enough as he went about his obviously illegal activities. In this case he was "lucky" enough to be able to dispose of the two women quickly and avoid any further distractions.

Once the basic premise of Holmes' aberrant morality has been grasped, these motives seem almost logical. As long as his readers understand that, in spite of his infrequent comments about how detestable his actions are, Holmes places little to no value on human life, then they make sense. A person might then indeed be sacrificed for money or in order for Holmes to keep his illegal dealings a secret, because, to Holmes, his own personal well-being is easily more important than others' lives. It is a dramatic shift from commonly accepted morality to this new way of measuring value but, once enacted, these motives become supremely logical.

This convoluted reasoning is also used to explain the death of Lizzie, a domestic who had caught the eye of Holmes' apparently irreplaceable janitor, Quinlan. Taking a long view, Holmes reasoned that, if his janitor's relationship with Lizzie became serious, he would lose that janitor and so, rather than risk "his leaving my employ I thought it wise to end the life of the girl."[10] This is not a case of Holmes decreeing that his own quality of life is worth the sacrifice of another life, but that, of two people in his employ, Quinlan was worth more than Lizzie. Quinlan himself was not implicated in any of Holmes' other crimes or given a reason for being so valuable that Holmes would rather murder his love interest than possibly lose him should the romance bloom.

Holmes does not report that Quinlan had come to him and informed him that he would be leaving his employment in order to marry or otherwise pursue Lizzie. It seems that Holmes only suspected it would be a possibility and this, added to the fact that he had already discovered in himself a propensity for murder, led him to choose Lizzie as his next victim. Her death sentence seems to have been based on shakier circumstantial evidence than even Holmes' own, although he does not concern himself with the particulars. She was, he reports, the first victim to die in the safe that he had previously denied owning at the time, but in which he further suffocated a number of his victims, once again proving the newspaper reports to be correct.

Emeline Cigrand's relationship was also "particularly obnoxious"[11] to Holmes, although not for the same reasons as Lizzie's. Cigrand worked for him as a stenographer but was also his mistress, and it was her engagement—not merely a potential romantic involvement—that upset him. The fact that he describes her as being only "almost"[12] indispensable to his work seems secondary to his jealousy, considering the course of action he chooses. It seems that Holmes could bring himself to cope with losing Cigrand, so long as no other man would have her since, after multiple attempts to murder her fiancé, Holmes decided to instead murder Cigrand herself on her wedding day. She had apparently stopped by on her way to the ceremony in order to bid Holmes farewell, at which time he asked her to step into the vault that had already been used to claim Lizzie's life.

Although airtight, the vault itself was apparently not soundproof since Holmes was able to hold a conversation with Cigrand once she had been locked inside. He reports that he extracted a promise from her to write a letter to her fiancé stating that she cannot be happy with him, and a further promise that she would move to a new city with Holmes and act as his wife, although Holmes—perhaps suspecting that promises made under the threat of death are worth little—kept her in the vault until she suffocated all the same. Even though she had agreed to do all he asked, apparently very willingly, his request had not been entirely realistic as far as his own business dealings and arrangements, although it is understandable why Cigrand would have attempted to gain her own freedom no matter what she was asked to say. Her death, it seems, was a simple matter of Holmes not wishing to give her up when it meant someone else could have her, even though it meant the loss of a stenographer who was so vital to his business.

Miss Anna Betts and Miss Gertrude Connor, listed as fourteenth and fifteenth in Holmes' recitation of murder not by dint of their chronological order but because of the similarities of their deaths, are not given a relationship status. Holmes was not interested in them as mistresses or for the work they could perform for him, but because he thought that, after he had given them poison instead of medicine, he "should be called to witness"[13] their deaths. In the first case, Miss Betts had her own physician in attendance, and in the second, Miss Connor had already returned home and was out of reach by the time she died. Holmes only deliberately poisoned their prescriptions for the chance of attending their deaths, either for the emotional thrill or the professional recognition, and he admits that "[p]erhaps these two cases show more plainly than any others the light regard I had for the lives of my fellow-beings."[14] He was not set to make any monetary profit off their deaths, and there was no romantic involvement or professional employment that would complicate or embarrass him. Holmes simply confesses taking this risk in order to watch the women die.

This is especially disconcerting since, in *Holmes' Own Story*, he reported having initially come to Chicago after an incident in which it was reported that a prescription he had prepared had in fact killed someone. When Holmes arrived in the city, it seems he was more or less fleeing from this accusation, which he earlier did not credit since it had no support and he personally had not learned of the patient's fate. It was merely a child who had come to the pharmacy to report on what had happened, which Holmes easily dismissed even when he was not confessing to murder after murder or presenting himself as a man who indeed rated other lives lower than material goods. That victim, like Julia Connor's baby, is not counted among Holmes' twenty-seven and is in fact not mentioned in his confession at all.

Miss Betts and Miss Connor have names, however, unlike the nineteenth victim who is identified as "a Female Boarder." Holmes freely admits that he does not recall her identity, and neither does he name the married tenant who became obsessed with this widowed and wealthy female boarder. The tenant, however, seemed to know that, when his infatuation with the boarder was becoming difficult due to his own married status, Holmes was the man to consult about such things, and Holmes was more than willing to do the tenant a favor in anticipation of the ways he might be repaid later. Holmes apparently suggested that the lovelorn tenant live in his Castle with the boarder until he discovered that she was actually boring, and that Holmes would then help him kill the woman and split her riches. Apparently the tenant was not offended by either the thought that his infatuation would be fleeting or that he would soon be murdering the woman he lusted after, since he agreed, and it was not long before he came to Holmes for help with the murder. This one involved neither a violent blow nor being locked in the vault, since Holmes suffocated her with chloroform—the same chemical known to have been Benjamin Pitezel's cause of death.

This single-use accomplice was more than willing to follow Holmes' scheme and may have even thought of such things himself before consulting Holmes. At the very least Holmes and this man share similar morals since the tenant did not balk or protest at the suggestion of murder and robbery, nor at the idea that he might leave his wife for a while to live with another woman. It seems that this anonymous tenant shared many desires and principles with Holmes, which both served Holmes' needs for having a man in his debt that he might be able to call upon at a later date—he does not mention if he actually did seek such repayment—and helps make his own behavior seem normal.

Although this accomplice is not presented as a multi-murderer, the way Holmes has been named, the fact that Holmes has been able to find so many people—men and at least one woman—willing to assist him in his endeavors is disturbing. He names none of them and does not offer to identify even the worst, who may be more of a horror than Holmes himself, but he does mention a handful of people willing to assist him in his various endeavors. Holmes, it seems, is not the only man in possession of such priorities. He has found many willing to help him along the way.

By not naming his accomplices, Holmes makes it impossible for anyone to confirm his story. Through mentioning them, however, he normalizes his thought process. Even those who are only willing to engage in death a single time, and then solely because he forced their hands, were shown to be malleable enough to be convinced to act like Holmes if even for a moment. While Holmes was considered deviant because he continued to murder with various justifications for his crimes, even those who were otherwise upstanding citizens could be put in situations that would make them also choose murder as the solution to their immediate problems. Holmes may have been the one to suggest the idea in the first place, but he still argues that, in each case, the others agreed. The threat of a man like Holmes is therefore not only to the people he murdered, but to those he either recognized as being similar to him, or to those he could manipulate into a difficult situation where murder seemed the only way out. Although some of his accomplices are presented as being fully guilty in their own right, some of the others are living victims who must deal daily with the consequences of their guilt.

Adding Devilish Details

In his recitation of the murders, Holmes sporadically provides more detail surrounding either the manner of his victims' deaths or the ways in which he ensured that their absence would be overlooked as long as possible. He does not, however, dwell on scenes or particulars that had already emerged in crime writing by the end of the nineteenth century. Holmes is not interested in the body discovery scene, first used in the Beadle *Narratives* of 1783, in which the story begins with a description of the murder victims, their wounds, and their location. Granted, since Holmes was the murderer he would not have needed to begin with the body and work backward in order to determine what had happened, but he often does not describe the condition of his victims at all. Readers are asked to note that, unless he states otherwise, the bodies were processed by his unnamed compatriot who paid him per corpse, but there is no indication of what, exactly, that processing entailed.

Holmes also gives few details when describing the murders themselves, and the only emotion he admits to is annoyance when someone's pleading becomes constant and repetitive. These would be the people he convinced to walk into his vault and then locked inside, since those who were hit—either by Holmes or an accomplice—are described as having been felled with a single blow, much in the same way *Holmes' Own Story* describes how Minnie Williams killed her sister, Nannie. Unless it is Holmes' intent to torture his victims, they die easily and quietly.

This is in contrast to the two women Holmes poisoned because he wanted to be called to be the attending physician at their deaths and does not align with twenty-first-century knowledge about serial killers and public perception of how easy it is to in fact murder someone. Shows like *CSI* and other police procedurals have led to wider awareness of real-life murder investigations and first-hand statements from killers about the difference between fictional accounts of murder and their own personal experiences. Holmes was a new kind of criminal, and he was personally willing to confess in print without an obvious intermediary in contrast to the way that execution sermons were penned by the ministers and not the condemned. He was giving his readers a direct look into the workings of his mind and a sequence of events that they would not have experienced personally nor read about previously. This was an audience who would accept his declaration that a single blow to the head was enough to kill someone.

The readers of Holmes' confession also made up an audience who were not continually reminded of Holmes' training as a physician. While his autobiography had reported on his training at the University of Michigan, and while Holmes himself reminded Judge Arnold of his education during his trial, only the two cases of Miss Betts and Miss Connor even reference his medical training. These two women died as a result of trusting Holmes to prepare their medication, pointing out the implicit faith customers must have in their doctors and pharmacologists that they will indeed first do no harm. Those in the medical field are of course meant to help people instead of harming—or killing—them, and Holmes continually reminding his audience that he had a medical degree would in turn remind them that any man they trusted to tend to their health could be just as twisted as he was.

Eight years earlier the world had already encountered the idea that a man—or possibly a woman—with medical training could potentially be a brutal murderer when it was suggested that the killer known as Jack the Ripper may have had medical knowledge. The organs missing from some of the bodies of victims attributed to the Ripper led to speculation that the killer was either a doctor or a butcher, since it seemed that he would have needed medical knowledge in order to work quickly in the dark. Holmes himself has in fact been suggested as a possible candidate for having been Jack the Ripper, although he is not one of the more popular suspects. At any rate, in 1888 newspaper headlines were already speculating negatively about the connection between physicians and murder, so Holmes' confession would not have been the first time such an association occurred. If he had wished to instill in his readers a genuine discomfort, he could have stressed this connection more and encouraged a distrust of all who had chosen that occupation, leading his readers to continue to feel unsafe even though he himself was behind bars.

Instead, Holmes' confession makes little reference to his title or level of education. He is at last confessing to having murdered multiple people and thus the distinction between him and his fellow inmates has collapsed, in spite of the quality of life he had been living prior to his imprisonment. Holmes is no longer an outstanding gentleman, but he might still be an outstanding criminal.

The Devil in the Details

For all the hedging and withholding of information surrounding the deaths Holmes purported to set out to reveal completely, there are moments in which he offers his readers a measure of detail. These instances are often stated matter-of-factly and almost coldly, in spite of the gruesomeness of their content. Charles Cole, for example, who was killed with a single blow, had his skull "crushed ... to such an extent that his body was almost useless to the party who bought"[15] it. For Holmes it was simply a situation in which he nearly lost out on any profit that could be obtained from Cole's murder, but his readers may make other associations, recalling articulated skeletons in doctors' offices of the kind Holmes referenced in his autobiography, or that, according to Holmes, he had once been terrified by such a skeleton. A crushed skull is an indication of incredible violence and, while he depicts this death as being quick, it would certainly have been messy.

Suffocation within the airtight safe would have likely made for easier cleanup. This method of death is at times reported without further detail, and other times made out to be even worse. Emeline Cigrand, for example, was dealt a "slow and lingering death"[16] inside that very vault when, it should be recalled, she had stopped by to bid Holmes farewell on the way to her own wedding. As Holmes' former mistress who had inconvenienced him with her engagement, she suffered instead of being killed quickly and quietly. The thought of Miss Cigrand, dressed in her wedding finery and slowly dying for lack of air instead of speaking vows to her intended husband, seems not to trouble Holmes, who does not dwell on it. At least the thickness of the vault—even though it allowed for conversation between Holmes and various victims as he extracted promises from them while indicating that such agreements would secure their freedom—prevented him from having to suffer through anything she might have said in pleading for her life.

Holmes' secret room, with its now-famous supply of gas, was not as soundproof, and thus Robert Latimer's lingering death included the

Thirteen. Details Revealed and Concealed

detail that "his pleadings had become almost unbearable"[17] to hear. Even so, it seems to be Holmes' need for the room and not his prisoner's pitiful cries that led him to finally kill the man. In order to stress Latimer's predicament, Holmes' adds that the state in which this secret room was found—its "partial excavation"[18]—was due to Latimer's desperate attempts to escape by clawing at the brick and mortar with his bare hands. This invokes the image of a common Victorian fear of being buried alive and the urban legend of people who woke up in their caskets and were later disinterred to discover bare bones at the ends of their fingertips from their attempts to break through the coffin lid. In spite of this horror, Holmes treats Latimer's death not as a mercy, but as a purely methodical choice due to his own need for the space.

Although Latimer's final pleas were merely irksome, Holmes reports that the final prayers of Miss Kate Durkee during her last hours suffocating in the vault were "something terrible to remember."[19] Apparently the infamous vault was not soundproofed, after all, although Holmes does not report on Emeline Cigrand's final words or indeed anything she may have said beyond making him a promise that should have secured her freedom. Miss Kate's death, like Miss Cigrand's and Latimer's, was not immediate.

Presumably these prisoners' cries would not penetrate to other, public rooms in the Castle, or else Holmes would have been caught much sooner. In order to either hear their final cries or to be sure that they made no such sounds, Holmes would have had to have been quite close to either the vault or the secret room the entire time. With their deaths being described as prolonged, and especially since Latimer was not in an airtight space and would have needed to have been gassed in order to induce suffocation, this presents readers with the thought that Holmes would have taken that time out of his life—his marriages, time with his mistresses, and business dealings—in order to simply wait out the remaining hours of their lives, listening attentively as he did so.

In *Devil in the White City*, Erik Larson depicts Holmes as listening at the door of the walk-in vault as his victims suffocated because it gave him sexual pleasure,[20] although Holmes himself does not discuss such a response. It would have possibly been one revelation too many for the late 1800s, or perhaps this was an instance in which Larson was influenced by the studies of serial killers undertaken a century after Holmes' execution and applied the newly-named common aspects of serial killers to Holmes' story. It would seem, at least, that Holmes did linger by the doors and was not disturbed by the pleadings or prayers of his victims, even if he did not state outright that they brought him any sense of pleasure.

Rogers, the young Englishman Holmes murdered with the help of the associate he would like to name, was also tortured, although in this case it was with the purpose of making him sign documents and not merely as some sort of game. The length of Rogers' imprisonment, which was punctuated by starvation and periods during which the room was gassed enough to make him ill, was determined by how long it took him to give in to Holmes and that associate. Once the documents were signed and the associate used his forging skills to convert them into cash, Rogers was no longer needed. This, then, was when Holmes forced his associate not only to suggest that they kill Rogers, but also to administer the fatal dose of chloroform himself. Holmes did not need to be the one to kill all of his victims, even if he was the one pulling the strings to ensure that they would die.

Generally when Holmes allowed his prisoners to live a while in either the vault or the secret room, rather than having them dispatched by blows to the head or, in the case of Minnie and Nannie's brother, a gunshot, it was because he still needed something from them in order to cover their sudden disappearance. Lizzie, murdered so that Holmes' janitor would not run away with her, was induced to write letters to her family and to the janitor explaining she had left the state for work and would not be returning. Mrs. Sarah Cook, who along with her niece had stumbled upon Holmes while he was taking care of Lizzie's body, wrote a letter that Holmes himself dictated, likewise explaining why she and her niece had left, in spite of her own pregnant state. Emeline Cigrand, his next victim, wrote to her husband-to-be in a similar vein. Once Holmes had elicited such documents, along with promises from these women that they would leave Chicago and never return or speak of what he had done, he had no further reason to keep them alive.

Holmes only reports this detail of having his victims provide documentation for their own upcoming absences in these three instances that occur one right after the other in his confession. Lizzie worked in the Castle and could be connected to Holmes not only as her employer, but because Holmes' janitor was interested in her. Mrs. Cook and her niece were both tenants, and Holmes admits that Emeline was not only his stenographer but his mistress. Each of these women could be traced back to him in some way so that, if they had simply disappeared without notifying their loved ones, Holmes would have been questioned. As it was, Emeline's father was not satisfied and letters were exchanged between the two men concerning Emeline's whereabouts and even the identity of her new husband.

Holmes does not indicate whether any members of Lizzie's family, the janitor Quinlan, or the tenant Mr. Cook inquired as to where Lizzie, Mrs. Cook, or her niece may have gone. There also seems to have been no investigation into their sudden disappearances, or any questioning of the reasons within the letters they wrote to various people. Had all of these absences been brought to police attention and the women connected back to the Castle, it seems likely that Holmes would have become a person of interest much earlier in his criminal career and might have been stopped before he had murdered even half of his purported victim count. However, were these accounts truthful, it seems that the letters written in the women's own handwriting were enough to convince their loved ones that they had moved on willingly, and that they did not wish to be pursued. Holmes' attention to detail while committing his crimes apparently surpasses his recording of those details for publication.

A Touch of Compassion

Along with these callous, offhand details of his crimes, Holmes does include a few gestures toward civility and accepted morality. While reporting his first murder, which he committed in 1886, he observes that he "had become wholly deaf to the promptings of conscience"[21] because of the numerous smaller crimes he had committed previously. Once he had killed someone for the first time, however, it seems that the metaphorical floodgates had opened. Holmes compares himself to a man-eating tiger who, as proven by the length of his confession, roamed far and wide in order to find victims with which to satisfy his bloodlust.

Holmes even marvels that someone like him "should have so long been allowed to live"[22] and continue to commit such horrific crimes. It seems to him that it is Providence's fault for allowing him to escape imprisonment time and time again so that he might continue to find and murder victims to satisfy his immoral desires. At this point, however, before moving on to a description of his second murder, Holmes also feels the need to beg his readers to only allow their negative feelings to fall upon him and not upon those who loved him, since they, of course, did not commit any of the crimes themselves, and none of them knew what he was up to. His loved ones—a category to which all three of his wives belong—were just as unaware of his actions as the general public.

Holmes shows another odd gesture of sympathy in his discussion of the murder of Miss Anna Betts, the first woman to whom he gave a poisoned prescription with the aim of being called to witness her death. He writes that authorities should check the prescription itself "if they are still inclined to attribute this death to causes that reflect upon Miss Betts' moral character."[23] He had apparently seen Miss Betts slandered in reports of her death and wished to clarify that all such accusations against her were untrue, thereby defending one of his chosen murder victims. Although she did fall prey to him, Holmes comes to her defense.

Lastly, in his discussion of an Unknown Chicago Man who had come to the city for the Exposition and whom Holmes thought would have been helpful to him, he pens the hope that either the man's name or handwriting might still be available so that his friends and loved ones might know what had happened to him. This concern is not only for the dead man, but for those who have missed him in his absence. In these two cases, Holmes seeks to bring justice to those he has murdered, not just by giving his confession but also by allowing the true facts concerning their lives and deaths to be known.

Miss Betts and the Unknown Chicago Man are not, however, the main victims whom Holmes wishes to respect by finally setting the story straight. He has by his own admission more greatly wronged others he has murdered not only through killing them, but through spreading tales about them after their deaths. Those who most deserve to have the truth printed in order to dispel all rumors and lies are, of course, Minnie and Nannie Williams and Benjamin, Howard, Alice, and Nellie Pitezel.

Fourteen

Those Hurt the Most

Many of the victims mentioned in Holmes' confession and discussed in the preceding chapter were not people he had previously associated himself with. Those who had been mentioned before were often briefly dismissed, more to acknowledge the rumors surrounding Holmes' deeds than to honestly claim innocence. Even then, with such little information provided in *Holmes' Own Story*, his confession must make corrections in order to provide readers of the *Inquirer* with the supposedly real version of the truth.

Three such cases are those of Emeline Cigrand, Robert Latimer, and Miss Anna Betts or Betz, mentioned briefly in *Holmes' Own Story* and also revisited now during his confession. Holmes' autobiography mentions Emeline Cigrand in his discussion of other disappearances, but in *Holmes' Own Story* Emeline left Chicago of her own free will and had been back to visit since her apparent disappearance while now, in his confession, he was her murderer. Robert Latimer and Miss Anna Betz, as he spelled her name in the previous text, also receive brief mentions in which Latimer has written letters to family members since his supposed disappearance and Holmes has been accused of killing Miss Betz during an illegal operation and not poisoning, as he writes in his confession. Holmes does, however, argue to his readers in his confession that Miss Anna Betts' death was not the result of her immoral character, although he fails to mention that he, personally, had a hand in disseminating this rumor.

These lies or omissions do not pain Holmes as much as the tales he has spread about the Williams sisters or members of the Pitezel family during his various attempts to argue for his own innocence. He had slandered Minnie Williams through his recitation of her apparent biography in *Holmes' Own Story* and by claiming that she had murdered her sister. Pitezel was misrepresented through Holmes' descriptions of his melancholy, alcoholic state, and his suicide. Alice, Nellie, and Howard had always been presented as being at the mercy of Holmes' manipulation as he took them between trains and boarding houses, but now the arch fiend confesses to child murder on top of his other crimes.

Because so much had already been printed about the Williams sisters and the Pitezel family, as opposed to smaller mentions of the other twenty-one victims named in Holmes' confession, it was not enough that Holmes would simply reveal the truth when it came to Minnie's and Nannie's murders. He also had the task of undoing the lies that had been built up around these people and their lives through the stories Holmes had told in order to make himself appear to be an innocent man suffering just as much as the others who had survived.

The Real Minnie Williams

In *Holmes' Own Story*, there seems to be nothing redeemable about Minnie Williams. She came to Chicago already a fallen woman, willing to tell Holmes of her past and then to live with him in an apartment as husband and wife. Due partly to her immoral ways and partly to her mental instability, Minnie murdered her sister, Nannie, because she thought that Nannie and Holmes had spent the night together. Then, after Holmes had taken care of Nannie's body and informed Minnie that they could no longer be a couple, Minnie left for another institutionalization. The next time they met, Holmes informed Minnie of his impending marriage. Although she seemed to accept the situation at the time, Minnie later used her new lover, Edward Hatch, to kill the Pitezel children while they were in Holmes' care so that he would become the subject of a murder investigation. Minnie was thus presented as unstable, immoral, vindictive, and homicidal, capable of both killing her sister with a single angry blow because of jealousy over a man and convincing another man to kill children for her.

Holmes thus begins his confession's discussion of Minnie with a full and complete retraction of all of this and more. He states that Minnie was not only a virtuous woman, but certainly had never attempted to blackmail a married lover. She was not responsible for Nannie's death, nor did she threaten the life of a nurse who cared for her during a period of insanity—especially since Minnie had not, in fact, ever had such an episode. Everything that Holmes had written or said about Minnie Williams up until this point was false, and he confesses that it gives him "a certain amount of satisfaction,"[24] to right these previous wrongs. Then, because all of it has been lies, he must start again at the beginning.

Minnie, like Holmes, apparently traveled often, since he first met her in New York and then Denver, giving his name as Edward Hatch each time. Hatch thus becomes not Minnie's lover and the murderer of the Pitezel children, but a name Holmes had once used for himself, and yet still no comparison is made between Edward Hatch and Edward Hyde. Hatch is not a separate personality from Holmes, but merely yet another pseudonym he has used in order to fulfill his various schemes and cons. In Chicago, when Minnie once again met him in order to take up the position of stenographer, much like Emeline Cigrand before her, he was finally introduced to her as Holmes.

Aside from being virtuous, Minnie was also rather naïve, and Holmes quickly exploited this to not only get money from her but to have her invite her sister to join them in Chicago, since Nannie had some property that Holmes decided he would like to have. In this new version of events Holmes met Nannie at the train depot and immediately took her to his Castle where he forced her to sign some pertinent documents and then locked her in the safe. Mr. Copps of Fort Worth, spelled Cops in *Holmes' Own Story*, is here vindicated in his assessment that the vault was used to kill people, since Holmes agrees that the bare footprint found etched inside the door was Nannie's.

According to the confession, Nannie was in Chicago for less than a day and never saw her sister. Holmes provided Minnie with "a delayed letter,"[25] perhaps written by Nannie in the hopes that she could exchange it for her life, saying that Nannie's trip had been canceled. He then took pains to intercept any letters written by friends and family from Texas who might be inquiring as to how the sisters were enjoying their visit, thereby keeping Nannie's arrival and almost immediate death a secret from her sister. Once Minnie had been wrung dry of all the money Holmes could leech from her, he decided to kill her, as well. This story, at least, retains some of the old adventure aspects of Holmes' first insurance scam from his autobiography.

Between Nannie's death and Holmes' decision that Minnie was no longer useful, the first fire had broken out at the Castle and thus Holmes did not have ready access to either his vault or his room with the poison gas. For reasons he does not explain he decided to take her to the city of Momence, Illinois, and register at a hotel as man and wife. Once again a train wreck features prominently in the unfolding of events, this time not stranding Holmes somewhere but causing him to run across someone who knew him and could later identify him. Since that man had only been present because of the wreck the curious Holmes had gone to see, it was reasonable to assume that he would recall both the date and place of their encounter, and Holmes decided it would be foolish to murder Minnie right then. Instead he later took Minnie to a different location, where he poisoned her before burying her body in a third place. All this was done because he had previously been recognized and did not wish to have himself, Minnie, the murder, or the burial site connected.

Holmes writes that he buried Minnie in the basement of a house that had been identified around the time Howard's body was found and expresses mild surprise that Minnie herself had not been. It seems to him that her remains would have been found, "if the detectives in reality went to that location."[26] The same detectives who were praised for their hard work at the beginning of Holmes' confession have now failed to locate one of Holmes' victims, even though her name had been connected to his from the beginning of the investigation and they were meant to have looked inside the house where she was buried. Although they saw through Holmes' lies when it came to the location of the Pitezel children, they could not find Minnie Williams even though she was more or less directly under their noses.

It is a criticism that leads Holmes to a moment of introspection. He laments the fact that Minnie Williams has not been properly buried; that he ruined her by turning her into his mistress; that he took so much money from her; that he killed both her sister and her brother; and that he "endeavored … to blacken her good name"[27] with the stories he told of her after his arrest. In spite of the fact that Holmes killed others for no reason beyond wanting to watch them die, he marks Minnie Williams as "the saddest and most heinous of any of my crimes."[28]

Fourteen. Those Hurt the Most

She was not his only mistress, nor the only person Holmes killed for money. Minnie was, however, the one Holmes chose to bring back to life in his second confession as the woman who had taken guardianship of the Pitezel children and would be difficult to reach since she had taken them overseas. The declaration that she had murdered Nannie was useful as an explanation as to why Minnie would be in hiding and therefore difficult to contact, as well as reluctant to personally return to the United States. It was also convenient for Holmes to have a female figure put in charge of the children, since two of them were girls and they were without their mother. Although Holmes himself had presented Minnie as a fallen woman, those who had known her argued strenuously for her virtue. Holmes needed her to be a woman who would not only have been romantically involved with him, but would have seduced him of her own free will and would therefore have reacted strongly against his leaving her. Although a virtuous woman would have been a better caretaker for the children, by the time Holmes wrote *Holmes' Own Story* he needed an explanation for the children's deaths and thus Minnie had undergone her complete transformation.

The change in Holmes' narrative from Minnie as seducer to Minnie as seduced repositions her from predator, first of Holmes and then of the children, to victim multiple times over. She was robbed of her virtue before she lost her money and then her life, since the other things Holmes took—her siblings and her reputation—were not known to her at the time of her death. Whereas so many of his other victims were valuable for the money they brought Holmes, Minnie continued to be useful to him long after her murder. Out of all the missing women he could have narratively resurrected to meet his needs as an alibi, Minnie was his choice. She had no parents and little close family—the sister who may have been a threat to Holmes had already become one of his victims. Minnie, like Holmes, apparently traveled a lot, and thus few people in Chicago would have known much about her and therefore would not have been able to contradict the person Holmes made her out to be.

Even with this freedom to craft a Minnie Williams to his own advantage, Holmes did not accuse her of having murdered the Pitezel children herself. He may have felt it was too much of a stretch for a woman whose friends and family had been protesting her morality, or perhaps it was the difference between the thought of Minnie killing

Nannie with a single blow while in hot blood as opposed to the systematic murder of children that stopped him. Holmes turned Minnie not into a multiple murderer in her own right, but into a dangerous figure who could use her feminine wiles to convince another man to commit those murders for her. Minnie therefore became a figure akin to Charles Manson: she was not physically present when people were killed, but she had convinced someone devoted to her—and who might not have been a murderer without her influence—to kill the three Pitezel children in the same way that Manson instructed his Family members to commit murder.

This had been the image of Minnie Williams that Holmes had been circulating for months, since the publication of *Holmes' Own Story*, and one that he now attempts to retract in a few inches of newspaper column. The fact that the *Inquirer* advertised the publication of Holmes' confession likely expanded the reading audience who would have seen this retraction, but the damage against Minnie's reputation had already long been done. She now occupies the position of one of Holmes' most famous victims, not by dint of anything that she had achieved but because of what he did to her name after her death. Although Holmes' confession includes mention of a handful of accomplices to some of his murders, one of them a woman, he had made Minnie more in his own image in *Holmes' Own Story* and presented her as a vengeful, conniving, murderous figure—the exact opposite of the role she fulfills in his confession.

Because Minnie is now a murder victim, she assumes a position of innocence that also includes the idea of naïveté. There is nothing she has done in her life to deserve her death, the way a fallen woman might—the trials for the murders of Helen Jewett and Maria Bickford in 1836 and 1846 clearly demonstrated the belief that sexual immorality was certain to end in death. Minnie Williams was, if anything, *too* innocent, since she came to the big city alone and was easily seduced and relieved of both her virginity and her inheritance. As her guilt decreases, Holmes' villainy increases so that his murder of Minnie is almost on the same level as his murder of the Pitezel children. While some of his other victims had engaged in illegal business dealings or otherwise shown themselves to be less than perfectly upstanding members of society, Minnie, like some of his other female victims, was only desecrated through her domination by Holmes.

"A Happy, Light-Hearted Man"

Benjamin Pitezel is another figure who must undergo a stark transformation from the man Holmes presented in *Holmes' Own Story*, although he, unlike Minnie Williams, was only accused of orchestrating a single death: his own. Since Holmes' second confession, Pitezel was indeed said to be dead and not in hiding somewhere with his children for the purpose of allowing his wife to collect his insurance premium. Holmes presented it as a suicide that Pitezel wished him to stage as an accidental death. In spite of the fact that he had been a depressed alcoholic during his lifetime, who had once awakened after a night of drinking to discover that he had taken a bigamous wife, Benjamin Pitezel cared greatly for the family he could not afford to support and thus had concluded that his own death was the only way he might provide for them. All that Holmes did after discovering his friend was dead, he did following Pitezel's orders.

Unlike previous instances in his confession where Holmes remarks that so many of the details have already been made public, he devotes a great deal of space to Pitezel's murder in spite of the fact that the story has been printed as far away as South Africa.[29] As with Minnie Williams, Holmes begins with their first meeting revealing that, even as early as that, he had already decided he would kill Pitezel. Holmes does not explain why he knew this beyond hinting that, by this point in his life, he had been so consumed with bloodlust that anyone he met could fulfill his depraved desires. He even indicates that, at the time he made this decision, he did not know that Pitezel was married and had children, thus broadening Holmes' scope of potential victims. It was simply unquestionable from day one that Pitezel would die, and thus all that Holmes did for Pitezel and his family—all the money he spent on them in appearance of caring for them—was to lull them into thinking that he was a true friend and deserving of their trust.

Since Holmes first met Pitezel during the construction of his Castle, this shows that he was capable of both patience and long-term planning. The delay between meeting Pitezel and murdering him may have been simply the same argument Holmes had continually put forward about Pitezel: that he was worth far more alive than he would be dead, even with an insurance policy to his name. In his confession, before he writes of the events in Philadelphia, Holmes admits that murdering various members of the Pitezel family was not, in fact, worth it to him. He had spent "seven long years"[30] cultivating his relationship with Pitezel, his wife, and their children through both physical exertion and monetary expenses, and whatever thrill or benefit Holmes had hoped to receive upon murdering them did not, in the end, cause the books to balance.

Here he confesses that all the kindnesses he tallied in *Holmes' Own Story* to present as evidence for reasons why he would not harm the Pitezel children were in fact carefully calculated maneuvers directed toward the eventuality of their deaths. While others, as Holmes muses, might dream of the delight of finding gold at the end of the rainbow, his fantasies involved murder. Holmes imagined that murder would fulfill him the same way sudden riches might fulfill any other man, although the dream far outstripped the reality. Whatever Pitezel was to Holmes in life, in death he was a great disappointment.

Instead of being the melancholy loser Holmes had earlier painted, he describes Pitezel as "a happy, light-hearted man, to whom trouble or discouragements of any kind were almost unknown."[31] He no longer has to be the sort of man who might indeed commit suicide, since this Pitezel will be murdered. He has also not betrayed his wife by marrying another woman while drunk, since, at the time Pitezel and Holmes leave for Philadelphia, he was not an alcoholic. Pitezel himself, therefore, seems to have few or no personal flaws, although Holmes quickly begins to work on him.

Holmes knew himself to be physically stronger than Pitezel, but he still deemed that it would be easier for him to kill the man if Pitezel were drunk at the time. Thus Holmes started sending letters to Pitezel that were supposedly from Carrie. He does not reveal the specific content, but whatever Holmes wrote caused Pitezel to start drinking. Holmes continued until he could be sure that he would find Pitezel drunk in the middle of the day, having turned him into the miserable alcoholic Holmes had previously said Pitezel became all on his own. Holmes' only concern at that point was that he needed to kill Pitezel in such a way that his clothes remained untwisted and would not reveal a struggle, since his death was meant to be staged as an accident.

In stark contrast to his previously published hesitation at harming his friends' corpse, Holmes confesses that, after tying Pitezel hand and foot, he in fact proceeded to burn his friend alive. Presumably any struggles against his bonds while this was happening could be attributed to the death Holmes wished to stage, or perhaps he assumed his friend would remain unconscious throughout the ordeal, although Holmes does not mention having any concern about whether the authorities would be able to conclude that Pitezel had been tied up at the time of his death. He does, however, report that he could not lie about Pitezel's death in this confession, since all the particulars had indeed been concluded and "to now make a misstatement of the facts would only serve to draw out additional criticism."[32] Apparently the detectives and others that Holmes praised had already known that Pitezel had been tied up, burned alive, and then had chloroform inserted into his corpse more than half an hour after he had died, so Holmes' earlier explanation in *Holmes' Own Story* was flawed and disproven from the start.

Unfortunately, Pitezel's drunken stupor did not last through this torture, and Holmes was once again assailed with cries, pleas, and prayers from a victim he was in the process of murdering, but whose death was not quick. The fire continued after his death, so that Holmes had to extinguish flames after he untied the ropes with which he had bound Pitezel. Then he inserted the chloroform into the dead man's stomach, an act that was highly questioned considering the improbability of completing it. Holmes explained it by saying that, if the chloroform was present during the autopsy, the death would indeed be ruled an accident and the insurance company would pay out a full claim. Since Holmes possessed a medical degree it seems that he should have been able to plan such things properly and he would have been aware that the coroner would be able to tell when the chloroform had been administered, and that the amount would be questionable.

Aside from this issue, the chloroform had another effect that Holmes, in his "limited medical experience,"[33] had not—and apparently could not have—foreseen: it reacted with Pitezel's body in such a way that the corner could not detect any alcohol in his system. It seems to the physicians who had viewed his body, therefore, that Pitezel had not only been alive at the time Holmes had set him on fire, but that he also would not have been drunk then or in the preceding twelve hours. Since Pitezel had been tied up at the time he was set on fire, Holmes must have therefore burned his friend not only alive, but fully aware.

Holmes argues against this supposition based on the fact that he would not have been able to subdue Pitezel if the other man had been fully alert. In spite of his previously mentioned superior strength, he could not have held Pitezel down long enough to tie him up—and perhaps he did not possess a cold enough heart to burn a man fully aware of his condition. Only the practicalities of the situation are mentioned, however, and Holmes mentions that Pitezel's condition at the time of his death was a main point of discussion at his trial, during which Pitezel's drunken stupor had been declared not only likely but necessary. Holmes may have been a monster who plotted the death of a man who, along with his family, had viewed him as a friend for years, but he was not so terrible as to burn him alive without any means of anesthetization. He did, however, leave the house afterward "without the slightest feeling of remorse for my terrible acts."[34] Holmes recognized his actions as terrible, but committed them—and hid or disguised the evidence—anyway, thus eliminating any chance of being ruled not guilty by reason of insanity.

In 1843 Daniel M'Naughten was put on trial for the murder of Edward Drummond, a case that led to the adoption of the M'Naughten—or McNaughten—Rule in multiple legal systems, including those of England and the United States. The McNaughten Rule states that the insanity defense may only be used in cases where the defendant was not aware that his actions would be seen as wrong by greater society. It was not enough for a defendant to stand in front of the judge and say that he, personally, did not believe that he had done any wrong. If he had hidden a body or, for example, attempted to disguise murder as an accidental death, this was an admission that he knew others would respond negatively to his actions. The fact that Holmes hid so many of his victims to the point where they were called disappearances instead of murders, along with the way he treated Pitezel's body, indicated that, even if his lawyers had mounted a defense at his trial, they would not have been able to have him declared not guilty by reason of insanity.

Holmes further argues that it would have been pointless for his lawyers to have pursued any sort of defense because of the case Detective Geyer had built up against him, going so far as to label any potential argument as "but a waste of my counsel's energies and my own."[35] That waste, however, was not merely due to the strength of the case against him, but also the fact that so many of the men in the jury box had been so deeply prejudiced against Holmes from the start. He argues that it would have been difficult, if not impossible, to sway even the most neutral of juries, but that was not the situation in which Holmes found himself. Instead, because he was faced with twelve men who would not in fact allow themselves to be convinced of his innocence, Holmes apparently made the decision alongside his lawyers to not even attempt a defense in the first place.

He asks his readers rhetorically if they can honestly question his decision to refrain from arguing that Pitezel's death was a suicide when nine of the jurors had already admitted prejudice before being selected, but Holmes does not acknowledge that such an argument would have, in fact, been a lie and should not have been believed in the first place. The fact that the jury had already decided Holmes' guilt was not the egregious miscarriage of justice he had previously argued, since Holmes is now confessing his full guilt not only to the murder of which he was charged, but to twenty-six other cases. He does not defend his lawyers' silence by admitting that anything they would have argued would have been an improvable lie, but because anything they said would not have been believed by the jury. His trial was thus unfair not because he was convicted of one of the murders he did in fact commit, but because the jury was—apparently rightfully—prejudiced against him from the start.

Holmes ends his discussion of Pitezel by saying that, although he assisted Holmes in crimes of property, Pitezel was innocent in any crimes against people. This includes his own family, since Pitezel honestly believed Miss Williams to be alive and capable of taking Alice in for schooling. Pitezel, Holmes argues, did not lie to his wife when he spoke to her of such plans.

Even when addressing the only case for which he stood trial, Holmes does not provide much supporting information or many details. His quick description of how he killed Pitezel tallies, as he says, with the information gleaned by the coroners and thus is not in and of itself entirely new. The change is simply that Holmes has now admitted that the experts were correct in their assessment and that he, although in possession of a medical degree, managed to make a few mistakes during the murder and subsequent staging of the body that the others were quick to discover. Once again Holmes bows to the superior knowledge of the men who laid out the case against him, admitting that he had done exactly what they had theorized in order to add credibility to their statements. He does not add details that they had not already supposed, or give more of an insight into why he chose to murder his longtime companion and subordinate. It is enough once again to admit that the prosecution was correct and to apparently unburden his soul, but not to insult the other men by suggesting that they had gotten any element of their argument wrong.

"The Saddest of All"

Holmes' final three murders—the mention of which was not allowed into the Philadelphia courtroom while he was tried for that of Benjamin Pitezel—are those of Howard, Alice, and Nellie Pitezel. Previously Holmes had concocted an elaborate tale in which all three deaths were attributed to the mysterious Edward Hatch, who looked almost exactly like Holmes and who was acting on the instruction of his current wife and Holmes' former lover, Minnie Williams. Holmes did his best to clear Minnie's name earlier in his confession by retracting everything else he had written or said about her and presenting her as yet another one of his victims, many times over. The deaths of the Pitezel children are, therefore, fully his own responsibility, as the detectives had already determined they must be.

Holmes' account of Howard's murder is disjointed. He describes renting the house outside of Indianapolis—indeed, he begins his recitation by saying that the "Irvington, Indiana, tragedy is next,"[36] marking it by location instead of using Howard's name—and the difficulty he faced in both having repairs made and getting furniture to the house. Since Holmes seems to have rented it purely for the express purpose of using it for the murder and then hiding Howard's body, this information seems to be presented solely to show Holmes' readers that he was indeed in possession of the wicked temper he had previously denied. Holmes goes so far as to marvel that he did not murder the man he had engaged to make the repairs, since the man's apparent indifference angered Holmes so greatly. Here he also admits that there are many people who could, and have, attested to his violent temper, and that they—and not *Holmes' Own Story*—were in the right.

Fourteen. Those Hurt the Most

In spite of his own medical training and admitted poisonings, Holmes explains that he stopped by the same drug store twice in one day in order to purchase what he needed to kill Howard. The second trip, a considerably risky one since it was so soon after the first, was because Holmes was not sure he had obtained enough supplies in order to complete the murder. Somehow his education and previous experience had failed him during that first visit and his behavior grew even more reckless. On that same day Holmes also explains that he retrieved a number of knives he had paid to have sharpened. Howard's murder, however, was delayed two more days until the arrival of the stove Holmes had ordered with the express purpose of disposing of Howard's body. This, unlike the furniture, actually had a use in a house that Holmes would abandon as soon as he had murdered the boy.

Howard's death is quickly passed over, since Holmes reports giving him "the fatal dose of medicine"[37] and then mentions that Howard had stopped breathing. Earlier the supplies were called "drugs," a much more neutral term than "medicine" for what was, in fact, "poison." Holmes the physician, however, administered medicine to Howard before cutting his body into pieces small enough to fit into the stove. This, Holmes states, he did as though he were dealing with an inanimate object. The stove was not entirely up to the task, however, since Holmes had to bury the pieces of Howard's body that Detective Geyer eventually found. Once other evidence of the crime was taken care of, Holmes recounts that he first checked his mail and then went to retrieve Howard's sisters to move them to Chicago, although he did return to the house in Irvington where he had been spotted. Once again Holmes admits it was foolish of him to continue insisting that it was Hatch the witnesses had seen. He also admits to creating "an excavation"[38] in the Detroit house— one Holmes immediately mentioned upon his arrest—in order to distract searchers from looking for similar things in Irvington and Toronto.

What Holmes does lament, however, is how his time has been spent in "days ... of self-reproaching torture, and ... nights of sleepless fear"[39] because even he cannot now understand his actions or what drove him to kill. Holmes cannot justify murdering Howard because he cannot see how it earned him any money, and he cannot ascribe to Howard any action that would make his death justifiable. There was no reason for this murder, or many of the others, outside of Holmes' desire to listen to what his victims had to say before they died or to simply be the cause of their deaths. He did not kill Howard because the boy was becoming an annoyance to him, or causing problems when he was left alone with his sisters, or for any reason other than his own murderous desires. These are not even explicable to Holmes himself anymore since, upon writing his confession, he declares he no longer understands that urge.

The deaths of Alice and Nellie, however, are the ones that Holmes believes his readers will label "the saddest of them all"[40] because their deaths, like Howard's, were a heartless act. Holmes adds that Alice's "death was the least of the wrongs suffered at my hands,"[41] confirming a suspicion that had arisen in the courtroom about the sleeping arrangements made directly after Alice and Holmes had helped to identify Pitezel's body. Although it was not then confirmed that Holmes had violated Alice, the suspicion had been present and publicized. Once again he works not to provide new information, but to confirm what has already been published or spoken as a strong suspicion.

In spite of the fact that so much had already been said or printed about the murders of the Pitzel children, Holmes declares his intent to continue to hold nothing in reserve and proceeds to lay out a timeline of his doings in Toronto, starting with boarding the girls at a hotel. He tells his readers about renting the house under an assumed name and furnishing it before the girls moved in, and of his accidental run-in with Mrs. Pitezel while he was in a department store. At that time Alice and Nellie were in the restaurant next door, and Holmes himself was holding boys' underwear even though he had already murdered Howard—a fact that turned out to be in his favor, since it allowed Mrs. Pitezel to observe the purchase and supported Holmes' earlier claims of innocence. It was quite the scare, however, since Holmes immediately thereafter locked the girls not only in the house but in a trunk he had bought for the express purpose of killing them in it. Although Holmes himself might have crossed paths with Mrs. Pitezel again after this, he ensured that she would not accidentally run across her daughters between then and the time he connected the gas to the hole he had already prepared in the trunk.

Holmes mentions opening the trunk and describes the condition of the dead girls' faces before explaining how he borrowed a spade and then proceeded to bury them in shallow graves in the basement. He does not, however, mention removing Nellie's feet so that her body could not be identified by her clubfoot, even though Geyer had clearly discovered her in such a condition. Holmes instead focuses on how he left the girls in the cold earth without even a scrap of clothing, focusing on how awful a person he must be while withholding details that were already proven. Once again Holmes' promise to tell all falls short.

Instead he revels in the retelling, calling upon his readers to "consider what an awful act this was!"[42] Having decided from the day he met their father that he must kill him, and having discovered that Pitezel had such a wonderful family who might also be murdered for his own pleasure, Holmes reminds his readers that, for many long years, he had acted as a second father to the children he had just heartlessly murdered and buried. Holmes in fact invites his readers to curse him—but him alone, since he acted of his own accord and even the children's parents had been unaware of what he was up to. This last is perhaps best illustrated by the short recitation of Holmes' attempted murder of Mrs. Pitezel and her two remaining children, in which he rented a house for them and put a "bottle of dynamite"[43] in the basement, along with a note asking Mrs. Pitezel to carry it up to the attic. Holmes had hoped she would obey and thus drop the bottle, killing all of them—a strange method of death when his previous instances indicate his preference to be the one personally committing the murder or at least present in order to witness the death. Carrie did testify to the presence of the bottle and the request, however, so it seems Holmes did in fact attempt to murder the entire Pitezel family before his incarceration.

Holmes brings his confession to a swift conclusion in which he acknowledges that any member of his audience who has managed to read all the way to the end could hardly expect him to honestly express remorse for his actions—and so he does not. He places himself as having been in solitary confinement for eighteen months and having only a few days left to live before his execution, presumably a position from which a man would little serve himself by lying. This confession is meant to be his final communication with the world, and Holmes ends it with the observation that, by openly saying he has no remorse, he cannot be criticized for the lack. Holmes' confession ends with his signature as H.H. Holmes with no acknowledgment of his medical degree or his birth name.

It is the final written communication Holmes will share, but it is not the last time he will address an audience. On May 7, 1896, when Holmes was led to the gallows, a number of witnesses had gathered to watch the execution. This, then, was Holmes' last chance to present himself, and he once again drastically changed his story. As these were his last words there would be no follow-up, no chance for an interview to clarify his statement, and no means of reconciling his final statement with all Holmes had written before.

Conclusion:
A Man of Mystery

On Thursday, May 7, 1896, Holmes left his prison cell for the final time. His walk to the scaffold was apparently a calm one, and he was accompanied by priests who prayed out loud. Before his death, Holmes spoke one final confession, apparently only because not speaking would make him "appear to acquiesce to my execution."[1] Now, mere weeks since his confession to twenty-seven murders and six more attempted besides, Holmes informed the spectators that he was in fact guilty of only two deaths, each of them women who had died as the result of his performing a criminal operation upon them. Then, in case he was unclear, Holmes firmly declared, "I am not guilty of taking the lives of any of the Pitezel family,"[2] in spite of both his conviction and his previous confession. By all accounts it seems that Holmes was calmer speaking there, waiting for the time to be hanged, than he had been while acting as his own attorney in court.

He attempted to leave the listening audience, as well as those who read about his execution later in the papers, with a feeling of guilt over the fact that they had not only allowed an innocent man to go to his execution but were continuing to let the murderer of children go free. Since the publication of his confession a number of his named victims had come forward to reveal that they were in fact still alive, calling all twenty-seven instances into question, and Holmes apparently decided to capitalize on this. Even though some of the murders were outright lies, the Pitezel deaths were the least likely to have been accepted as Holmes' embroidering of the truth in order to make his tale all the more fascinating. Still, his final word on the matter reverted to his argument in *Holmes' Own Story*, reducing him to a wrongly convicted innocent man and therefore far less than the most skilled criminal of the age.

After his execution, by previous arrangement made with his lawyers, Holmes' body was placed in a specially made oversized casket that was half-filled with concrete. Once his body was positioned, the casket was filled the rest of the way. This was due to Holmes' fears that he might be dug up by resurrection men, either for the purpose of becoming a medical specimen or to be examined by physicians who wished to determine once and for all how Holmes differed from his fellow men. He had rejected all monetary offers prior to his death in exchange for the study of his body or head, and this final burial in a double plot meant that, until the filming of the 2017 History Channel series *American Ripper*, he remained undisturbed. As part of the series Holmes was not only exhumed but identified in order to prove that he had not in fact escaped the gallows, in spite of the rumors to the contrary.

The Perils of Being First

In the twenty-first century, the label "serial killer" carries with it an entire narrative structure that orients an audience's expectations. Figures such as Ted Bundy, John Wayne Gacy, Jeffrey Dahmer, and others from the "Golden Age" of serial killing have added their own twist to the general biography, but, especially since the FBI took on the role of leadership and expertise with the practice of profiling, a serial killer is more or less a set figure in the American psyche for both professional and popular representation.

Starting with the interviews performed by Special Agents John Douglas and Robert Ressler, and then refined by continued study through the Behavioral Science Unit, the figure of the serial killer has been largely established as being male, white, and generally younger than middle-aged. His childhood likely includes incidences of torturing animals, starting fires, and bedwetting past the usual age—again, all of this based upon the interviews performed with those who had committed violent crimes and had been incarcerated for them. The serial killer's father is likely absent and his mother strict and abusive. Any romantic relationships he may have cultivated would have been unhealthy and awkward, generally with his ex-girlfriends admitting to deviant sexual practices or other questionable behavior, if they were willing to discuss their involvement with him at all.

Ted Bundy is the standout of the Golden Age serial killers in that he apparently presented as charming and intelligent, having graduated college and been accepted to law school while many others did not attain higher education or project confidence. The fact that early fictional serial killer Hannibal Lecter was also presented as charming and intelligent, with a certain upper-class sensibility to his homicidal and cannibalistic tendencies, has also swayed public and popular perception of the figure of the serial killer. In order to be considered interesting and therefore worthy of a book or other publication, a serial killer should align with the basic broad sweeps of this expected narrative of his life, while at the same time contributing something unique to catch and then maintain an audience's attention. Indeed, in the twenty-first century it seems that the search is not for another serial killer, but rather for one whose story is in fact interesting enough to make it to print.

Between the naming of the phenomenon as "serial killing," the media representation of factual serial killers, the FBI's representation of itself as an expert on the subject both internally and in congressional hearings, and the plethora of fictional serial killers who at times become confused with their real-life counterparts to the point where some researchers find it "irrelevant to distinguish between"[3] them, popular culture in the twenty-first century is saturated with stories about such people, men and women both. "Serial killer" is not a designation limited to law enforcement records and courtrooms, but a commonly used and popularly recognized term.

Although still separated from and elevated above criminals convicted of enacting a single crime, with their appearances slated for sweeps week in many crime procedural shows, the serial killer is no longer a figure of utter mystery. The genre of true crime even struggles with books about serial killers since they can indeed be so formulaic. One of the authors who has attempted to break this mold and expand the true crime serial killer narrative is, in fact, Erik Larson, whose crime stories run parallel to historical events, therefore broadening the focus of books such as *Devil in the White City* or *Thunderstruck*, which alternates between the story of Hawley Harvey Crippen's murder of his wife and Guglielmo Marconi's inventions that allowed for wireless communication across the Atlantic. For twenty-first-century readers, the extra historical hook is a necessity, since the serial killer seems to already be a known entity.

In the 1890s, however, this knowledge had neither been acquired nor disseminated. No one was a serial killer because the term had yet to be coined, and thus the story behind the label did not exist. When H.H. Holmes was arrested for the murder of Benjamin Pitezel and subsequently suspected of murdering his three children, along with the Williams sisters and many more unknown victims besides, he could not be easily categorized and therefore explained. The commonly retold background of the serial killer includes so much information about his childhood because it, in part, clarifies how a man could have committed such repeated atrocities against strangers.

A single murder, committed in hot blood, is generally explicable. A man who kills his wife and her lover upon finding them in bed together may not have been in the legal right, but his actions had a clear and immediate cause. In this example, his homicidal rage is directed at those who had wronged him in an immediate reaction to that offense. No such easily traceable motive was immediately ascribable to Pitezel's death at Holmes' hands, and the deaths of Alice, Nellie, and Howard Pitezel were even more troubling. A solid narrative would be absolutely necessary to convince the public of Holmes' innocence, and it would also be desirable should Holmes turn out to be guilty. When he was arrested in Boston in November 1894, Holmes needed that solid narrative in order to secure his freedom.

Adaptation and Expertise

Immediately after his arrest, Holmes encountered the first fight for control of his own story. He was able to give a spoken confession, later termed his first confession, but his name and speculation of his guilt were already being published in the papers and disseminated to a much wider audience than the one his own words could reach. Newspapers could run a new story about him with every edition, but Holmes was barred from communicating indiscriminately with the outside world. Although he was allowed to send multiple letters his first week as a prisoner, the bulk of Holmes' communication was limited to managing his business deals. Thereafter he was restricted in all of his communication, professional as well as personal. He was allowed to receive the newspapers and read what others were saying about him, but, being in prison, Holmes had lost control of his own narrative.

His ability to follow the popular version of his story, however, worked in his favor since, before 1894 was over, Holmes had already made his second verbal confession. Based on the information he had read in the newspaper, Holmes realized that there was a strong possibility that Pitezel's body would be dug up for a second time to prove his identity. Holmes' first confession indicated that Pitezel was alive and well, abroad with his children, and the news that his first version of events was being challenged was worrisome. If the body initially buried as B.F. Perry and subsequently identified as Benjamin Pitezel—falsely, according to Holmes' first confession—was indeed Pitezel, then Holmes' statement fell apart. This was when he revised his story to say that Pitezel was indeed dead, and thus Holmes had not substituted another body for his friend's. Any charge of insurance fraud, then, would have to be dropped were the body again identified as Pitezel.

Holmes' first two confessions came in quick succession, and each was spoken and relatively short. In the first especially he responded to questions that were put to him, therefore able to react immediately to his audience's confusion and reassure them of Pitezel's safety and Holmes' own concern for Carrie and her children. His second confession was given more than once, with the second time being in the presence of a stenographer, and was thus more of a monologue, presumably incorporating any questions he may have been asked the first time through. Considering his past as a conman and a swindler, it should be of no surprise that Holmes was able to adapt so readily to his audience's reactions, be they in the same room with him or those who had written and disseminated information pertinent to his case. He was clearly able to respond to others in order to sell his most valuable asset: himself.

Very little of Holmes' past had been recorded in writing and thus little was verifiable, but this also meant that Holmes had plenty of leeway when it came to constructing his own biography. He was also not constrained to the title of "serial killer" or its expectations, allowing him to shape his past in the way that he saw fit. On the one hand this meant he was working without an established framework, being "America's first serial killer" and uniquely the most dangerous criminal of the age, and thus he had to create this explicable—and innocent—version of himself from scratch. On the other hand, however, Holmes had almost complete freedom to construct himself from birth to the present-day, and he continued to receive as much reading material as he requested. Holmes could therefore follow how the headlines and articles changed and adapted his story and, since newspapers were written with the express purpose of selling copies to eager readers, he could track what audiences were responding to.

The newspapers also helped Holmes keep up with the ongoing investigation into the whereabouts of Alice, Nellie, and Howard Pitezel. Although his first confession put them abroad with their father, his second admitted that Benjamin Pitezel was dead and placed the Pitezel children in the care of Miss Minnie Williams, who was meant to see to their education. They were still meant to be out of the country and difficult to contact, so Holmes himself was not concerned with the fact that he had not heard from them. He assumed that all parties were fine, but that they did not want to advertise their current location. Throughout the first half of 1895 various detectives had attempted to follow the path along which Holmes had dragged his various hostages during the fall of 1894, but it was only when Detective Frank Geyer decided to do the same that Holmes' second confession was threatened.

Just as Geyer had utilized the newspapers to prepare various real estate agents for his visit and his inquiry into whether or not they had rented a house the previous fall to someone who looked like Holmes, Holmes made use of the headlines to protect himself. When he heard a commotion outside of the prison, he called for the morning paper and was thus aware that the girls' bodies had been found in Toronto before anyone arrived to question him about it. Again, as in the case where the newspapers told him that Pitezel's body would likely soon be disinterred for another identification, Holmes was aware of the situation with enough time to prepare himself for confrontation. When it came to Pitezel's body, he was able to initiate the change in his narrative by asking to give a second confession, and when it came to the discovery of Nellie's and Alice's bodies, he had some time to review the known facts and to piece a new story together between them.

These are two obvious instances in which Holmes' consumption of the daily paper assisted him in his presentation of himself and his argument of his own innocence, but they are not the only examples that show Holmes used his knowledge of how others were presenting his story to his advantage. While sitting in prison in Philadelphia, Holmes would have been able to track the most repeated and therefore intriguing elements of his supposed biography and crimes and thus incorporate them into his own version if they had proven to be interesting. Much of what was being printed about him was, of course, negative, and Holmes clearly wanted to present himself in a positive light in *Holmes' Own Story*, but a book about a completely innocent, wrongly accused man could hardly compete with those articles. Instead of throwing out the titillating elements completely, Holmes assigned those he could not part with to others instead.

Contrasts in Character

In his first widely published work, disseminated before his trial in the fall of 1895 and meant to convince a wider audience of his innocence, Holmes struggles with presenting himself as the blameless, wrongly accused hero of his tale. Blameless, wrongly accused heroes do not often find themselves in headlines because the media generally prefers to focus on sex and violence, and those newspaper articles were his competition. In order to make sure that *Holmes' Own Story* sold and was discussed just as much—if not more—than the newspapers, he had to include those tabloid-style elements in some way.

The components of the newspaper articles that were apparently too good to pass up were thus assigned to secondary players in *Holmes' Own Story*. Holmes himself was being painted by reporters as a womanizing bigamist with a dark past that included murder and abortion. He may have been educated and well enough off, but he was a callous man who used others and was skilled at cons and scams. On top of this, a man who committed so many apparently senseless murders had to have been mentally deviant, as well. A biography that did not include plot elements just as tantalizing would not have sold.

Minnie Williams comes off the worse for this adaptation. In *Holmes' Own Story* she is given a number of these negative traits. It seems that she cannot go anywhere without attracting the attention of attached men, and an affair with one of them results in her need to seek an abortion for her own mental health. As a fallen woman, Minnie apparently reveled in relationships and convinced Holmes to live as her husband, until her sanity was once again threatened and she suffered a mental breakdown. Minnie accused Holmes of having cheated on her with Nannie, and she is bundled out of the narrative and into an institution after she murdered her sister.

Instead of being the bigamist who took mistress after mistress and defiled them, Holmes has transformed himself into an unmarried young man who might, in fact, be more naïve than Miss Williams. He did nothing but comply with her wishes as a weaker-willed man confronted with a sexually-charged woman, and who could blame him? Minnie's *Holmes' Own Story* past turns her into the sort of person Holmes himself had been presented to be, and positions him as the victim of their relationship. Holmes had to extricate himself from any emotional and romantic entanglements with Minnie not only because she had proven to be a murderess, but because she was emotionally unstable, and Holmes then had to ensure that Minnie would not cross paths with Georgiana once the latter became his wife. Minnie Williams became a reminder of Holmes' unsavory past that he had forcefully left behind, but which clung to him all the same. Minnie was presented as not only the sexually predatory, unstable former lover, but the mastermind behind the deaths of the Pitezel children, meaning that Holmes was not the only victim laid at her feet. Indeed, Holmes took the major accusations that had been leveled at his character and assigned them to Minnie in his autobiography, which allowed him to make himself look all the better when placed in comparison.

Benjamin Pitezel, too, acquired a number of negative traits in *Holmes' Own Story* that were not necessarily borne out elsewhere by others who had known him. As part of his argument that Pitezel had indeed been suicidal, Holmes made Pitezel out to be a drunk who was unable to retain employment or properly manage his finances. Pitezel therefore became an irresponsible husband and father, often away from his family and unable to send them any money to support them since he so often spent it on drink. Further, while in Texas, Pitezel somehow managed to find himself in a bigamous marriage after a long night of drinking—a failure that, as Holmes presents it, led to an initial suicide attempt. Pitezel is therefore not only incapable of providing for his family, since he is too much of a dreamer to hold down a job, but also incapable of pulling off a proper scam, so has failed them completely.

Holmes, of course, had been shown through the newspapers and the story rehashed and printed by Robert Corbitt to have had not two, but in fact three wives, all with different last names depending on the pseudonym under which he had wooed them. He also had two children, one by each of his first two wives, who presumably did not see him often, if ever. His first wife, known as Mrs. Mudgett, was living back in Maryland with their son, and Holmes had bought his second wife and their daughter a house near Chicago in order to keep them out of the way of his business and romantic dealings. The only wife to which he admits in *Holmes' Own Story*, Georgiana Yoke, thought herself to be Mrs. Howard, did not know of his other wives, and was unaware of his children.

The fathering of multiple children by multiple women does not make an appearance in *Holmes' Own Story*, but Benjamin Pitezel takes up the mantle of being a negligent father and terrible husband. Alice, Nellie, and Howard are thus to be pitied not only because of their deaths, but because of the character of the man who had fathered them, and the conditions in which they were raised. Carrie Pitezel may not be in such a heartbreaking position, however—although she has lost her husband and her children, women were often blamed for the actions of their husbands, and readers who accepted Holmes' version of events might accuse Carrie of causing her husband's alcoholism and depression the way she was condemned for not having stopped his insurance scam. As much as Holmes claimed he was working for Carrie's freedom and peace of mind, by changing Pitezel to be more like the newspaper articles being printed about himself, Holmes may have turned public opinion more staunchly against her.

Since the character of Edward Hatch was merely a figment of Holmes' imagination, Hatch's story is not changed for *Holmes' Own Story* but rather invented out of whole cloth. He must, out of necessity, remind others of Holmes strongly enough that purported misidentification could happen but, at the same time, must stand apart from Holmes. Hatch was the sort of man who appeared to be a gentleman but could in fact murder three children in cold blood, all because of his infatuation with Miss Williams, who had ordered him to do so. Hatch, then, must align with the sort of person the newspapers imagined Holmes himself to be, since that type of man had been publicly accepted as capable of such homicidal acts. While it is unclear whether Hatch's past has included marriage, mistresses, or children, he is still the sort of man who would present himself as being married to Minnie Williams, and thus the sort of man who would staunchly stand by a loose woman.

Holmes himself had taken up with Minnie in the past, but he ended their relationship when murder became a factor. Hatch, on the other hand, is convinced to enact the murders himself, as part of Minnie's plan to get back at Holmes for being unwilling to continue as her lover once she had murdered her sister. It is a strong distinction that Holmes does not in fact stress. During the bulk of *Holmes Own Story* he presents Hatch as a stalwart companion who is willing to do his part to help the children, even worrying about Hatch's overall mood lest the other man sink into a depression that mimicked Pitezel's. Holmes simply cannot comprehend Hatch as a murderer, especially since he did not seem to have had the opportunity to commit the crimes even if it had been part of his character. It is only during the Prison Diary Appendix that Holmes lays out how Hatch must have committed the crimes.

This was a narrative move that Holmes may not have entirely thought through. After all of the comparisons between himself and Hatch, who was clearly capable of presenting as a gentleman of class and intelligence to the point where he could fool even close companion Holmes for months, he fails to clearly distinguish between Hatch, who was faking it, and himself, a true gentleman. Any argument Holmes presents as to how Hatch could have managed the deception could easily apply to him as well, especially since Holmes, earlier in *Holmes' Own Story*, has documented numerous cases in which he committed cons and scams. The difference seems to be that Holmes' schemes—which are generally amusing vignettes in which Holmes, as the underdog, must outmaneuver the detective hot on his heels—do not involve murder. He may deal in death through his work as a doctor and used his medical connections in order to procure "material" for these schemes, but Holmes himself would not take a life.

The adventure and excitement Holmes ascribes to himself in *Holmes' Own Story*, then, is innocent fun. Even in his successful insurance scam, it is only a faceless corporation that must suffer in paying out the $20,000 policy. Holmes' adventures show off his intelligence, wit, and skill while at the same time remaining lighthearted and engaging, presenting him as a rascal but certainly not a criminal. Hatch, for all his public image as a gentleman, is far worse. Hatch is the man the newspapers want Holmes to be.

Making His Own Myth

The narrative elements of *Holmes' Own Story*, then, could not ignore the newspaper variations completely. The story of Pitezel's death and the odd multi-city travels in the fall of 1894 had caught audiences' attention, and readers continually paid for any new information that might be forthcoming. Much of the legend that has since grown around Henry Howard Holmes began in those initial newspaper articles, especially when his "Murder Castle" was being excavated. Gruesome finds were documented on the front page and then, days later, retracted in much smaller, more hidden articles so that the rumors remained in public memory. Even before his trial, Holmes was far more interesting as a legend than as a factual human being.

Through his two verbal confessions—not to mention his previous cons and multiple marriages and extramarital relationships—Holmes had proven himself willing to change his backstory or mold his presentation of the events in order to suit him best. A large part of this ability might be attributable to personal charm, but Holmes was no amateur as a rhetorician, either. He was able to work within the constraints of a given situation in order to attain his goals, most of which involved a lack of persecution for his questionable, if not outright illegal, dealings. By the time Holmes was arrested in Boston, he had already slipped out of myriad situations that should have ended with him in jail but, either because he had convinced his opponent otherwise or because Holmes had simply filibustered and confused the other party until charges had been dropped, he had remained a free man. This willingness to change his story depending on the audience and situation, as well as the talent for incorporating fixed points of reference, is also apparent in Holmes' various confessions.

One of these changes has been referenced in the above discussion of how Holmes took the traits most often publicly ascribed to himself and transferred them to others within his biography, retaining the intrigue while at the same time removing his own culpability. This strategy not only allows him to present the same intrigue and sensation as the newspapers, but also lets Holmes raise himself up as he pushes the others down. In comparison with Minnie Williams, Benjamin Pitezel, and Edward Hatch, Holmes cannot help but appear to be a fine, upstanding gentleman—in spite of his admitted previous scams and cons.

In this quest to present himself as incapable of murder, Holmes is willing to change what he must about his own past. He is, presumably, the person in the best position to share information about H.H. Holmes, having lived through his own experiences, and thus can center himself as expert of his own life. If there are others who contend that any stories he tells are false, Holmes might dismiss that person and once again claim his expertise. Even when someone from his past, such as one of his wives, wished to speak up, Holmes took control of his own narrative by simply ignoring her existence in his autobiography. As the presented sole author of this written document, Holmes does not need to contend with interruptions or questions from an audience when he, personally, wishes to ignore the existence of such people or claims completely.

In making Minnie Williams, Benjamin Pitezel, and Edward Hatch major players in the convoluted plot of the fall of 1894, however, Holmes positions himself as expert on their lives, too. Whether dead, in hiding, or imaginary, none of them are present for comment, and none can be asked to share their own version of events. In the case of Edward Hatch this presents little issue, since no one can be found who can support the argument for the man's existence, much less come to his defense. Indeed, Holmes eventually admits that he created Hatch entirely from his own imagination, confessing to the Pitezel murders alongside twenty-three others, although he does not take the time to bluntly state how all of the negative attributes he ascribed to Hatch must now be applied to himself. No matter how terrible Holmes made Hatch out to be, there was at least no real-life reference with which he had to contend—or rather, none outside himself.

Minnie Williams and Benjamin Pitezel, on the other hand, had friends and family not only worried about their extended absences, but vocal about their character. Minnie's loved ones rallied mightily against

Holmes' depiction of her as seductress, arguing instead that she was in fact childlike and incredibly naïve. Holmes needed Minnie to be worldwise and generally capable, aside from her intermittent mental instability, so that he could position himself as having been taken in by her and then turn her into the mastermind behind the child murders. It was known and provable that Minnie had access to money and land, and, since Holmes freely admitted to being a bit of a con man and swindler, presenting Minnie as a naïve, rich young woman in *Holmes' Own Story* would have shifted the balance of power between the two of them and made it all too believable that he could indeed have taken advantage of her, if not also taken her life.

In order to combat the argument of Minnie's having been an innocent victim, Holmes crafted a backstory for her that she would credibly not have revealed to her relatives out of shame. Holmes' Minnie fairly slinks away from an engagement in order to abort her married lover's baby, and neither the fiancé nor the lover may have been fully aware of that situation. Further, since Minnie moved to a new city in order to reinvent herself under a new name—another facet of Holmes' own background that he displaced onto another—she could indeed conceivably have hidden her state as a fallen woman from her family. Additionally, her murder of her sister was meant to have taken place with a single blow in hot blood, so violence was not presented as a constant component of her character and yet no one else would necessarily be able to confirm it.

Minnie was meant to have revealed all of this to Holmes in a confessional monologue that he remembered so well as to present seemingly word for word, situating him differently than any of her other friends or her own family. While her loved ones outside of Chicago were unaware of Minnie's dark past, Holmes had been her confidant and then her conspirator in hiding Nannie's murder. Presumably it is only the fact that he knows Minnie to have orchestrated the children's deaths that leads Holmes to reveal her every secret in his autobiography, since he otherwise apparently kept this knowledge to himself. Even in the case of another person, with Minnie's own fixed points and other voices clamoring for control of her biography, Holmes dismisses the protestations of outrage and simply presents his own version of Minnie—at least until his newspaper confession, in which he concedes that Minnie

Williams was in fact largely as naïve and childlike as previously advertised.

Benjamin Pitezel's backstory is perhaps easier to manipulate since Holmes also had the tools to control Carrie Pitezel, as well. She had, after all, been arrested in Boston when he was, and prior to that she had shown herself willing enough—or perhaps bewildered enough—to follow Holmes from city to city, always with the hope that she would see her husband and her absent children, utterly pliable to Holmes' suggestions. It comes as little surprise, then, that he attempted to murder her and her remaining children via a simple note asking her to take a jar from the basement to the attic of a house, hoping that she would drop the unstable nitroglycerin along the way: Carrie had complied with all of his strange orders up until that point, and Holmes was either oblivious to her growing frustration and suspicion, or saw it and did not care.

Pitezel was also not a genteel young woman who had a small fortune attached to her name. He was merely a day laborer, and one who had a record of being unable to hold a job. Not all of Holmes' negative claims about Pitezel were as unsubstantiated as those he made about Minnie, and Pitezel's checkered employment history could speak for itself. Added to this was the fact that Pitezel had indeed been away from his family for long periods of time, and that Carrie would have been told that he was off on business for Holmes, so Holmes might indeed have a better grasp of Pitezel's character and mental state than his family did.

By giving Pitezel the vice of alcoholism, Holmes ascribed his "friend" with an addiction seen at the time as a mark of weak character. This dependence on drink fed both Pitezel's money problems and his relationship woes, leading to his depression and his suicide. Once again the negative traits of one of his compatriots placed Holmes in a predicament: just as Minnie's pleas pushed him to dispose of Nannie's body and not report it to the authorities, Pitezel's suicide note guilted him into staging it as an accidental death and then lying to Carrie about her husband's whereabouts. Holmes would never have engaged in such illegal activity on his own, and only does so when he feels cornered and unable to act in another way.

What Holmes does not question, however, is his own continued association with people who keep putting him in such situations. The poor character of Miss Williams, Pitezel, and Hatch apparently does not rub off on Holmes at all, nor even threaten his genteel status. Nannie's death, and then those of the children, prey upon his conscience, but Holmes does not pause to contemplate his own active culpability in those murders even as he presents the events in *Holmes' Own Story*. His role is minimal, and his hands are clean.

A Singular Fiend

In constructing his narrative for his autobiography, then, Holmes carefully selected what to include and what to ignore in order to craft a book that would be appealing enough to audiences to sell, while at the same time supporting his argument for his own innocence. This bid to make the story of an innocent man interesting also includes tales of previous insurance scam attempts, both failed and successful, in which Holmes tries to demonstrate his main argument for his innocence: if a man as intelligent and cunning as himself had begun such a scam at least twice before, and only succeeded on the second try through much difficulty, then why in the world would he agree to go along with Pitezel when the other man suggested just such a thing? Holmes recounts his adventures with his "dead friend" and the pursuing "Secret Service Agent" with glee and delight, but even this vignette that focuses solely on himself shows many of the same narrative missteps he displayed in his portrayals of his compatriots.

Up until *Holmes' Own Story* and his prison diary, Holmes seems to have largely dealt with others in adversarial situations using verbal communication instead of written. Written communication leaves a trail, which a confessed con man would likely do his best to avoid if at all possible. Clearly intelligent enough to have earned his medical degree, Holmes was also capable of cunning during verbal sparring in order to extract himself from legal entanglements. The ability to read people and either change their minds or wear them down enough to drop any charges, however, does not necessarily translate into the ability to present a long, complicated case purely in writing without the benefit of immediate audience feedback.

Because he was presenting himself as a new kind of criminal, one whose unique traits required the best and brightest detectives to best him, Holmes was not working off of a given narrative structure. He did not have to worry about whether his story would be "just another true crime" book, but he also did not have guideposts as far as what information should be stressed repeatedly or stated outright. Unlike Ted Bundy, Holmes was clearly not a lawyer, and the structure and format of *Holmes' Own Story* reveals inconsistencies, gaps, and vague allusions when a clear and logical statement would have served him better in his argument for innocence.

Along with simply ignoring people and events that did not fit his representation of himself and a reshuffling of personal traits among himself and his closest companions, Holmes struggled with maintaining a coherent narrative throughline. He especially wrestled with timelines, since although *Holmes' Own Story* starts with his childhood, the various recounted scenes jump around throughout the book. Although Holmes' Michigan insurance scam comes immediately after Nannie's death within the text, he presents it as having occurred many years previously—and yet, even though Holmes had not yet met Georgiana Yoke at the time Nannie had died, the insurance papers had been signed in favor of his wife. During his initial attempt at an insurance scam Holmes recounted that he kept portions of "the material" in barrels for over a year, in the basement of a building in Chicago, without clarifying how he had managed to store them so easily in spite of the fact that, during his second scam, a purpose-built trunk failed to contain the odor of a relatively fresh body. Each incident is presented as its own story, almost independent of the events around it, with the express purpose of showing how difficult such a scam would be and proving why Holmes would not have attempted it yet again with Pitezel.

Readers who are caught up in the adventure elements of the story or the thrill of the chase between Holmes and his "Secret Service Agent" might well overlook these slips and not question who, exactly, was meant to have received $20,000 or why they should be so concerned about Georgiana Yoke if she had indeed inherited such an amount at some point previously. Similar embellishments arise during pieces of Holmes' confession in the *Inquirer*, marking further instances in which Holmes could have benefited from the presence of a live audience able to ask questions and have him clarify why, for example, his murder of Minnie Williams involved so many curious locations, or who his unnamed assistants were. Holmes simply gets so caught up in his conception of himself at the center of the story, either as wronged innocent or as arch fiend, and trips himself up in some details while forgetting to mention others completely.

There are also many instances that have since been incorporated into the Holmes mythology that Holmes himself did not state outright, although he likely should have in order to strengthen his argument. In *Holmes' Own Story* it is actually questionable whether or not Hatch was meant to have resembled him closely. Holmes observes that Hatch did indeed shave during their travels with the Pitezel children, presumably so that their similarity would be even more convincing, but he does not describe Hatch's appearance and at times even seems to backtrack and admit that Hatch did not look very much like him at all. Part of this might be a struggle with the belief of the day that a man's dark and twisted soul would be revealed in deviant physical features, while Holmes himself was meant to be an attractive man, and he could not therefore make Hatch both attractive and a child murderer. A large segment of the overarching problem, though, seems to be that Holmes had never anticipated being captured, and thus did not have his story prepared from the start.

Upon his arrest and his first round of questioning concerning Pitezel's death, Holmes presented his interviewers with the story that, presumably, Carrie Pitezel would also have been sharing: that her husband had spoken of committing an insurance scam and had decided that he should stay in hiding and keep his continued existence a secret from their children lest the fraud be discovered. Some of the known facts helped support Holmes in this argument, especially since he himself had been called upon to identify Pitezel's disinterred body. Were Holmes in on the scam, he certainly could have lied at the cemetery, and it was already suspicious how he had offered to make himself available for it. He might also have managed to coerce Alice into agreeing with this identification, considering the length of time that the body had been buried and Alice's youth. Since the fate of Alice, Nellie, and Howard was not to be called into question for some time yet—and since the focus was solely on whether or not insurance fraud had been committed—Holmes apparently decided that sticking with his original story was his best bet.

However, the chance that Pitezel's body might be disinterred for a second identification, even so many months after his death, was enough to prompt Holmes to change his story and apparently come clean. Perhaps Holmes believed that this new variation, in which Pitezel committed suicide and the only possible fraud would lie in his staging of the body, would secure his own release from prison. No murder had occurred, no corpse had been stolen, and perhaps the insurance policy Pitezel had insisted on holding did not, in fact, include a suicide clause. Once again timelines become Holmes' enemy, although now in real life instead of in his fictional construction of the past.

In his prison diary Holmes reports that he first attempted communication with Miss Williams around this time, at the end of 1894, although there is no documentation that he actually made any such moves until months later in the late spring of 1895. In December, at the time of Holmes' second confession, there is no mention of the cipher he and Miss Williams had agreed upon, and no attempt to place an ad in a London paper in order to catch her eye and reassure Carrie Pitezel and the larger public that the children were safe. It would seem that Holmes had not yet fleshed out his narrative enough in order to include such details even though a man who was so concerned about the children would have wanted them contacted straightaway. Although he had enough of a tale concocted to keep Carrie following along, it was not nearly as convincing to the men who first interviewed him after his arrest.

The fact that he was not immediately released, then, would have been an enormous failure for a man who had been able to talk his way out of so many previous situations. Although the narrative he had constructed for Carrie had been more or less accepted by a woman who seemed to have no other choice, it did not convince the detectives. Holmes was lucky in that he was able to read the newspapers during his imprisonment and adapt that tale in order to argue for his own innocence, although even then, in *Holmes' Own Story*, the situation of his wrongful imprisonment is not resolved. Holmes constructs the tale that Hatch murdered the children, under orders from Minnie Williams, which means that both the murderer and the mastermind behind those murders are still walking free.

Man or Monster

In both *Holmes' Own Story* and his confession in the *Inquirer*, Holmes struggles with the question of motive. The newspapers had already painted him as having murdered Pitezel in order to take most of his $10,000 insurance policy, although the explanation for the subsequent murders of the three middle Pitezel siblings are less clear-cut. It would seem that only a monster would murder children, and the whole zigzagging journey among various Midwest cities and even into Canada is difficult to explain without including questions of mental deviance. A man who could murder Pitezel and then keep his widow in suspense as he took her offspring from her would quite simply be a monster and, according to *Holmes' Own Story*, that monster was still on the loose, as well as the woman who had controlled the monster.

Holmes' Own Story is therefore not a reassuring tale. Instead of the guilty party being captured, Holmes argues that he, an innocent man, has been imprisoned instead—and, moreover, had also been fooled by Hatch to the point where it took him months of reflection to conclude how Hatch had managed the murders, and why. Although Holmes indeed tries to downplay his resemblance to Hatch in spite of his argument that many who saw Hatch thought he was Holmes, Holmes himself should have been close enough to recognize the deviance in Hatch.

Once he had created Hatch, however, Holmes was left with the difficulty of explaining why this stranger would at all be interested in murdering the Pitezel children. Although audiences in the twenty-first century have become accustomed to serial killers as selecting strangers as their victims in order to fulfill their own personal desires, nineteenth-century readers had no such points of reference. Part of the role of the crime narrative is to reassure the public that justice has been done and that they, themselves, are not in danger of becoming the next victim. Many true crime books since the boom of the late twentieth century are only written once someone has been convicted of committing the crime, thereby assuring their audience of their own safety since the criminal has been apprehended, and include descriptions of the crimes that allow readers to comfort themselves that they would be able to recognize such a fiend and would be able to prevent a similar travesty from befalling their own families.

In the case of *Holmes' Own Story*, mothers might have been able to console themselves that they, at least, would not let their husband's best friend take their children, or that they would have prevented their husbands from concocting such an insurance scam in the first place. Hatch, however, is still free and very much a threat to whomever else Minnie Williams deemed worthy of her wrath. According to this version, the Pitezel children died because of a woman scorned, and Minnie was able to take her revenge slowly and at her leisure. She was also capable of convincing her purported husband to enact that revenge for her, and successfully, since Holmes must write his biography from prison. The police have not believed Holmes' explanation and thus have chosen not to look for Hatch, thereby increasing the danger to the general public.

By the time of Holmes' confession in the *Inquirer*, however, he has changed his story yet again in order to admit to the murders of four members of the Pitezel family, the Williams sisters, and twenty-one other people besides. Law enforcement may now be praised for having captured the right man and not having listened to his false stories, and Holmes even describes his face as having changed and devolved so that he now looks like the deviant he always was inside. After having resisted the accusations for over a year, changing his defense in order to avoid embarrassing situations in which his story would be proven to be untrue and also to compete with the wider market of newspapers and their own versions, Holmes owns up not only to the murders of which he had been accused, but a few more besides. He now takes on the mantle of the arch fiend, the most dangerous criminal of the age, and all the energy he had previously put into his indignant defense is newly directed toward sharing murderous details. Since he is both irredeemable and rightfully sentenced to hang, it would seem that Holmes has no reason to hold himself back—especially since this was one more chance for him to reach a wider audience and place himself at the center of the story.

In spite of the fact that Holmes now praises law enforcement for having captured the right man, he still does not leave his readers with overwhelming reassurance and feelings of safety. Here Holmes introduces the idea of various accomplices, some he forced to comply with his homicidal wishes, some who readily agreed, and at least one who eagerly descended into a life of crime once Holmes had given him that first taste. Although Minnie Williams is dead—and was never a criminal mastermind—and Hatch does not exist, Holmes introduces these other threats. He is not, in fact, the only man who thinks the way he does, or the only man who would turn to murder in order to solve his problems. He is rather one of many, and although he has encountered so many others in his life, he does not name any of them. The arch fiend chooses to stand alone even as he indicates that he may not actually be the "greatest criminal of the age"-there are already others who are poised to take up the mantle.

In the *Inquirer* confession, at least, Holmes does not highlight his medical degree. Previously in *Holmes' Own Story* he emphasized the fact that he was a doctor, especially since this meant he had access to corpses for his planned insurance scams. In his printed confession, however, he does not remind his readers that he was in fact a physician, trusted to fill prescriptions and diagnose illness when he in fact used much of what he learned in order to commit murder and dispose of the resulting bodies. Holmes does not, therefore, work to instill within his readers a mistrust of all medical professionals, even as he casually refuses to identify people who apparently have the same morality as he does. He works against both his claim to be the greatest criminal of the age and his stated intent to reveal all in this confession, leaving out many details or bowing to past newspapers articles that he had previously claimed to be false.

In a sense it seems as though the *Inquirer* confession is, in fact, Holmes giving up and presenting himself as the monster he has so long been accused of being. Although he does give more details and names than had previously been revealed or even suspected, Holmes is now the creature the public initially made him out to be. There is no need for him to explain himself more, since it has already been printed. With his execution looming, Holmes in essence surrenders to the public image that has been created for him and of him, at least for the purposes of having one more publication and one more chance to make money before his death.

Conceding the Story

This capitulation is evident at many points in the *Inquirer* article when Holmes states that a murder or a person has already been written about and he has nothing more to add runs counter to the fight he had been putting up for over a year to take control of his own biography. The same lack of a narrative structure that therefore gave Holmes no hard and fast rules about which elements of his story to stress and which to leave alone also meant that he was not constrained to follow generic expectations, since the true crime genre had yet to be established. Holmes had the ultimate freedom to present himself the way he wished and to adapt his story as he liked depending on what he thought would sell. Directly after his arrest and in *Holmes' Own Story* he fought to voice his own version of events in a way that reversed the dominant narrative. Although Holmes wrote a response to his guilty verdict claiming that he would challenge it given enough time, during the trial and now in his *Inquirer* confession no counternarrative is presented. Holmes is simply the man everyone has said he is, and they have all been intelligent enough to figure out what, exactly, he did, even apparently in cases where contradictory versions had been published. He does not select the "correct" variation but rather dismisses many of these murders completely as having already had enough printed about them.

Between his two spoken confessions, *Holmes' Own Story*, and the accompanying tales of fraud, Holmes has clearly shown the willingness and ability to change his tale based on the specific needs of the audience and the moment. This is especially true when such adaptability could net him something—money, for example, or his life as a free man thanks to a sentence of "not guilty." When his confession was published, mere weeks before his scheduled execution, Holmes was likely no longer able to cling to hope of the second, but the first was still a possibility. If the goal of *Holmes' Own Story* was to save his life and the *Inquirer* confession was just for money, then this could explain the change not only in Holmes' profession of his guilt, but the time and effort devoted into crafting the narrative. The men responsible for Holmes' imprisonment are meant to be validated, and the addition of further details or the correction of any currently suspected methods would simply undermine Holmes' claims of their skill and intelligence.

Perhaps Holmes was not satisfied with his capitulating written confession, or perhaps it was merely the next step in his long-term marketing plan, since his last words contradicted the *Inquirer* article completely and returned to the argument stressed in *Holmes' Own Story*: Holmes himself was not a murderer, having only lost two patients during illegal procedures, and thus the murderer of the Pitezels was still out there, walking free. The man whose lawyers had not presented a counternarrative during his trial, and who had since had his name put to a confession of twenty-seven murders, went to his death claiming innocence once again. The detectives he had praised mere weeks before had, apparently, gotten it wrong after all.

This was a clear attempt by Holmes to surround his death with an air of mystery and the ploy seems to have worked. Between his last words being a confession of his innocence and his strangely elaborate concrete burial, rumors swirled that varied from the supernatural—Holmes was meant to have cursed those who had wronged him—to the sleight of hand. Indeed, the History Channel series *American Ripper* went so far as to open Holmes' concrete-filled coffin and compare the DNA of the body found inside with Holmes' great-great-grandson in order to confirm his identity. More than a century after his execution, it was concluded that Holmes had not escaped the noose that day, although the legends surrounding his life were even more spectacular than those claiming he had avoided death on May 7, 1896.

Life After Death for the Greatest Criminal in History

Although not nearly as popular as his contemporary, Jack the Ripper, or the serial killers of the twentieth century's "Golden Age" and the focus of the true crime boom, the mythology surrounding H.H. Holmes continues into the twenty-first century. As the records of his verbal statements show, Holmes was a man willing to change his story in order to fit with the information currently available, all with the purpose of presenting himself as an innocent man caught up in the plans of others in a situation out of his control. *Holmes' Own Story* and the confession published in the *Inquirer* also bear his name, although they may have been heavily edited—or perhaps not written by Holmes himself at all. They do, however, contribute to the myth surrounding the man.

The figure of H.H. Holmes evolved during his lifetime in such a way as to make him a pliable, moldable figure. Verifiable facts about his life are sparse, and during his lifetime Holmes himself worked to change his representation of himself depending on the demands of the situation. He had already demonstrated numerous ways his story could be twisted around the fixed points confirmed by others in order to meet his goals of coming across either as innocent of all wrongdoings or guilty of more than he had previously been accused. As the twentieth century progressed and the term "serial killer" was coined and applied to more and more men, Holmes' story could be retroactively adapted in order to being sensation to him not only as a murderer, and not simply as a serial killer, but as "America's first serial killer" with an ascribed victim count higher than most of those who came after him. As the FBI and other experts cemented the serial killer narrative, Holmes's character and biography could be molded to fit.

Whereas Holmes had no such framework to use in his own presentation of himself, authors such as Harold Schechter and Erik Larson knew of the expected biography of men who were labeled "serial killers" and thus had guidance in how to structure their narratives of Holmes' life. Certain vignettes related in *Holmes' Own Story* or Holmes' *Inquirer* confession were retained and repeated because they fit in with the new understanding of such murderers, while others have been discarded for being both unverifiable and for deviating from the expected narrative. If Holmes' variations lacked sufficient detail for audiences in the late twentieth or early twenty-first century, authors could add it based on the larger body of knowledge obtained about serial killers in order to fulfill the generic expectations of true crime. These myths and apocryphal tales about Holmes have become popular knowledge to the extent that Adam Selzer had to carefully work to dismantle them in his 2017 book *H.H. Holmes: The True History of the White City Devil*, which then ran the risk of being less fascinating and certainly less morbid than prior versions.

H.H. Holmes was in fact his own first myth-maker, and the elements he included in *Holmes' Own Story* and his *Inquirer* confession, chosen in order to entice audiences of the day, largely align with narrative fundamentals still incorporated in popular true crime books of the twenty-first century. Even as Holmes himself recognized his "first" status and acknowledged his unique position in the world of criminality, he was able to draw on the newspaper narratives being written about him in order to isolate the components that would make his story a "good" one—that is, one that sold and was widely read. His adaptability to newly discovered evidence and information allowed him to change and shape his story and laid the groundwork for others coming after him to do the same. Although his tales show gaps and inconsistencies when compared with today's narratives, Holmes managed to establish himself as a malleable, adaptable, scoundrel whose story can easily be shaped to rival that of even the Golden Age's biggest stars. The threads of contemporary true crime are present in his often-dismissed autobiography and confession which, although rightly disparaged for a lack of veracity, present the rhetorical and generic evolution that helped shift American crime narratives from their beginnings as Puritan execution sermons to the true crime genre of today.

Chapter Notes

Introduction

1. Peter Vronsky, *Serial Killers: The Method and Madness of Monsters* (New York: Berkley, 2004), 328.
2. Mark Seltzer, *True Crime: Observations on Violence and Modernity* (London: Routledge, 2006), 35.
3. Jean Murley, *The Rise of True Crime: 20th-Century Murder and Popular Culture* (Westport, CT: Praeger, 2008), 132.
4. Harold Schechter, *Depraved: The Definitive True Story of H.H. Holmes, Whose Grotesque Crimes Shattered Turn-of-the-Century Chicago* (New York: Pocket Star Books, 2008), 285.

Chapter One

1. H.H. Holmes, *Holmes' Own Story: in which the Allged Multi-Murderer and Arch conspirator tells of Twenty-two Tragic Deaths and Disappearances in which he is said to be Implicated, with Moyamensing Prison Diary Appendix* (Philadelphia: Burk & McFetridge Co., 1895), 11.
2. Selzer, *H.H. Holmes: The True History of the White City Devil* (New York: Skyhorse, 2017), 138.
3. Ibid., 3.
4. Schechter, *Depraved*, 13.
5. Selzer, *True History*, 28.
6. Ibid., 52.
7. Ibid., 30.
8. Schechter, *Depraved*, 68.
9. Ibid., 29.
10. Ibid., 57.
11. Ibid., 114.
12. Ibid., 161.
13. Frank P. Geyer, *The Holmes-Pitezel Case: A History of the Greatest Crime of the Century and of the Search for the Missing Pitezel Children* (Philadelphia: Publishers' Union, 1896), 135.
14. Schechter, *Depraved*, 377.
15. J.D. Crighton and Herman W. Mudgett, M.D., *Holmes' Own Story: Confessed 27 Murders—Lied Then Died* (Murietta, CA: Aerobear Classics, 2016), 277.
16. *American Ripper*, History Channel (2017), Season 1, Episode 8.
17. Peter Vronsky, *Sons of Cain: A History of Serial Killers from the Stone Age to the Present* (New York: Berkley, 2018), 286.

Chapter Two

1. Geyer, *The Holmes-Pitezel Case*, 88.
2. Ibid., 97.
3. Ibid., 75.
4. Ibid., 81.
5. Ibid., 67.
6. Ibid., 65.
7. Ibid., 98.
8. Ibid., 136.
9. Ibid., 153.
10. Ibid., 142.
11. Ibid., 164.
12. Ibid., 165.
13. Ibid., 167.
14. Ibid., 115.
15. Ibid., 126.
16. Ibid., 171.
17. Schechter, *Depraved*, 248.

Part II

1. Patricia Cline Cohen, *The Murder of Helen Jewett: The Life and Death of a Prostitute in Nineteenth-Century New York* (New York: Vintage, 1998), 15.
2. Robert L. Corbitt, "The Holmes Castle: A Story of H.H. Holmes' Mysterious Work," in *The Strange Case of Dr. H.H. Holmes* (West Hollywood, CA: Waterfront Productions, 2005), 404.

Chapter Three

1. Wayne C. Minnick, "The New England Execution Sermon, 1639–1800," *Speech Monographs* 35, no. 1 (1968): 78.
2. Holmes, *Holmes' Own Story*, 5–6.
3. *Ibid.*, 199.
4. *Ibid.*, 10.
5. *Ibid.*, 202.
6. *Ibid.*, 7.
7. *Ibid.*, 10.
8. *Ibid.*, 12.
9. *Ibid.*, 19.

Chapter Four

1. Holmes, *Holmes' Own Story*, 24.
2. Crighton and Mudgett, *Holmes' Own Story*, 36.
3. Ann Rule, *Green River, Running Red: The Real Story of the Green River Killer—America's Deadliest Serial Murderer* (New York: Pocket Star Books, 2005), 583.
4. Holmes, *Holmes's Own Story*, 33.
5. *Ibid.*, 39.
6. *Ibid.*, 42.
7. *Ibid.*, 46.
8. *Ibid.*, 56.
9. *Ibid.*, 57.
10. *Ibid.*, 187.
11. *Ibid.*, 206.
12. *Ibid.*, 207.
13. *Ibid.*, 211.

Chapter Five

1. *Ibid.*, 27.
2. *Ibid.*, 93.
3. *Ibid.*, 96.
4. *Ibid.*, 113.
5. *Ibid.*, 122.
6. *Ibid.* 138.
7. *Ibid.* 132,
8. *Ibid.*, 51.
9. *Ibid.*, 158.
10. *Ibid.*, 168.
11. *Ibid.*, 181.
12. *Ibid.*, 187.
13. *Ibid.*, 186.
14. Schechter, *Depraved*, 315.

Chapter Six

1. Holmes, *Holmes' Own Story*, 64.
2. *Ibid.*
3. *Ibid.*, 65.
4. *Ibid.*, 66.
5. *Ibid.*, 70.
6. *Ibid.*, 71.
7. *Ibid.*, 72.
8. *Ibid.*, 74.
9. *Ibid.*
10. *Ibid.*, 75.
11. *Ibid.*, 76.
12. *Ibid.*, 79.
13. *Ibid.*, 82.
14. *Ibid.*, 84.
15. *Ibid.*
16. *Ibid.*, 85.

Chapter Seven

1. Holmes, *Holmes' Own Story*, 97.
2. *Ibid.*, 107.
3. *Ibid.*, 87.
4. *Ibid.*, 111–112.
5. *Ibid.*, 117.
6. *Ibid.*, 138.
7. *Ibid.*
8. *Ibid.*, 129.
9. *Ibid.*, 132.
10. *Ibid.*, 128.
11. *Ibid.*, 127.
12. *Ibid.*, 134.
13. *Ibid.*, 128.
14. *Ibid.*, 142.
15. *Ibid.*, 155.
16. *Ibid.*, 159.
17. *Ibid.*, 175–176.

18. *Ibid.*, 169.
19. *Ibid.*, 191.
20. *Ibid.*, 182.
21. *Ibid.*, 194-195.
22. *Ibid.*, 187.
23. *Ibid.*

Chapter Eight

1. Holmes, *Holmes' Own Story*, 212.
2. *Ibid.*, 235.
3. *Ibid.*, 213.
4. *Ibid.*, 105.
5. *Ibid.*, 213.
6. *Ibid.*, 213-214.
7. *Ibid.*, 214.
8. *Ibid.*, 219.
9. *Ibid.*
10. *Ibid.*
11. *Ibid.*, 234.
12. *Ibid.*
13. *Ibid.*, 222.
14. *Ibid.*, 235.
15. *Ibid.*, 236.
16. *Ibid.*, 236-237.
17. *Ibid.*, 236.
18. *Ibid.*, 240.
19. *Ibid.*, 256.

Chapter Nine

1. Holmes, *Holmes' Own Story*, 212.
2. *Ibid.*, 215.
3. *Ibid.*, 216.
4. *Ibid.*, 215.
5. *Ibid.*, 212.
6. *Ibid.*, 213.
7. *Ibid.*, 214.
8. *Ibid.*, 216.
9. *Ibid.*, 214.
10. *Ibid.*
11. *Ibid.*, 217.
12. *Ibid.*, 225.

Chapter Ten

1. Holmes, *Holmes' Own Story*, 225.
2. *Ibid.*, 225-226.
3. *Ibid.*, 226.
4. *Ibid.*, 228.
5. *Ibid.*, 230.
6. *Ibid.*, 232.

7. *Ibid.*, 237.
8. *Ibid.*, 241.
9. *Ibid.*, 242.
10. *Ibid.*
11. *Ibid.*, 234.
12. *Ibid.*, 240.
13. *Ibid.*, 231.

Chapter Eleven

1. Holmes, *Holmes' Own Story*, 251.
2. *Ibid.*
3. *Ibid.*, 252.
4. Schechter, *Depraved*, 334.
5. Holmes, *Holmes' Own Story*, 253.
6. *Ibid.*, 243.
7. *Ibid.*, 245.
8. *Ibid.*
9. *Ibid.*, 246.
10. *Ibid.*, 249.
11. *Ibid.*, 255.
12. *Ibid.*, 256.
13. *Ibid.*

Part IV

1. Schechter, *Depraved*, 326.
2. *Ibid.*, 354.
3. Selzer, *The True History*, 289.
4. Schechter, *Depraved*, 382.

Chapter Twelve

1. H.H. Holmes, "Holmes Confesses 27 Murders," *Philadelphia Inquirer*, April 12, 1896, 1.
2. Selzer, *True History*, 319.
3. Holmes, "Holmes Confesses," 1.
4. *Ibid.*
5. *Ibid.*
6. Schechter, *Depraved*, 385.
7. Holmes, "Holmes Confesses," 1.
8. *Ibid.*
9. *Ibid.*
10. *Ibid.*
11. *Ibid.*

Chapter Thirteen

1. *Ibid.*
2. *Ibid.*
3. *Ibid.*

4. *Ibid.*
5. *Ibid.*
6. *Ibid.*
7. *Ibid.*, 8.
8. *Ibid.*, 1.
9. *Ibid.*
10. *Ibid.*
11. *Ibid.*
12. *Ibid.*
13. *Ibid.*
14. *Ibid.*
15. *Ibid.*
16. *Ibid.*
17. *Ibid.*
18. *Ibid.*
19. *Ibid.*
20. Erik Larson, *The Devil in the White City: Murder, Magic, and Madness at the Fair That Changed America* (New York: Vintage, 2004), 296.
21. Holmes, "Holmes Confesses," 1.
22. *Ibid.*
23. *Ibid.*
24. *Ibid.*, 8.
25. *Ibid.*
26. *Ibid.*
27. *Ibid.*
28. *Ibid.*
29. Crighton and Mudgett, *Holmes' Own Story*, 236.
30. *Ibid.*
31. *Ibid.*
32. *Ibid.*
33. *Ibid.*
34. *Ibid.*
35. *Ibid.*
36. *Ibid.*
37. *Ibid.*
38. *Ibid.*
39. *Ibid.*
40. *Ibid.*
41. *Ibid.*
42. *Ibid.*, 9.
43. *Ibid.*

Conclusion

1. Crighton and Mudgett, *Holmes' Own Story*, 277.
2. *Ibid.*
3. Michael Arntfield and Marcel Danesi, *Murder in Plain English: From Manifestos to Memes—Looking at Murder Through the Words of Serial Killers* (New York: Prometheus Books, 2017), 140.

Bibliography

American Ripper. History Channel (2017), Season 1, Episode 8.

Arntfield, Michael, and Marcel Danesi. *Murder in Plain English: From Manifestos to Memes—Looking at Murder Through the Words of Serial Killers.* New York: Prometheus Books, 2017.

Cohen, Patricia Cline. *The Murder of Helen Jewett: The Life and Death of a Prostitute in Nineteenth-Century New York.* New York: Vintage, 1998.

Corbitt, Robert L. "The Holmes Castle: A Story of H.H. Holmes' Mysterious Work." *The Strange Case of Dr. H.H. Holmes.* Dimas Estrada, ed. West Hollywood, CA: Waterfront Productions, 2005.

Crighton, J.D., and Herman W. Mudgett, M.D., *Holmes' Own Story: Confessed 27 Murders—Lied Then Died.* Murietta, CA: Aerobear Classics, 2016.

Geyer, Frank P. *The Holmes-Pitezel Case: A History of the Greatest Crime of the Century and of the Search for the Missing Pitezel Children.* Philadelphia: Publishers' Union, 1896.

Holmes, H.H. "Holmes Confesses 27 Murders." *The Philadelphia Inquirer,* April 12, 1896.

_____. *Holmes' Own Story: in which the Alleged Multi-Murderer and Arch conspirator tells of Twenty-two Tragic Deaths and Disappearances in which he is said to be Implicated, with Moyamensing Prison Diary Appendix.* Philadelphia: Burk & McFetridge Co., 1895.

Ladwig, Dane. *Dr. H.H. Holmes and The Whitechapel Ripper.* CreateSpace Independent Publishing Platform, 2014.

Larson, Erik. *The Devil in the White City: Murder, Magic, and Madness at the Fair That Changed America.* New York: Vintage, 2004.

Minnick, Wayne C. "The New England Execution Sermon, 1639–1800." *Speech Monographs* 35, no. 1 (1968): 77–89.

Murley, Jean. *The Rise of True Crime: 20th-Century Murder and American Popular Culture.* Westport, CT: Praeger, 2008.

Schechter, Harold. *Depraved: The Definitive True Story of H.H. Holmes, Whose Grotesque Crimes Shattered Turn-of-the-Century Chicago.* New York: Pocket Star Books, 2008.

Seltzer, Mark. *True Crime: Observations on Violence and Modernity.* London: Routledge, 2006.

Selzer, Adam. *H.H. Holmes: The True History of the White City Devil.* New York: Skyhorse, 2017.

Vronsky, Peter. *Sons of Cain: A History of Serial Killers from the Stone Age to the Present.* New York: Berkley, 2018.

_____. *Serial Killers: The Method and Madness of Monsters.* New York: Berkley, 2004.

Index

American Ripper 28, 242, 263
Arnold, Judge Michael 26, 76, 177, 191, 192, 193, 219

Behavioral Science Unit (BSU) 3, 242
Belknap, Myrta *see* Holmes, Myrta
Betts, Miss Anna 188, 210, 215, 216, 219, 224, 225
Betz, Miss Anna *see* Betts, Miss Anna
Bickford, Maria 230
Bundy, Louise 57–58
Bundy, Ted 2, 5, 10, 26, 29, 57–58, 182, 191, 192, 211, 242–243, 256
Burke, William 13

chloroform 38, 39, 40, 216, 222, 233
Cigrand, Emelie 16, 17, 20, 69, 186–187, 188, 214–215, 220, 221, 222, 223, 225, 227
ciphers 38, 41, 44, 146, 184, 258
Cole, Charles 207, 208, 209, 211, 220
Columbian Exposition 1, 2, 9, 16, 17, 72, 87, 182, 187, 224
Conan Doyle, Arthur 14
Connor, Gertrude 210, 215, 216, 219
Connor, Julia 15, 16, 69, 70, 182, 206–207, 209, 211, 213
Connor, Ned 15, 69
Connor, Pearl 15, 16, 69, 206–207, 209, 211
Cook, Mrs. Sarah 213, 222, 223
Copps, Mr. *see* Cops, Mr.
Cops, Mr. 183, 184, 185, 186, 227
Corbitt, Robert L. 51, 54, 135, 249
Crawford, Jack 4
Crippen, Dr. Hawley Harvey 36, 165, 243
"the CSI effect" 4

Dahmer, Jeffrey 2, 57, 242
Devil in the White City (book) 7, 221, 243

Devil in the White City (nickname) 1, 182
Douglas, John 3, 242
Durkee, Miss Kate 212, 221

execution sermon *see* Puritan execution sermon

Federal Bureau of Investigation (FBI) 3, 10, 12, 57, 242

Gacy, John Wayne 2, 10, 18, 242
Geyer, Detective Frank 25, 26, 33, 37, 38, 40, 47, 94, 124, 129, 150, 152, 155, 157, 163, 166, 167, 170, 174–175, 198, 199, 234, 237, 239, 246

Hare, William 13
Hatch, Edward 6, 7, 74, 87, 88, 89, 90, 91, 92, 93, 120–126, 127, 128, 129, 147, 150, 153, 157–158, 176, 178, 185, 189, 190, 203, 226, 236, 237, 249–250, 251, 252, 254–255, 256, 258, 260, 261; as one of
Hedgepeth, Marion 20, 25, 33, 38, 111, 112, 133, 144
Holmes, H.H.: acting as his own attorney 26, 192, 194; "America's first serial killer" 1, 9, 12, 28, 182; anonymous accomplices 97, 106, 206, 207, 208, 209, 210, 211, 217, 218, 222, 256–257, 260, 261; childhood 11–13, 55–64, 132–133, 168; criticizing law enforcement 133, 134, 136, 142, 172, 187, 228; euphemisms for "corpse" 65, 66, 97, 102, 104, 250, 255, 256; feelings of guilt 83, 91, 114, 165; first confession 32–37, 131, 152, 244, 245, 251, 256; insurance fraud 60, 65, 94, 96–109, 256; medical training 65, 95, 148, 177, 219, 233, 235, 236, 239, 250, 255, 261; money as care 42, 43, 44,

57, 71, 80, 81, 83, 84, 85, 89, 92, 108, 113, 119, 120, 121, 133, 152, 169, 179; "monster" 7, 259–261; motive 129, 159, 179–182, 190, 197, 211–217, 244, 269; Mudgett, Herman Webster 1, 11, 14; other pseudonyms 31, 163, 174, 177, 187, 189; parents 11, 55–58; praising law enforcement 75, 167, 197, 198, 199, 200, 201, 203–204, 205, 206, 235, 260, 262; pseudonyms 227; second confession 37–42, 146, 152, 156, 171, 231, 245, 246, 251, 258; timelines 123, 124, 125–126, 127, 153, 172, 189, 256, 258
Holmes, Lucy Theodate 15, 249
Holmes, Myrta 15, 69, 76, 135, 193, 249
Holmes, Sherlock 14, 176
Holton, Dr. 14
Howe, Jeptha 22, 23, 32, 40–41, 84, 117–118
Hyde, Edward 92

Jack the Ripper 1, 2, 9, 10, 28, 92, 219, 263
Jewett, Helen 49, 230

Ladwig, Dane 10
Larson, Erik 7, 10, 14, 18, 221, 243, 264
Lattimer, Robert 213, 220–221, 225
Leacock, Dr. Robert 212
Lecter, Hannibal 2, 4, 243
Lizzie (surname not given) 214, 215, 222, 223
Lovering, Clara *see* Mudgett, Clara

Mansfield, Richard 92, 93
Manson, Charles 230
McNaughten Rule 234
Morgan, Dexter 2
Mudgett, Clara 12–13, 69, 249
Mudgett, Robert Lovering 13, 249
"Murder Castle" 1, 15, 17, 18, 19, 25, 28, 31, 51, 52, 158, 182, 187, 206, 209, 211, 213, 216, 221, 222, 223, 231, 251; vault inside 183, 186, 214, 215, 218, 220, 221, 222, 227
Murley, Jean 3, 4

newspapers 7, 8, 25, 26, 29, 37, 48, 49, 51, 52, 54, 95, 124, 125, 127, 131, 135, 137, 138, 141, 142, 150, 167, 170, 171, 175, 181, 182, 193, 194, 201, 210, 219, 244, 246, 247, 250, 251, 258, 259, 264

Parkman, Dr. George 50, 54, 192
Pinkerton Detective Agency 25, 33, 36

Pitezel, Alice 2, 7, 22, 23, 24, 25, 26, 27, 35, 41, 43, 45, 48, 52, 84–85, 86, 87, 89, 118, 119, 120, 122–124, 125, 129, 138, 147, 150, 157, 158, 159, 162, 163, 166, 169, 170, 185, 190, 200, 226, 235, 238–240, 244, 246, 249, 257
Pitezel, Benjamin 2, 6, 23, 24, 25, 27, 37, 42, 49, 50, 51, 52, 76, 90, 92, 94, 105, 108, 111, 126, 129, 135, 146, 147, 152, 157, 165, 181, 193, 194, 200, 213, 216, 231–236, 244, 246, 251, 252, 255, 256, 257; acting as mastermind 34, 35, 36, 81, 84, 106, 112, 115, 116, 117, 122, 144, 180, 254; and alcoholism 19, 20, 34, 43, 44, 46, 80, 82, 83, 85, 226, 248, 249, 254; "B.F. Perry" 21, 22, 33, 37, 39, 41, 118, 171, 245; suicide 26, 38, 39, 43, 44, 46, 55, 60–61, 79, 81–82, 83, 85, 91, 113, 114, 116, 158, 161, 171, 189, 226, 248, 254, 258
Pitezel, Carrie 19, 20, 22, 23, 24, 25, 26, 27, 32, 33, 34, 35, 36, 37, 38, 39, 41, 42, 43, 45, 46, 47, 48, 75, 76, 84, 85, 86, 87, 92, 106, 108, 116, 117–118, 119, 120, 121, 122, 124, 125, 132, 134, 136, 138, 151–152, 153, 154, 157, 163, 166, 171, 190, 193, 198, 232, 238, 245, 249, 254, 257, 258
Pitezel, Howard 2, 7, 24, 25, 27, 32, 35, 41, 43, 44, 47, 50, 51, 52, 86, 87, 88, 120, 122, 126, 127, 129, 138, 157, 158, 162–163, 166, 169, 170, 171, 185, 200, 226, 236–238, 244, 246, 249, 257
Pitezel, Nellie 2, 7, 23, 25, 26, 27, 35, 36, 41, 43, 48, 86, 87, 89, 120, 122–124, 125, 129, 138, 147, 150, 157, 158, 162, 163, 166, 169, 170, 185, 190, 200, 226, 238–240, 244, 246, 249, 257
Puritan execution sermon 6, 53, 54, 78–79, 127, 140, 179, 201, 218, 265

Quinlan, first name unknown 214, 223

Ressler, Robert 2, 3, 242
resurrection men 13, 33
Ridgway, Gary 29, 182
Robinson, Richard 49–50
Rogers, first name unknown 208, 209, 211, 212, 222
Rotan, Samuel 191, 192, 195; as "Holmes' lawyer" 26–27, 28, 235, 263

Schechter, Harold 9, 10, 12, 14, 15, 17, 21, 92, 177, 199, 264
Seltzer, Mark 3
Selzer, Adam 10, 12, 14, 17, 18, 29, 196, 264

Index

serial killer 2–6, 8, 9, 10, 12, 28–30, 57–58, 59, 80, 203, 211, 218, 221–222, 242–244, 245, 259, 263–264
Shoemaker, William A. 154, 191, 192, 195; as "Holmes' lawyer" 26–27, 28, 155, 235, 263
The Silence of the Lambs (movie) 4
Smith, Eugene 21–22, 23, 192
Starling, Clarice 4
Stevenson, Robert Louis 92

trial reports 6, 49, 54, 127

University of Michigan 13, 14

Vronsky, Peter 28

Warner, first name unknown 212
Webster, John 50, 54, 192

Williams, Minnie 6, 7, 16, 24, 38, 41, 42, 45, 46, 52, 69–70, 71–74, 80, 86, 88–89, 90, 91, 93, 95, 96, 120–123, 127, 146, 151–152, 153, 157–168, 176, 178, 184, 185, 186, 189, 190, 203, 226–230, 231, 235, 236, 244, 246, 247–248, 249, 250, 252, 253, 258, 260; as murderess 43, 51, 72, 87, 114, 132, 147, 183, 199, 218, 225–226, 248, 253
Williams, Nannie 6, 16, 41, 43, 51, 71–73, 83, 87, 90, 91, 94, 95, 96, 114, 138, 159, 160, 180, 199, 218, 226, 227, 244, 248, 255, 256

Yoke, Georgiana 6, 7, 20, 24, 31, 32, 35, 36, 39, 48, 54, 74–77, 78, 84, 88, 90, 91, 95, 96, 119, 120, 126, 127, 128, 130, 131–142, 145, 146, 148, 149, 151, 155, 161, 163, 168, 172, 190, 193, 203, 248, 256

www.ingramcontent.com/pod-product-compliance
Ingram Content Group UK Ltd.
Pitfield, Milton Keynes, MK11 3LW, UK
UKHW041930140426
5217IPUK00014B/404